Buy, Buy Baby

Buy, Buy Baby

How Consumer Culture Manipulates Parents and Harms Young Minds

Susan Gregory Thomas

MARINER BOOKS
HOUGHTON MIFFLIN HARCOURT
BOSTON • NEW YORK

First Mariner Books edition 2009

Copyright © 2007 by Susan Gregory Thomas

www.hmhbooks.com

Library of Congress Cataloging-in-Publication Data

Thomas, Susan Gregory.
Buy, buy baby : how consumer culture manipulates parents
and harms young minds / Susan Gregory Thomas.
p. cm.
Includes bibliographical references and index.
ISBN 978-0-618-46351-0
1. Child consumers. 2. Advertising and children. I. Title.
HF5415.32.T46 2007
339.4 70830973—dc22 2006030498

ISBN 978-0-547-23795-4 (pbk.)

PRINTED IN THE UNITED STATES OF AMERICA

Book design by Robert Overholtzer

DOC 10 9 8 7 6 5 4 3 2 1

FOR ZUZU, FRANKIE, AND TIN

Contents

Everyone [in America] is in motion, some in quest of power, others of gain. In the midst of this universal tumult, this incessant conflict of jarring interests, this continual striving of men after fortune, where is that calm to be found which is necessary for the deeper combinations of the intellect?

—ALEXIS DE TOCQUEVILLE, *Democracy in America*

Buy, Buy Baby

Introduction

T IS A MIDSUMMER DAY, about one o'clock, at the midtown Manhattan power-lunch landmark Oceana. The dining room conveys the quiet, streamlined elegance of a stateroom on a luxury liner, the ideal backdrop for the muted, intent conversations that typically take place here. It is not unusual to spend upward of one hundred dollars per person for lunch at Oceana, but the typical guest does not pay out of her own pocket for meals here. This is a place where executives capitalize on their corporate tabs to lay the unofficial foundations for deals that will be inked in boardrooms later. On this particular day, a man who is one of the premier kids' marketers in the United States is perusing the restaurant's tasting menu. An executive who has been in the field for more than twenty years and done business with Mattel, Hasbro, and Procter & Gamble, he clearly finds this a comfortable milieu; indeed, it is one of his favorite lunch haunts.

For the purposes of my conversation with him, he does not want his name divulged. If the details of what he is about to discuss were attributed to him in print, he chuckles, he "would most likely end up being forced to testify about them in a Senate subcommittee." His tone is calculatedly offhand, but he is serious about the inflammatory nature of the issue on the table. He is here to discuss how marketers target babies and toddlers as customers. It is, he admits, very controversial to market to such a young group, and most marketers and advertising agencies will tell you they don't do it. But don't believe them, he says: they do.

The executive tells me that the moment a baby can see clearly, she becomes a consumer. What he calls the "mini-me" phenomenon encourages children to be brand sensitive at an early age. Today's infants are crawling and toddling billboards for America's big brand names, he says, citing the successful business strategies of the Gap and Nike to expand their adult apparel lines to hip clothing for babies and toddlers. Furthermore, he says, all developmental milestones of early life are punctuated by brand names. Babies don't travel in plain old strollers; they ride in Maclarens, Graycos, or high-end Bugaboos. Their car seats have Eddie Bauer labels. Their nipples are Nuks, their bottles are Playtex or Avent. Their diapers are Huggies with Disney's Winnie the Pooh or Pampers with *Sesame Street* characters. He maintains that as soon as a baby or toddler points to McDonald's Golden Arches, the "brand request" is born: words aren't required. Even supermarket managers are becoming aware of toddlers' influence as consumers. At many chains, products for toddlers are placed at their eye level; the child simply grabs the box and hands it to mom, who drops it into the shopping cart.

The kids' marketing consultant points out that today's babies and toddlers spend more time in preschool or daycare than they ever have in the past, either because their upper-middle-class parents worry about "socializing" an only child or because both have jobs. The result, from a marketer's point of view, is that even a toddler is developing a public persona. Peer pressure, a prime medium for marketing to children, starts earlier than ever. But if the executive were forced to name the single most powerful force in targeting toddlers as a market? Easy, he says: television. *Sesame Street* may have started the revolution in what he calls "toddler TV," but that show is scrambling to keep its place now. In fact, toddler television has made it possible to calibrate market segments to one-year intervals. It's *Teletubbies* for one-year-olds, *Blue's*

Clues for twos, *Barney* for threes. If you talk about *marketing* to babies or toddlers, you are "seen as evil," he says, but so-called educational television for little children wears what he calls an "acceptability halo." A marketer who establishes "educational credit" can get away with anything.

THE BIRTH OF A BABY CULTURE

In the majority of American households with children between the ages of zero and three years old, popping in a baby video or flicking on the TV set to a preschool program is as mundane a routine as tooth brushing or bath time. It is not so much a parenting decision as a national reflex. Such videos and TV programs are marketed as educational for babies and toddlers, and it is generally accepted that on some level they are educational. Noggin, a cable channel for preschoolers, touts its tag line: "It's Like Preschool on TV." There's little reason to question that claim. The channel was started as a joint venture of Nickelodeon and Sesame Workshop, both trustworthy institutions. Many preschoolers have mastered mousing skills by their second birthday, and the Web sites of their favorite shows have games and activities for toddlers. The term "preschooler" is understood by many sources, including the Nielsen ratings, to refer to two- to five-year-olds; some include eighteen-month-olds in that category.

Elitists may find it tacky, but few Americans — and not just parents of very young children — register it as unusual that at chain bookstores, discount behemoths such as Wal-Mart, and libraries, many of the most popular books for infants and toddlers are based on licensed television characters or snack foods, such as General Mills' Cheerios or Pepperidge Farm's Goldfish. Few eyebrows are raised when daycare chains and even pre-K programs adopt curricula based on TV characters, with their licensed cartoon likenesses emblazoned on posters, books, videos, take-home handouts, coloring books, and other materials marketed as educational. Many of these programs are produced in collaboration with Scholastic, a company whose reputation is synonymous with education. There is little reason to question the claims by makers of baby toys and equipment that their products "stimulate" babies' cognitive abilities with blinking lights or classical music. The packaging explains why such features are educational, and parents are sure that they read or saw something that an expert said about them. In any case, most people buy these products because that's what is on the market.

The world of infants and toddlers did not look like this even fifteen years ago. Babies and toddlers were generally used by the media only as stars in daytime television commercials. (Enter the wobbly tot, lurching around the house as a frazzled mother follows with a roll of paper towels and a happy, defeated smile for her irresistible little monster.) Mothers were the target consumers. Very young children were simply considered too young to grasp basic advertising pitches; moreover, the industry generally viewed pushing products on little children as unethical. But much has changed in a very short time. Until very recently, for example, "preschooler" referred to four- and five-year-olds; those younger than three were considered babies or toddlers. Today the "zero-to-three" market has become the first segment in "cradle-to-grave" marketing, representing more than $20 billion a year. Selling to this age group is a rapidly growing industry manned by a battalion of specialized and sophisticated advertising firms; child psychology researchers, often funded by companies interested in building a consumer base of very young children; and cross-marketing campaigns that deliberately intertwine educational messages with subtle commercial ploys. As the zero-to-three market has grown, so has a popular culture revolving around babies and toddlers. It includes formal classes and school (gymnastics, music, art, academics), the use of machines previously reserved for adults and older kids (computers, VCRs, TV, DVRs, cell phones, digital cameras), and rigorous schedules to ensure that every moment offers an opportunity to "learn."

The emergence of the zero-to-three market has, both directly and indirectly, compelled the toy, food, and apparel industries, as well as every major media conglomerate, to reconfigure their long-term marketing strategies. Brand recognition starts much earlier than one might think. Marketing studies show that children can discern brands as early as eighteen months; by twenty-four months they ask for products by brand name. In fact, a study conducted in 2000 found that brands wield as much influence on two-year-olds as they used to on children of five and up. Nearly two-thirds of the mothers interviewed for the study reported that their children asked for specific brands before the age of three, while one-third said their kids were aware of brands at age two or earlier. Brands that kids knew best included Cheerios, Disney, McDonald's, Pop-Tarts, Coke, and Barbie.

The phenomenon of cradle-to-grave marketing can, in some ways, be seen as the ultimate, inevitable step in the phenomenon that kids' marketers have long referred to as KGOY: Kids Getting Older Younger. Since the 1980s, marketers have been refining ways of mining the 'tween market: children between the ages of six and eleven. This age group has always been brand-conscious, but as one longtime marketer put it, "It's dribbled down" to even younger children. But how has this happened, and why?

No Special Talents

In the late 1990s, a *New York Times Magazine* feature article titled "Test-Tube Moms" marveled at what had become "a neurotic national pastime": "raising a scientifically correct child." If any one event triggered this neurosis, it was the Clintons' 1997 White House Conference on Early Childhood Development and Learning, later famously referred to as the "brain conference." With the goal of impressing on both Congress and the public the importance of funding early-child-care programs, the conference called on neurobiologists and experts in the field of early childhood development to explain how the brain grows during the first three years of life. Presenters emphasized that the brain develops more rapidly, and makes more significant connections, in these years than it ever will again. A massive public relations campaign bolstered by celebrities, most notably Rob Reiner, echoed the importance of the years from zero to three, and the campaign was publicized by all the major press outlets.

Within a month of the conference, the Baby Einstein Company was founded by Julie Aigner-Clark, a stay-at-home mother of a toddler. Aigner-Clark launched an educational video series for babies with $18,000 of her own savings, seed money for a business that she, having paid attention to timing and cultural trends, had good reason to believe would take off. Aigner-Clark saw that Baby Boomers were having their first children later and were applying the well-known yuppie drive to baby-rearing. Products that promised to stimulate early literacy — such as giant earphones designed to straddle pregnant bellies — had been hot for a few years. Generation-X women were now starting to have babies, too, and were bringing some of their technology know-how to lap time, spawning a new category of software for babies called lapware. Also, they had grown up watching *Sesame Street* and were comfortable using television as a babysitter. The Mozart Effect, though ultimately debunked, was more or less accepted as fact in the popular culture. Of course, Aigner-Clark knew about the brain conference. She also noted that for this generation of new mothers, taking a shower or making a grilled cheese sandwich had become a high-stakes proposition. The new mom felt it was not an option to leave her baby in his cradle while she bathed or prepared a meal; the baby required stimulation, entertainment, or soothing.

Aigner-Clark tapped a real gold vein with the title of her company. Although she would later insist that she "honestly had no idea what a great marketing name it was," Baby Einstein is widely regarded as one of the most ingenious product names in marketing history. It was inspired, Aigner-Clark says, by a remark attributed to Albert Einstein: "I have no special talents. I am only passionately curious." Highlighting babies' natural passionate curiosity, the company's publicity materials and public statements insist that its products are not genius-makers but are grounded solely in the principle that "every moment of every day in these early years is an opportunity for discovery." But it is clear that the reason the company name has worked so well is that Einstein is famous for his genius as a scientist, not for his emotional temperament. Similarly, the other historical namesakes in the Baby Einstein pantheon — Babies Mozart, Beethoven, Bach, Van Gogh, Shakespeare, Galileo, da Vinci, and Newton — are creative geniuses. The obvious genius of the company name is the power of its suggestion: parents implicitly understand the insinuation that their babies can be made smarter or more creative by watching these videos.

It is not surprising that Aigner-Clark had a hit on her hands. She could have walked away after a year or so with a profit of well over six figures and the satisfaction of achieving the postfeminist All by making a bundle from a fulfilling, home-based business. But her timing was more than good. In just five years, she sold the Baby Einstein Company to the Walt Disney Company for an estimated $25 million. Aigner-Clark nailed the zeitgeist completely.

Some people in kids' marketing suggest that Aigner-Clark played the wholesome milkmaid for effect. She knew she had a cash cow, and she milked it dry. If this is true, her act is almost scandalously good. But she does not seem like a steamroller executive, nor is she unsophisticated — she's smart and savvy. Moreover, she seems genuinely nice (though she works at home, she frets that she sees even less of her children than if she worked outside because she is compulsively drawn to her office). There is nothing out of the ordinary in this. In fact, her whole comportment seems utterly ordinary — which, in a sense, makes it still stranger. One has the impression, in talking with her, that she feels like Luke Skywalker after the fluky, fateful pull of the trigger that detonated the Death Star's central nerve: How did I do it? Did I do it, or was the Force with me? A hint of supernatural awe crept into the title of a speech Aigner-Clark gave at a marketing conference in a recent year: "Can Lightning Strike Twice? The Personal Quest to Find a Sequel to Baby Einstein." The title was poignant. It suggests that she credits fate for the success of her product rather than herself. She had, without a doubt, deliberately walked out into the field on a rainy day, but she hadn't known that the weather patterns that afternoon would make it *the* rainy day. Furthermore, finding a sequel to Baby Einstein misses the point. Its impact has been so profound that it is hard to discern where the product ends and the culture of early childhood in America now begins.

ALLEGIANCE TO A BRAND

Baby Einstein and the raft of imitators it spawned helped transform the culture by addressing a seemingly simple issue. As *People* magazine wrote in 2000, in a piece marveling at the self-made millionaire mom, "It's one of life's great mysteries: How did parents of toddlers eat dinner in peace before videos? Julie Aigner-Clark, thirty-three, founder of the Baby Einstein Company, can't answer that — but she has helped moms and dads feel less guilty about their VCR habit." It is remarkable to think of it today, but Aigner-Clark was the first person to broker the merger of what now seem like two relatively obvious ideas: that a video or TV program can be a good baby toy and that a well-designed toy might boost a baby's brain power. In a decade, this convergence has, perhaps permanently, transformed the everyday experiences of all but the most insulated American children between the ages of zero and three.

This merger has caused a major shift in the child-rearing style and core beliefs of the majority of American parents, cutting across social and economic boundaries. It is not just that more babies and toddlers watch TV, videos, and DVDs, though they certainly do. It is estimated that nearly 30 percent of American homes in which young children live own a Baby Einstein video. According to Disney market research, Baby Einstein has 82 percent brand awareness. Three out of four pregnant women say they are "likely to buy Baby Einstein products." In a groundbreaking 2003 study of the media habits of America's children under six, the Henry J. Kaiser Family Foundation reported that more than half of the parents surveyed believed that educational TV and baby videos such as those produced by Baby Einstein were "very important" to their babies' intellectual development. President George W. Bush underscored this widely held conviction in his 2007 State of the Union address, commending Aigner-Clark for "represent[ing] the great enterprising spirit of America." Perhaps because of the belief that a video can raise their babies' IQ, or can at least be "educational," more than a quarter of American children under the age of two have a television in their room, in spite of an appeal by the American Academy of Pediatrics that children under two not watch television at all. On a typical day, 61 percent of children six months to twenty-three months watch television; by age three, 88 percent do. The median time that children from zero to three spend watching some form of media on the screen is slightly under two hours — about as much time as they spend playing outside and about three times as much time as they spend being read to.

What might be called the baby genius phenomenon — the widely held notion that infants and toddlers can be made smarter via exposure to the right products and programs — has spread throughout the toy industry. Today, to be competitive in the baby and toddler business, a toymaker's products must encourage "learning," or at least claim that they do. The fastest-growing segment of the $3.2 billion infant and preschool toy business is represented by "educational" products, which are advertised as stimulating babies' and toddlers' cognitive abilities. Indeed, the demand for such playthings has completely transformed the toy industry. It has helped catapult dot-com-era start-ups such as LeapFrog into the major leagues and drastically shifted the business strategies of longtime players such as Mattel's Fisher-Price and Hasbro's PlaySkool. Wholesale buyers, who follow no educational guidelines in their decisions, are governed only by how they believe customers will respond to packaging claims. It is now standard for anyone marketing to very young children and their families to make certain that his product — and brand — wears what the kids' marketing executive called an educational "halo." As he said at Oceana, if you can get educational credit, you can pretty much get away with anything.

The end game is getting a customer. Just two years after Baby Einstein's launch, network and cable television began to produce shows for toddlers because they saw a chance to hook kids to their channels early on. Asked why so many cable channels were diving into the preschool market, Nick Jr.'s top executive, Brown Johnson, said, "It's about building allegiance to a brand."

KGOY

This book looks at the development of what has become the youngest segment in American youth culture. This is not a culture, clearly, that babies and toddlers invented, but rather one constructed by parents, child-care providers, television, and marketers. The effects of this culture on young children are surprising, sometimes shocking, and profound — though academic and marketing researchers alike are only beginning to understand just how deeply the effects run, or even precisely what they are. They are rarely what they seem. To some extent, this is an examination of what marketers call "age compression" or KGOY. Although the nuances are slightly different — the first implies that adults apply the force, the second shrugs that kids getting older younger is an inevitable consequence of living in our times — they both refer to the fact that today's grade-school children are dealt with the way teenagers were ten or more years ago, and so on down the age scale. Both phenomena, which date back at least to the 1920s in the United States, have been consciously manufactured and maintained by marketers. Since the beginnings of what is generally considered the American youth culture — that point where the media and children's public lives intersect — KGOY has been a source of parental alarm as well as a business opportunity. Parents have always rebelled against the commercialization of their children initially, but over time they, the children, and, ultimately, American society, internalize the new standard of KGOY as the social norm. Anyone on its periphery is considered quaint, odd, or rigid. KGOY is the ever-changing heart of American youth culture.

KGOY takes on a different meaning when applied to babies, however. Whereas even slightly older children may not feel as old as they act, or are called on to act by a variety of forces, all but the most cloistered have some cultural frame of reference for what the KGOY performance might look like. Babies and toddlers do not. Babies and toddlers are not little kids; they do not think like little kids. The developmental gap between an eighteen-month-old and a four-year-old is as wide a gap as exists in human development; indeed, a teenage girl has more in common, cognitively speaking, with an elderly man than a toddler does with a four-year-old. Babies and toddlers have no prior experience of the world; as the Swiss psychologist Jean Piaget first showed in the 1920s, the picture of the world they are working to assemble is categorically different from older children's, and certainly from adults'. As research is showing, babies and toddlers are astonishingly concrete thinkers. What they may *seem* to be learning from the stimuli and experiences they encounter in the new baby culture is very different from what they are *actually* learning.

This book also looks at the important social and historical forces that converged to create the new baby culture. The rise of the child-rearing expert in the United States, the "professionalizing" of motherhood, drastic changes in material culture and work-family patterns in the 1970s, and the vastly different childhoods and parenting styles of Baby Boomers and Generation Xers have all contributed to the formation of today's zero-to-three market. Toddler TV may have been the tipping point, but momentum had been building for as long as a century.

PROBLEM-SOLVING DEFICIT DISORDER

Still, in the past decade something unique, and uniquely concerning, has been unfolding with the past decade's development of a baby and toddler market. For one, the long-term impact of the baby genius phenomenon may be anything but educational. Many in the field of early child development suspect that babies and toddlers reared on TV, videos, and blinking, beeping "smart" toys may ultimately suffer from cognitive problems. Diane E. Levin, a professor in the early childhood education department at Wheelock College in Boston, calls the phenomenon "problem-solving deficit disorder." Levin contends that such products essentially overstimulate very young children, so that instead of using their own resources to solve a problem or an uncomfortable feeling — Mom is in the shower, boredom, and so on — they apply those resources to processing the dazzling object that has been placed before them. Over time, Levin says, babies and toddlers accustomed to getting this kind of sensory "hit" when they feel uncomfortable may not just become dependent on having that hit but may even lose the ability to work through feelings and ideas independently or with the help of a trusted friend. Marie Anzalone, who is on the faculty of Columbia University's occupational therapy program, reports that she frequently treats very young children from low-income as well as upper-middle-class families who appear glazed over and numb, which she believes is an ingrained response to overstimulation from technology toys and television. These toddlers simply cannot integrate the sensory overload to which they are routinely subjected; to cope, they begin to tune out.

Constant distractions are known to impair children's cognitive development in other ways, too. A University of Massachusetts study conducted by the preeminent academic researcher Daniel R. Anderson on the effects of television on young children showed that even the seemingly benign practice of keeping the television running in the background at home can be disastrous for toddlers' development because it interferes with their ability to concentrate on their own activities. The study reported that one-year-olds' focused play is reduced by half when the television is on, even if the children are not specifically tuning in to the programming. Focused play — which, as the celebrated preschool pioneer Maria Montessori pointed out, is the work of childhood — is essential for normal cognitive development. In other words, it is essential for little brains to grow.

INCREASED DEPRESSION

The baby genius phenomenon has paved the way for the commercialization of early childhood, and that has raised the stakes higher still. In 2004 the American Psychological Association strongly recommended that advertising and marketing to children under the age of eight be restricted. The reason for the organization's admonition was that children in that age group do not understand persuasion. They may recognize that an ad looks different from a television show or a magazine article, but they do not grasp its intent to persuade an audience to buy something. They don't understand that what the ad suggests may not be entirely true or that the product depicted in an advertisement may not look the way it is presented. Their capacity to think abstractly on this level has nothing to do with intelligence; it is indicative of a developmental milestone corresponding with age level. If a seven-year-old cannot understand that SpongeBob is there to sell her junk food, how can a baby understand this? What are the long-term effects of being raised in such a marketing culture, not only to one's mind but to one's sense of self and spirit?

It is clear to see how these effects are manifested as children grow older. In her extensive study of Boston-area children between the ages of ten and thirteen, Juliet B. Schor, a sociologist and the author of *Born to Buy: The Commercialized Child and the New Consumer Culture,* sought to determine whether involvement in consumer culture had any effect on children's general well-being. Over a period of three years, Schor and her team of graduate students administered a questionnaire consisting of more than 150 questions covering media use, consumer values and involvement in consumer culture, relationships with parents, demographic variables, and measures of physical and mental well-being. Defining "consumer involvement" on a spectrum of identifiers ranging from "I feel like other kids have more stuff than I do" and "I care a lot about my games, toys, and other possessions" to "I like watching commercials," the study's results were striking. Regardless of the participants' socioeconomic, educational, or cultural background, Schor found that "high consumer involvement is a significant cause of depression, anxiety, low self-esteem and psychosomatic complaints." She also found a clear causal and reflexive relationship between consumer involvement and health: "Less involvement in consumer culture leads to healthier kids, and more involvement leads kids' psychological well-being to deteriorate." Finally, "Higher levels of consumer involvement result in worse relationships with parents, which also leads to increased depression, anxiety, lower self-esteem and more psychosomatic complaints."

THE INFLUENCE OF MARKETING

My research for this book began in the mid-1990s, when I was a senior editor at *U.S. News & World Report*. At that newsweekly, many of the editors in title are reporters in fact, and it was my job to cover technology as it related to consumers as well as business.

In 1997 I started to get calls from consumer software companies wanting to set up press appointments to demonstrate what they were calling "lapware" — educational software for infants and toddlers, who would sit on a parent's lap while they used the software. The lapware that most companies showed me seemed to be digital versions of cause-and-effect toys. Instead of twisting a plastic key to release a pop-up plastic animal, infants would bang on the keyboard for the reward of seeing stars and shapes sparkling across the monitor. The lapware for toddlers — largely aimed at children between the ages of two and five — was more overtly academic. It was easy for parents to assume that software with titles such as JumpStart and Reader Rabbit was "educational," and what's more, it seemed to provide an important computer experience. According to the software firms, new scientific research on the brain had shown that a person never learns more than in the first three years of life; after that the window closes, and opportunities to grow new neurons and build the foundation for future brain power are lost. As the White House Conference had shown, they argued, failure to stimulate a growing brain could have serious consequences down the line.

At that point in technology history, computers enjoyed a virtually unimpeachable reputation as educational instruments. The overwhelming sentiment at the time was that by using computers even for the most mundane tasks, children were not only learning a particular skill but were also becoming *smarter* in the process. A great many people, of great social and economic influence, seemed to believe that "kids today" were smarter because they could do things like insert a CD-ROM into the appropriate disk drive and build Web sites using HTML software. But the archaeological and anthropological record shows that children have always begun using the predominant tools of their culture at around four or five years old. Kids were no more sophisticated for using computers in Newton, Massachusetts, in the mid-nineties than for learning how to use bows and arrows in the prehistoric Lenape nation. The real change, it seemed, was the influence of marketing: people believed it.

That was certainly true for the technology industry as a whole. Ingenious marketing and public relations campaigns could take a great deal of the credit for the heady success of the tech economy of the nineties. I was especially impressed by the Palm marketing team, which did a phenomenal job of convincing not just harried dot-com CEOs but everyone else who had relied on paper datebooks that they would not be able to get organized without a hundred-dollar hand-held digital gizmo. It was common knowledge that Microsoft and Intel kept upping the ante with new versions of Windows that demanded ever-faster processors; then PR departments helped drive the fear of becoming obsolete, which accelerated the upgrade cycle. Internet providers fed concerns that if you didn't have a Web site, you would be denied access to the digital age.

But while PR and marketing firms may have boosted unit sales, they were not entirely responsible for a massive change in cultural sensibility. The Web itself was doing that. It is easy to forget that until the mid-nineties, e-mail was still a clunky mode of communication employed mostly by techies and academics. Most other e-mail correspondence was restricted to private systems, such as internal corporate networks. The Web changed all that. When the Web took off, so did viruses — and not just hard-disk-munching e-bugs. Viral behavior itself seemed to find parallels in the world the Web had wrought. In his provocative treatise *Media Virus! Hidden Agendas in Popular Culture*, Douglas Rushkoff argued that ideas and trends were not just taking on viruslike qualities of replication, dissemination, and adaptation. They *were* viruses. Just as a biological virus that causes the common cold or AIDS attaches itself to a healthy host cell with a sticky protein shell, a media virus first hooks into a person's mind via a titillating news event, scientific theory, or new technology. Then, just as a biological virus injects its own genetic code to turn healthy cells into virus-replicating machines, a media virus infects thoughts with ideological code: "Like real genetic material, these [ideological codes] infiltrate the way we do business, educate ourselves, interact with one another — even the way we perceive reality." In both cases, the weaker the host, the more susceptible to viral infiltration. Soon Rushkoff's book became required reading at major marketing firms; Rushkoff himself became one of the hottest speakers on the business conference circuit. Marketers around the country wanted to learn how to unleash their own media viruses.

THE BABY GENIUS VIRUS

With the emergence of lapware, a new media virus seemed to be taking form: a baby genius virus with several major components. One was the notion that "technology makes you smarter and better." While the fertile conditions of the dot-com era fostered a particularly virulent strain in the nineties, that sentiment had been around for a long time.

Historians have pointed out that America's confidence in technological progress is probably as old as the nation itself. The ingenuity of Benjamin Franklin, Thomas Jefferson, and many other iconic figures in American history has always been touted and mythologized. In his prescient nineteenth-century work *Democracy in America*, Alexis de Tocqueville remarked on Americans' "addiction" to the uses of "practical science." Confidence in technology has become inextricably linked with many of the traits we associate with the American character: the pioneering ethic, self-reliance, self-improvement, reinvention, pragmatism, and optimism. The faith that the correct application of science and technology can somehow transmit such values is central to the American outlook. From the Eisenhower-era film loops featuring the can-do star Our Friend the Atom to the Reagan administration's deep faith in the Star Wars defense system to Silicon Valley's conviction that the Internet-driven "New Economy" would coincide with the new millennium, the promise that technology would bring about a brighter tomorrow has inspired Americans even as it has disappointed them.

Such pitches and promises are key to our consumer economy, too. Most advertising campaigns rely on targeting the "aspirational," often the spark of hope ignited when we learn of the amazing "technology," "advance," or "breakthrough" embedded in the new car, computer, phone, face cream, razor blade, dishwashing soap, saucepan, or coffee maker. Such commercials work because, however embarrassingly or unconsciously, we have internalized the suggestion that this new technology is the conduit for self-improvement, reinvention, optimism — manifest destiny itself. We want to believe.

The other major component of the baby genius virus, the emphasis on the profound importance of the first three years of life, was propelled by the Carnegie Foundation's report and the White House brain conference. Although the conference organizers intended to convey the necessity of government-funded, standards-based child care for infants and toddlers, the event's lasting legacy was a resurgence of the national preoccupation with raising babies the right way. These two forces united to produce an extremely potent germ. Because online communities of mothers were growing exponentially — and Gen-Xers relied on them for information as well as moral support — the baby genius virus began to multiply like crazy. If it is true that our American consumer economy takes our concerns, commodifies them, and sells them back to us (a notion attributable, I believe, to Noam Chomsky), then the baby genius zeitgeist was clearly a case in point. The brain conference raised concerns about the importance of babies' first three years, which was being sold back to parents in the form of brain "stimulators" such as lapware, baby videos, "learning" toys, and so on. What was most remarkable about the baby genius media virus was that, like the flu, it infected everyone. It started in a population of upper-middle-class parents on the East and West Coasts, but over the next several years it spread across the country and across ethnic and socioeconomic backgrounds. Also remarkable was how little resistance there was to the idea. There was no evidence that any of these products was any more educationally stimulating than shaking a rattle, playing with blocks, mucking around in the backyard, or just hanging out, playing with a beloved caregiver or parent. Indeed, there were no studies available on how babies and toddlers even processed screened media or electronic toys. *There was no reason to believe any of it.*

PERSONAL CONVERSATIONS

In 1999 I began reporting on online privacy. At the time the two biggest concerns were the possibilities that hackers would tunnel into people's hard disks and steal their financial information and that pedophiles would lure children into lurid conversations by pretending to be children themselves. But during my work on this beat, I learned about another worrisome practice that was far more widespread: marketers using children's personal information to target them as customers. I had been covering the Federal Trade Commission (FTC) guidelines for the Children's Online Privacy Protection Act of 1998, which required commercial Web sites targeted at anyone younger than thirteen to take certain steps to maintain children's privacy online. The steps outlined were pretty flimsy. For example, the FTC required sites to state clearly to users that they were collecting personal data and to declare how they were planning to use it; sites were supposed to get verifiable parental consent before collecting and using that information and to allow parents to screen their children's personal information and stop marketers from using it again. However, it was easy for children to duck such hurdles; any kid old enough to type competently could forge the consent forms. Furthermore, while the guidelines emphasized children's safety, they did nothing to protect children from marketers. Sites were not required to get parental permission before collecting children's e-mail addresses or names if they were procured in response to kids' e-mails or to contest entries or e-newsletter subscriptions.

What alarmed critics was the ability of marketers to use "spokescharacters" to develop personalized relationships with children. The Center for Media Education feared that sites with branded characters could conduct ongoing "personal" conversations with young children through e-mail or personalized Web sites. And through the use of basic tracking software, sites could register each child's online footprint and use a simple algorithm to determine his habits, fears, likes, and tastes; such techniques were already widely used in targeting adult customers. An automatic program could then produce irresistible messages tailor-made for each child. Child development professionals, such as Michael Brody of the American Academy of Child and Adolescent Psychiatry, were concerned that young children's emotional investment in cartoon spokescharacters would make them especially vulnerable to these intimate marketing messages. Such figures were celebrities to children, Brody said, and could have a powerful psychological impact.

As the psychologist Bruno Bettelheim argued in his 1976 book *The Uses of Enchantment,* it is through iconic fairy tales that young children unwittingly explore their unconscious fears of abandonment or the death of a parent; such narratives help children process these abiding fears without talking about them directly, which would be overwhelming — and, developmentally, almost impossible. Turning fairy tale characters into corporate spokespeople robs children of a vital part of their inner lives, of a rite of passage fundamental to human development. It has been proven that children under the age of eight are not cognitively able to understand persuasion, even in the blatant form of a TV ad. This kind of personalized character marketing is far more subtle and insidious than a TV ad. Brody said bluntly, "Marketers have become child experts, just like pedophiles."

Behind That Friendly, Furry Face

By the time I was pregnant with my first child in 2000, baby genius tech toys had come to dominate the market. Now especially curious about the efficacy of such products, I wrote a story about "smart" toys, trying to assess the value of such gizmos as the Babbler, an electronic plush baby toy that spoke in Japanese, French, and Spanish phonemes when babies whacked it, and VTech's Muzzart, a cuddly dog that played tinny Mozart. For the story, I had interviewed a broad range of child development experts, including Jerome and Dorothy Singer at Yale's Edward Zigler Center in Child Development and Social Policy and Alison Gopnik, a professor of psychology at the University of California at Berkeley. Along with her colleagues Andrew Meltzoff and Patricia Kuhl at the University of Washington, Gopnik wrote *The Scientist in the Crib*, a fascinating look at the newest research on how babies learn. Every one of the experts I consulted said that such toys offered no special advantage. They were products of marketing, not research.

By the time my child was born, shows such as *Blue's Clues*, *Dora the Explorer*, and *Clifford the Big Red Dog* ruled the preschool airwaves, and the starring characters were licensed everywhere. Baby Einstein videos had become some of the most popular baby shower gifts in the country. As I, along with all the other new moms in my New York neighborhood, struggled into our new parental skin, I noticed that many were turning on these shows or videos of the baby-genius variety for their babies and toddlers. The general response in my urban, liberal, educated group seemed to be: "I don't know if it's going to make my baby into a genius, but he *loves* it, and it lets me take a shower." The consensus was that it couldn't hurt: *we* were all raised on TV, after all, and we didn't turn out to be completely brain-dead. Many of the parents were uncertain that the Baby Einstein–type videos really *would* help stimulate their babies' budding neurons. But if there really was something magic in them, how could we *not* show it to them?

You might think that because I had already done a fair amount of reporting in this area and interviewed experts at the top of this field I would be immune to such questions. You would be wrong. I was freaking out. Maybe those experts were just cynical academics, elitists who would rave about the virtues of wooden blocks until your eyes rolled. Maybe, in spite of my years covering technology, I was finally becoming a Luddite myself. And maybe it was better to let young children share the culture of their peers so they wouldn't feel like hothouse orchids: pure and precious, unable to survive outside a rarefied environment. Finally, maybe mother really did know best. Maybe moms could sense something in their own children's responses that no research psychologist would ever be able to tease out or interpret properly. That is, maybe Julie Aigner-Clark's maternal instincts *were* better qualifications for grasping the infant mind than all those people with Ph.D.'s in child psychology.

But my background as a technology journalist seems to have saddled me with the curse and gift of extreme suspicion of marketing come-ons. Having learned over the years that most marketing and PR campaigns are based on a lot of illusory fluff — and knowing what a sham lapware was — I couldn't help wondering if the wool was being pulled over our newly maternal eyes with this stuff, too. Also, my memory was that television had generally been the purview of older kids, starting at around four. What, exactly, was the effect of toddler television and babies' videos on the *really* little watchers?

But it wasn't until my seventeen-month-old toddler first saw an Elmo video and within minutes memorized the "Elmo's World" theme song and within days spotted Elmo on every licensed packaged product we encountered in the supermarket, bookstore, toy store, and library — and begun referring to these Elmo products as "Elmo diapers" or "Elmo books" — that I knew there was definitely something behind that friendly, furry face. I didn't know what it was, but I felt it was worth looking into. This book is a report of what I found.

1

Learn Something New
Every Day

I T IS MARCH 2004, around nine o'clock on a Tuesday morning in the Bay Area's industrial-chic city of Emeryville, California. Although Beth, a producer at the technology toy company LeapFrog, is in the final stage of pregnancy — the bulky, drowsy stage — she is sharp and energetic as she discusses the features of a new toy prototype. Beth is one of the top producers in the LeapFrog Baby division, launched in 2004, and all eyes — both internally and in the business world at large — are watching closely. As with its products for older children, LeapFrog must protect its brand integrity by ensuring that its toys for infants and toddlers are designed for optimal learning. The prototype Beth is describing is an interactive plush frog that she and her team have been working on for several months. Some people who work here say that you can feel a high-pitched vibration in the air when a new product presentation is in progress. Then again, you can sense that vibe just about anytime at LeapFrog.

Walk by any cubicle in LeapFrog's loftlike headquarters, and you see casually dressed product designers and producers gripping oversize stainless steel coffee mugs as they discuss a current project or weigh in with verve on someone else's. Whiteboards are inscribed with diagrams and flow charts. There is something of a time-capsule feeling at Leap-Frog, as if all the creative, manic, Ivy League energy that was evenly distributed throughout the Bay Area during the e-business era of the 1990s were preserved in these offices. Then that energy was largely directed at convincing Wall Street that Web-based business-to-business (B2B) companies would be the pillars of the New Economy. Now, at LeapFrog, it is aimed at making toys that enhance children's cognitive development, or, as the company consistently styles it, *learning*.

Beth is clearly on this wavelength as the group begins describing the prototype's features. It is designed to be a toddler's special buddy, helping him through tricky transitions or prompting him to reach important milestones that research says are critical features of socioemotional learning. When the child is struggling to settle down for a nap, for example, he can squeeze the doll's arm and hear a particularly soothing voice — his mother's — urging him to nod off. A simple voice recorder embedded in the toy allows the child's mother to record herself expressing encouraging commands: "Potty time, Aidan!" or "Would you like an apple or raisins for snack now?" or "Night-night, lambchop!" An important feature of the voice recorder is that the doll can convey the family's own particular language instead of the canned terms that LeapFrog producers might record. That is, one family might say "potty," while another might use "toilet." This kind of personalization is key, Beth emphasizes, because the research says that when toddlers are repeatedly exposed to terms with which they are familiar, their learning is enhanced. Her colleagues nod.

After a period of silence, a perplexed visitor raises a question: might it be unsettling for a toddler to hear his mother's disembodied voice channeled through the toy? Toddlers are famous for their phobias: could this set off fears that his mother has somehow embedded herself in the toy? What will he think when the voice doesn't answer him as his mother does, but in these prerecorded snippets? The eminent child psychoanalyst Donald W. Winnicott argued that a young child who becomes emotionally attached to a stuffed animal is projecting the feelings of love and security he feels with his mother onto this inanimate creature when she is not present. If that is the case, what are the psychological ramifications of channeling her voice through a toy? Beth looks at her boss uncomfortably. He twiddles his pencil. "Well," he says after a few moments, "I guess we have to say that we put the mother's voice in because the research said that babies' and toddlers' social interaction with the mother enhances learning."

Smart Toys

Over the past decade, the emphasis on offering learning experiences to babies and toddlers has created a dizzying array of industries, both cottage and well beyond. Today thousands of classes are offered for infants and toddlers, ranging from sign language to early music training to gymnastics, as well as classes that teach new mothers how to simply relax and do nothing with their infants. Parents often view these classes as prerequisites for getting into a good preschool, according to market research groups conducted by the Gymboree Corporation. Classes are often supplemented by videos or DVDs marketed as being developmentally appropriate for a toddler audience. In 2003 Amazon.com listed 140 videos or DVDs aimed at children aged two and younger; three years later, there were 750. According to the NPD Group, sales of toys billed as educational were up 50 percent in 2003 over 2002, the only toy category whose sales increased in a relatively slack market. Indeed, while overall toy sales have been flat or slightly declining in recent years, infant and toddler toy sales are seeing single-digit growth year after year.

To get a visceral sense of how the baby genius phenomenon has saturated the marketplace, you need only meander through the aisles of any baby superstore in the United States. Such is the demand for baby gear that even as massive toy-store chains like Toys "R" Us fold, baby-only emporiums such as Babies "R" Us and buybuy BABY flourish. There you'll find a huge selection of cognitively stimulating mobiles, developmentally appropriate rattles, vibrating bouncy seats, educational baby videos, and crib attachments that soothe with classical music — all with packaging that highlights the lessons or special advantages that each product claims. LeapFrog can take a great deal of credit for pushing the baby genius movement forward, and its history and corporate culture offer a window into the anatomy of that world.

LeapFrog's advertising tag line is "Learn Something New Every Day!" and it is admittedly religion within the corporate walls. At LeapFrog you hear the word "learning" invoked so often, by everyone from public relations assistants to high-ranking executives, that you wonder if the word means something more formal and monolithic here than it does elsewhere, the way "enlightenment" is used in a general way by most of us but has quite a specific meaning for practitioners of Buddhism or yoga. Founded by a former technology company executive, LeapFrog, launched in 1995, made its meteoric mark as one of the first companies to capitalize on crossing the educational toy market with the technology industry, producing what are often called "interactive toys" or "smart toys." In the most basic sense, these are playthings with low-cost electronic chips embedded underneath a layer of soft material or plastic. When the chip is activated, the toy gives an aural or visual response; this cause-and-effect dynamic represents interactivity. What this translates to in toyland is generally gizmos that beep, play electronic ditties, and flash colorful lights, usually with numbers or letters emblazoned on them.

Presenting early academic skill activities in an electronic toy has come to define LeapFrog's specific brand of learning. But it has also played a substantial role in transforming the definition of "learning" in the minds of consumers as well as the major toy producers. Today, when consumers are asked in surveys to describe an "educational" or "learning" toy, many mention an electronic gadget that displays a sequence of numbers or letters. Only a small segment of consumers prefers crafts or open-ended playthings, such as building blocks or dolls, to learning toys. According to analysts and marketers, LeapFrog's marketing efforts have convinced customers from all walks of life that an electronic device is not just *an* educational toy but *the* educational toy. Such toys attract a wide customer base — what marketers call "mass and class" — low-income buyers as well as well-educated upper-middle-class consumers. According to LeapFrog's own market research, and also focus groups conducted by Scholastic, LeapFrog products are especially popular with foreign-born Latina and Asian mothers for whom English is a second language, who believe that the toys will teach their children to speak English. These mothers are willing to pay a premium for Leap-Frog products, often forgoing other toys or educational materials, such as books.

LeapFrog's success, and its brand of "learning," has had monumental repercussions in the toy industry. Just seven years after it was founded, LeapFrog became the third-largest toy maker in the country, behind Mattel (number one) and Hasbro. LeapFrog's popularity forced the hands of Mattel's and Hasbro's early childhood divisions, Fisher-Price and Playskool, respectively. Largely because of LeapFrog's popularity, Fisher-Price and Playskool now offer toys for babies or toddlers that feature electronics and claim to offer some type of academic lesson. According to toy-business executives and analysts, buyers for the large retail stores have come to believe that infant and toddler toys claiming to teach early academic skills produce the most profit. Toy makers explain that when they show toys that don't promise to help a child learn, the buyers refuse to stock them. One high-level toy designer showed a group of major chain buyers a stuffed animal whose body parts — eyes, nose, and so on — were named on labels stitched into the fabric. The primary purpose of the toy was to help parents teach their babies the parts of the body. But, the designer said, the buyers balked: "They said, 'Mothers don't want to teach their children about their *bodies*. That's not *learning*. Mothers want their babies to know the alphabet. Put ABC on it, and we'll think about it.'" The company acquiesced, even though letters and numbers had no relation to the focus of the toy. It is sold today as a toy that promotes learning.

No "Learning" Toys

LeapFrog producers cringe at stories like this, even though they may ostensibly be good for business. The producers argue that slapping numbers and letters on a toy does not lead to learning. The company prides itself on the research behind each toy. Starting with the flagship product, the LeapPad, for which it is still best known, all LeapFrog's subsequent learning products — ranging from TurboTwist Handhelds for middle-schoolers to Leap's Phonics Railroad for toddlers — have been based to some degree on academic research. LeapFrog producers are passionate about research. They read stacks of educational journals and attend academic conferences. The company pays a number of professors in the field of education to consult on toy design. In fact, the LeapPad was inspired by a Stanford professor's research on preliteracy. While launching LeapFrog, the founder, Mike Wood, consulted with the reading specialist Robert Calfee (who has chaired LeapFrog's Educational Advisory Board since the company's founding) and learned that preliteracy skills depend on "phonetic awareness." That is, before children can learn how to read, they need to develop the specific understanding that words are composed of strings of smaller sounds. Supporting phonetic awareness is what adults versed in reading to children are doing, usually without thinking about it. As they read, they listen for the child to repeat a word she finds interesting; when she does, they enthusiastically repeat the word, too, and they sound it out slowly and clearly. For example, a child might point to a picture of a ladybug in a book and try to pronounce the word herself: "Yay-dee-buh!" In response, the adult might happily affirm: "Yes, that's *right!* That *is* a LAY-dee-bug! A *LAY*-dee-bug!"

With the LeapPad, Wood set out to replicate electronically that encouraging of phonetic awareness and, beyond that, to achieve electronically what every book-loving adult does when reading to young children: sound out words, ask questions about characters, repeat favorite sections over and over again. Physically, the LeapPad is a booklike hardware and software unit designed for four- to eight-year-olds. A plastic base houses a touch-sensitive web of electronics as well as a low-cost sound chip. The software component is not a disk containing a program but a series of interactive books made of specially coated paper, similar to the material used for shipping pouches. The books fit into the plastic base and the two components work in tandem. When a child uses the stylus tethered to the base and touches one of the pictures or icons in the book, she can have the book read to her or hear each word, as well as its phonemes, pronounced. A child can use the stylus to point to an assortment of icons to activate even more reading-related activities.

But replicating what has always been a fluid, enjoyable experience for adult readers and young listeners turned out to be a very complicated technological task and a major graphics design challenge. Where a parent or other caregiver would naturally follow a child's interest, asking her spontaneous questions about a particular appealing character, for example, the inert LeapPad can only simulate interactivity. To do this effectively, product designers had to presume that the child using it might be interested in *everything*, so they had to anticipate every question, or as many as possible. A great deal of stuff — icons, instructions, questions — had to be packed onto every page, with the result that a LeapPad "book" resembles a children's book only in that it has pages.

Engineering the maximum percentage of learning per square inch of toy became the mission of LeapFrog under Wood's leadership (he was ousted in 2004). All the effort that went into LeapPad's design also meant that it cost more than the average children's toy. The first LeapPad debuted as the Phonics Desk in 1995, with some success. But in 1999 it was relaunched as the LeapPad Learning System and became the industry's top-selling toy in December 2000 — the first for an educa-

tional toy in more than fifteen years. Today LeapPad's hardware component has a list price of fifty dollars, with LeapPad-compatible "books"
listing for fifteen dollars apiece. This makes the LeapPad one of the
most expensive mass-produced toys on the market, but that has not im-
peded sales. According to the company, 77 percent of U.S. households
with young children own a LeapPad.

Quickly, LeapFrog sought to reach even younger consumers. In 2001,
the company released My First LeapPad, which is shaped like a bus and
geared to three- to five-year-olds; in 2003, the LittleTouch LeapPad (list
price thirty-five dollars) debuted, aimed at babies and toddlers from six
to thirty-six months. LeapFrog's product line had always been geared to
the age range from prekindergarten — four-year-olds — to the tail end
of junior high school. But its forays into the baby and toddler toy category were so successful that LeapFrog officially launched its LeapFrog
Baby line in 2004 with great fanfare at the International Toy Fair, the
annual trade show held in New York City. By 2006 the lineup had
grown far beyond the LittleTouch LeapPad and plush interactive dolls
to include more than three dozen toys, including the Learning Piano,
which offers three "LeapStages" activity cards that trigger different musical and voice recordings (names of instruments and how they sound;
snippets of songs like "London Bridge"; and a counting song featuring
a cow, two pigs, three sheep, four cats, and five ducks); the Learn &
Groove Musical Table, which plays forty "learning songs" and introduces letters and numbers in English or Spanish; the Learn & Groove
Alphabet Drum, which, with each bang, displays letters from A to Z in
lights while a recorded voice identifies each one (again, in either English
or Spanish); and the Learn & Groove Counting Maracas, which count
from one to ten, name colors, and pronounce vocabulary words with
each shake.

The highlight for LeapFrog at the 2006 toy fair, where the product
was placed center stage in a mock living room complete with comfy
leather chairs and a large-screen TV, was Baby's Little Leaps Grow-
With-Me Learning System. The product includes a console base/DVD

player connected to a TV and a wireless controller with two sides: the baby side, recommended for infants from nine to twenty-four months, has oversized buttons; the toddler side, twenty-four months and up, features a joystick. Press materials explained that the infant or toddler affects what happens onscreen by "exposing" himself to "active learning experiences that change with every touch, slide and toggle." A brand manager explained that the product's goal was to "bathe the child in language." Like other LeapFrog products, the manager said, the Little Leaps system is "about giving Moms and Dads the tools they need to help children learn." Indeed, LeapFrog Baby's mission from the outset was to support parents in helping their babies and toddlers learn. It came from a key piece of market research, a product line manager explained: "We talked to moms, and they told us there were a lot of developmental toys for baby out there, but that there were no 'learning' toys."

STARTING POINTS

Ask a child developmental psychologist or an early childhood educator to discuss the distinction between a "developmental" and a "learning" toy for infants and toddlers, and you will be met with a puzzled look. In early child development, the commonly accepted understanding is that there is really no difference between development and learning for infants and toddlers: they are one and the same. While it may be possible to tease apart cognitive learning from socioemotional learning from physical learning starting with the late twos and three-year-olds — when toddlers begin to become more social and, therefore, developmentally capable of practicing empathy — it is not possible to separate these types before that age. A physical milestone, such as learning to walk, is inextricably linked with the socioemotional milestone of learning to separate from the mother or other regular caregiver; this independence is, in turn, inextricably linked with the cognitive milestone of learning to assign words or gestures to specific things or personal needs. Furthermore, "learning" takes place in a social context — that is, between a young child and a caregiver. It is specifically through this interaction that young children create what Lev Vygotsky — generally considered to be Piaget's counterpart in child development — called "mental tools." After a child has acquired these mental tools, she may apply them in a wide variety of situations. That is, an eight-year-old who has mastered fine motor skills, has the ability to think abstractly and understand symbols, and has a certain level of comfort with technology can use a computer effectively. A baby cannot.

The idea that there is a difference between "learning" and "development" may have taken root with the 1994 publication of a Carnegie Corporation report focusing on the care of infants and toddlers — children from zero to three years old. The report was called *Starting Points*, and, like other federally commissioned reports before it, this one underscored the need for high-quality child care and health care, as well as parent education and support for families with young children. But this report was different from its predecessors in that it highlighted neuroscience as a justification for providing federally funded services for babies and toddlers. The Carnegie task force maintained that between the ages of zero and three, neural synapses formed far more quickly than scientists had previously understood. The way the brain developed in the long run depended profoundly on a child's experience during these first critical years. Moreover, young children subjected to severe neglect would suffer irrevocable neural damage. At least, those conclusions could be surmised from the extant data. Actually, the report admitted, "researchers say that neurobiologists using brain scan technologies are on the verge of confirming these findings."

While it was accurate to say that a gust of synaptic connections are made in the baby brain, some in the field said that this was not news; such findings were at least a decade old at that point. Also, the report did not emphasize that the very young brain was doing the equally important work of pruning *back* the thicket of synaptic connections. Without this editing process, the brain would be continuously and in-

tolerably overwhelmed, unable to make meaningful connections or draw conclusions — in short, unable to make sense of the world.

The report briefly acknowledged that no neuroscientific research substantiated the suggestion that babies and toddlers raised in impoverished circumstances were doomed to long-term cognitive deficits. Nor was there any evidence proving that an "enriched" environment in early childhood led to increased social, emotional, and intellectual prowess later in life. Studies had shown that mice kept in a state of privation grew far fewer brain synapses than those raised in stimulating, nurturing environments. But the brain-scan technologies that the Carnegie task force referred as "on the verge of confirming these findings" could not be used on healthy infants. Positron emission tomography (PET), one of the brain-imaging technologies that allows scientists to observe neural activity in living subjects, requires the injection of radioactive substances that scientists are legally and ethically forbidden from administering to normal, healthy children. The other technique, functional magnetic resonance imaging (fMRI), requires absolute stillness. There were simply no data on normal, healthy infants or toddlers, nor were any parents likely to give permission for their children to be studied under such circumstances.

TOXIC OR NONTOXIC

The report did, however, impress two heavyweights: Rob Reiner and Hillary Clinton. The actor-writer-director launched the child advocacy group I Am Your Child (since renamed Parents' Action for Children) in 1997, a campaign to publicize what his promotional materials characterized as the latest "breakthroughs in brain research" in children from zero to three. Reiner's efforts were driven by the conviction that if America's parents and policymakers realized the importance and lifelong impact of neural activity in the first three years, the result could be a cultural transformation. As Reiner proclaimed in a 1998 address to the National Association of Counties: "Whether or not a child becomes a toxic or nontoxic member of society is largely determined by what happens to the child in terms of his experiences with his parents and primary caregivers in those first three years . . . justice begins in the high chair, not the electric chair."

What leading researchers studying the infant mind *had* been discovering since Piaget was that babies and toddlers are, in a sense, another species: fascinating and categorically different from adults. Instead of focusing on adults as the product of childhood development, the research suggested that offering babies and toddlers the most supportive care possible is the right thing to do because they are society's most vulnerable *people* (and, arguably, its most delightful). "Children aren't just valuable because they will turn into grownups but because they are thinking, feeling people themselves," wrote Alison Gopnik, Andrew Meltzoff, and Patricia Kuhl in *The Scientist in the Crib.* "Child abuse isn't evil because it may produce neurotic adults but because it abuses children."

Yet as Reiner clearly recognized, in the past American legislators and the public have been unconvinced by such idealistic sentiments. What did it matter what happened to children under three if they would never remember any of it as adults? What was the return on the investment? If neuroscience could prove that early childhood experiences had a measurable effect on the final product — the adult — then perhaps the public and Congress would understand that nurturing babies is good because it creates confident adults who can contribute productively to the workforce. Offering the very young high-quality, standards-based, government-supported daycare would be in society's best interests in the long run. Conversely, neglecting or abusing young children would create angry, violent adults who deplete the tax base and threaten the quality of life. When Reiner made a call to the Clinton White House in the mid-1990s, he found a more than willing collaborator in Hillary Rodham Clinton.

THE BRAIN CONFERENCE

Reiner's collaboration with the Clintons culminated in the White House Conference on Early Childhood Development and Learning, which convened in April 1997, to unprecedented press coverage and celebrity fanfare. In the months leading up to the event, *Time* ran a cover story entitled "How a Child's Brain Develops and What It Means for Childcare and Welfare Reform." *Newsweek* devoted an entire issue to "Your Child: From Birth to Three," with Reiner and White House staff members as editorial consultants and Johnson & Johnson as the exclusive corporate advertiser. The special edition sold about a million copies worldwide, setting a record for the magazine; indeed, the issue was so popular that it went through several printings. ABC aired the prime-time special *I Am Your Child*, directed by Reiner and starring Roseanne Barr, Mel Brooks, Billy Crystal, Tom Hanks, Charlton Heston, Rosie O'Donnell, and Robin Williams.

White House planners divided the conference into two parts, the first of which was devoted to "the new brain research." Only one neuroscientist spoke. Dr. Carla Shatz, a neurobiologist at Berkeley, summarized the existing research on infant brains, which was not new. She offered a Brain Wiring 101 talk, which covered much of the same ground as the Carnegie report by explaining that it was the brain's job to build and then prune synaptic connections during the first three years and that loving caregivers along with life itself seemed to do an excellent job of facilitating this process.

The only other scientist who spoke at the conference was the clinical psychologist Patricia Kuhl of the University of Washington, the leading specialist on how infants acquire language. Kuhl described babies as eager communicators who required no special "input" to learn language, other than the typical mutually enjoyable interchanges of baby and caregiver. Her research had shown, Kuhl said, that while infants are born with the remarkable capacity to discriminate all the sound contrasts used in any language of the world, they begin to tune in particularly to the phonemes of their native language or the languages spoken regularly at home or in daycare. When President Clinton urged her to designate "some minimum threshold vocal interplay" or provide some evidence that leaving the TV on didn't provide adequate verbal stimulation, Kuhl said that wasn't possible. Kuhl was pretty confident that a recorded voice would not enhance language development because babies are so sociable and because that's part of what helps them learn about language — to say nothing of love. Indeed, Kuhl's 2003 experiment proved that nine-month-old American infants who were spoken to in Mandarin Chinese by a native speaker for less than five hours in a laboratory setting were able to distinguish phonetic elements of that language. In a companion study, Kuhl showed that another group of American infants exposed to the same Mandarin material via DVD or audiotape showed no ability to distinguish phonetic units of that language.

Within weeks of Kuhl's comment at the 1997 conference, Aigner-Clark had launched Baby Einstein, complete with a soundtrack featuring disembodied voices speaking words in foreign languages. She told the press she had been inspired by Kuhl's research.

THE MOZART EFFECT

A few weeks later, a former choral instructor named Don Campbell popularized the Mozart Effect in a book of that title, which claimed that listening to classical music is a panacea. *The Mozart Effect* was based on a research paper published in 1993 by the British journal *Nature,* in which two professors at the University of California at Irvine reported that after listening to eight minutes and twenty-four seconds of Mozart's Sonata for Two Pianos in D Major, thirty-six college students scored eight to nine points higher on a set of spatial reasoning problems in the Stanford-Binet intelligence tests than students who had not listened to the sonata. The boost, which the researchers called the "Mozart Effect," lasted ten minutes. The same researchers published a follow-up study a year later reporting that the effect could be produced only by listening to Mozart, not other music (namely, works by Philip Glass or British technopop). To determine if music in general could offer more lasting results for spatial learning in young children, the UC Irvine researchers also studied a group of three-year-olds in a Los Angeles public preschool program. Of the thirty-three children, twenty-two received eight months of fairly rigorous music training, including daily group singing instruction, weekly private lessons on electronic keyboards, and daily keyboard practice and play.

The researchers reported that when tested on a spatial reasoning task — putting puzzles together — "the children's scores dramatically improved after they received music lessons." The preschoolers who had not received the training showed no change in their spatial test scores. From this study, the researchers theorized that spatial reasoning, like musical performance, "requires forming an ideal mental representation of something which is eventually realized." They said they had "shown that music education may be a valuable tool for the enhancement of preschool children's intellectual development."

The original Mozart Effect study seemed odd, and the results marginal and of dubious value. By 1999 follow-up experiments published in *Nature* and *Psychological Science* could not reproduce the findings, which the scientific community took to mean that the originally published Mozart Effect was an anomaly. No research had shown that the Mozart Effect applied to children, and the follow-up study suggested that music lessons, not just listening to music, was an engaging and complex activity that stimulated many cognitive functions. No research of any kind had been done on infants and toddlers.

But in the wake of the White House Conference and the national focus on zero- to three-year-olds, the promise of building better brains through classical music became a media virus. Don Campbell capitalized on the success of his book and the zero-to-three zeitgeist by starting a virtual publishing franchise, featuring CDs such as *The Mo-*

zart Effect— Music for Children, which was a fixture on *Billboard*'s Top Classical Albums chart for over six months, followed by the chart-busters *The Mozart Effect— Music for Babies* and *Love Chords— Music for the Pregnant Mother and Her Unborn Child,* featuring baroque compositions and a twenty-four-page companion book. Copycats followed. Delos Records mined the effect with *Baby Needs Mozart,* featuring flutists Eugenia Zukerman and Jean-Pierre Rampal, pianist Carol Rosenberger, and clarinetist David Shifrin, and a follow-up, *Baby Needs Baroque.* Mozart and other classical composers inspired entire lines of baby toys.

Perhaps nowhere was the Mozart Effect more potent than in Georgia. In 1998 governor Zell Miller asked the state legislature to approve funding for classical music CDs to be distributed to all parents leaving the hospital with their newborn babies. At the press conference to launch his "Build Your Baby's Brain Through the Power of Music" campaign, Miller, flanked by representatives of Sony Music Entertainment, announced: "No one doubts that listening to music, especially at a very early age, affects the spatial-temporal reasoning that underlies math, engineering, and chess." Soon Florida, Colorado, and other states followed suit.

THE BIG HURRY

The Clintons' brain conference and the Mozart Effect never would have taken root if they had not fallen on fertile soil. The relationship between young children, learning, and marketing in America was forged long before the 1990s. Piaget himself once famously complained after one of his lecture tours to the United States: "Why is it that when I come to America and give lectures on children's development and cognitive stages, there are always three of four people who get up in the audience and say, 'That's great, but how can we make kids do it sooner?' What's the big hurry?" The hurry may have started more than a hundred years ago.

In *Raising America: Experts, Parents, and a Century of Advice About Children*, a comprehensive history of child-rearing advice, Ann Hulbert cites the 1899 convening of the National Congress of Mothers in Washington, D.C., as marking the start of the "professionalizing" of child-rearing. For the first time, such topics as proper nutrition, appropriate stimulation, and general infant care were discussed in scientific papers rather than simply passed down at home from one generation to the next. Advisers in child-rearing were now nationally known pediatricians issuing dictums from lecterns, rather than grandmothers demonstrating burping techniques in the nursery. Science, not sentimentality, was to be mothers' new guiding principle. The experts at the conference made it clear that "the superior stage of the race" was at stake. In that era of Teddy Roosevelt's trademark "strenuosity," women were for the first time in history exhorted to take on the role of motherhood not just as an avocation but as a vocation, and the seeds for today's approach to motherhood were sown. Some practices of that new scientific motherhood bear a distinctive ancestral resemblance to those in contemporary America.

The expert advice presented at the 1899 meeting of mothers was well publicized, and articles on scientific motherhood and its methods became staples of women's magazines. Except for some tweaking to modernize the language, the headline in the April 1910 issue of *Cosmopolitan* magazine could easily have run as the lead feature in any parenting magazine of the past twenty years: "What Is to Become of Your Baby? Will children reared under the new, scientific methods be superior mentally and physically to those reared in the old-fashioned ways of our mothers?" Child developmental experts became important public figures, and toy companies began hiring developmental psychologists to approve the educational aptness of their products. Companies that hired experts may not have had children's best interests at heart so much as a return on their investment by capitalizing on the obsession with expert child-rearing research and advice. Experts, in turn, depended on good relations with the press to drive home their messages, and the press made them celebrities. The experts' theories on infant care became regular features in newspapers, parenting magazines (*Parents* was founded in 1926), and even educational films screened at department stores in tandem with product promotions.

The supply of, and demand for, expertise began to make a neat loop from expert to press to parent to product. As some pediatricians became celebrities, advertisers and marketers were quick to recognize that their endorsements would be invaluable. And these pediatricians realized that they could transmit their messages more effectively by endorsing a product than by preaching from a lectern. Arnold Gesell, director of the Yale Clinic of Child Development in the 1930s and '40s, may have been the first nationally known pediatrician to recognize the power of marketing. It was in part Gesell's willingness to promote his ideas in commercial forums that inspired many toy manufacturers to hire child psychologists to endorse their infant and toddler toys.

At the turn of the century, child experts had proclaimed that the way young children were treated had a demonstrable effect on their adult personalities, and thus the very future of humanity, and that following scientific methods of child-rearing was paramount in securing that future. The emergence of the Roosevelt era's "scientific motherhood" reflected the culture's break from the past and a clear-eyed march into modernity; ads directed at young mothers appealed to their own expertise by promoting products that might help them do the job conferred on them by the 1899 National Congress of Mothers. But by the mid-1940s, part of mothers' responsibility was to instill a sense of patriotic spirit and moral fiber in their young children. Ads now claimed that toys would enhance not only the intellect but civic duty as well. At the war's end — and the official start of the Baby Boom — the banner headline of a 1946 Playskool advertisement in *Parents' Magazine*, featuring a drawing of a baby happily fitting the final ring on a stacker toy, read: A CHILD AT PLAY TODAY . . . A RESPONSIBLE CITIZEN TOMORROW. The ad copy promoted Playskool toys' credentials: "Playskool educational toys are designed in co-operation with child psychologists. They direct the play instincts into channels that build muscular control, eye-hand coordination, color and shape perception."

These ads conferred expert status on the product itself. Instead of being touted for its ability to help a parent help her child, the toy could channel the experts all by itself. The cult of the child-rearing expert and the marketing industry were beginning to merge. The message running through articles on child-rearing was: leave it to the experts. And on facing pages were ads exerting an even more powerful commercial undertow: leave it to the expert-endorsed products.

SUPERBABY

Nobody took this advice more seriously than Baby Boomers, those Americans born between 1946 and 1964. In the 1970s and '80s, this group became parents, bringing to the experience an obsession not just with child-rearing expertise but also with academic research on infants. Research on babies and toddlers came into its own as an academic field in the 1980s. What would come to be known as the golden age of infant research in the United States came about in part because more women were working in academia, forcing universities to consider seriously the study of infant and child development. Moreover, technology had improved on Piaget's primary tools of pen, paper, and observation; video had become less expensive and made precise recording and analysis possible. Researchers in the 1980s were beginning to discover that infants were not only capable of constructing pictures of the world but were much more precocious from the very start than anyone had previously appreciated. Often comparing babies to phenomenally powerful computers, academics reported that infants were born with a nuanced capacity for interacting with parents and caregivers. The infants' specific responses were in fact part of an evolutionary strategy to help adults tailor teachings particularly for them. A baby was actually designed to teach his parents. The coo that his mother found so adorable was engineered to be adorable so that its message — "You are on the right track here" — would be understood. The new buzzword was "competent," used to describe the ingenious babies, whose parents, many studies found, often failed to engage them adequately.

In an era in which power-suited mothers were analyzed at every turn — from *Newsweek*'s 1980 cover story "The Superwoman Squeeze" to the 1987 Diane Keaton movie *Baby Boom* — working women were now struggling both to achieve competence in their careers and to be competent enough to stimulate their competent babies. The struggle became ever more public, as coverage of the academic findings on the infant brain became standard not just in women's and parenting magazines but also in *Time, Newsweek,* and the *New York Times.* Superwoman was, it seemed, no match for her offspring, dubbed by the press "superbaby."

The rate at which scientific findings about infant learning made their way from academic journals to mainstream press reports to product cycles was more compressed than ever. The findings themselves were also becoming ever more compressed. Academics, though pleased in many ways to share their work widely through a newspaper or newsweekly, were disturbed by how much of the nuance in their research was lost in the process.

The problem that worried experts most was age compression, or what would ultimately become known as Kids Getting Older Younger. The term "superbaby" *should* have conveyed that infants are a lot more alert and aware than previously thought. What the popular press conveyed, however, was that superbaby was a miniature 1980s superwoman, a baby yuppie ready to embark on a course of bourgeois self-improvement and achievement — not when she graduated from Harvard but right now. The 1980s saw the marketing of infant flash cards, designed to drill little geniuses on their ABC's and 1-2-3's. Yuppie mothers had step aerobics classes; yuppie babies had Gymboree classes.

PRENATAL UNIVERSITY

Some of the most bizarre innovations in baby products emerged from 1980s academic research focusing on the origins of literacy. The established assumption had been that children are ready to start learning to read when they first receive formal instruction at about age six, usually from their first-grade teacher. That timetable made it almost impossible for teachers to diagnose and attend to reading-related learning disabilities at an early enough age. Because children were assumed to be blank reading slates before school age, teachers had no context to draw on when a child showed signs of reading difficulties in school. Did the trouble stem from developmental issues, or were there cultural barriers that could be addressed? In looking for answers to that question, academics discovered that reading skills began far earlier than first grade; in fact, the foundations of literacy clearly began in infancy. The research revealed that children who were "bathed" in language from the start — spoken to, read to, encouraged to tell their own stories and share their thoughts — were far more likely to be able to read by school age than those who weren't. In short order, academic terms such as "pre-reading skills," "emergent literacy," and "prerequisites to reading" were introduced into the popular lexicon via newsweeklies and parenting magazines devoted to keeping anxious Boomers abreast of the latest baby research.

An outfit based in Hayward, California, that called itself Prenatal University was among the first to capitalize on the burgeoning compulsion to raise literate children. Founded in 1979 by an obstetrician-gynecologist named F. Rene Van de Carr, the course taught expectant parents how to channel a fetus's attention, help her build a useful vocabulary, and learn lullabies. In the fifth month of pregnancy, for example, students were taught how to engage in the "Kick Game," an activity requiring parents to massage the area of the mother's belly where the fetus had kicked, wait for a response, and then massage again to set up a sort of in utero Morse communication. After two months of this conditioning, the curriculum expanded to teaching the fetus Dr. Van de Carr's "primary-word list," which included words such as "pat," "rub," "squeeze," "shake," "stroke," and "tap." Parents were instructed to use a rolled-up newspaper as a megaphone to direct their voices at the fetus while conveying the associated actions via her pregnant tummy at least twice a day. Three or four weeks before birth, the fetus's curriculum was further enriched with a "secondary-word list," since, according to the Prenatal University's president, the fetus was now ready to learn words she "might need to know in the first few months after birth," including "tongue," "powder," "burp," "yawn," "ice cream," and "throw up." As extra credit, really ambitious parents could teach Infantspeak, ten words Van de Carr deemed critical for early talking: "dada," "mama," and "bye-bye," as well as "din din" (for food other than milk) and "poo poo" (for diaper change). At birth, the baby received her degree: "Baby Superior." At this point, explained Van de Carr in a newspaper interview, "the child is already a success, has already achieved, is already a winner . . . the parents' expectations have already been met." Now, he said, parents "can just relax and enjoy their baby."

Fetal conditioning was just the start for many 1980s superbabies. The importance of auditory stimulation in utero was further emphasized in the parenting book *How to Have a Smarter Baby*. Written by a professor of nursing and a lay writer, the book counseled expectant parents to play recordings of their own voices or soothing music, which, the book's jacket copy misleadingly claimed, would be part of "an easy 15-minute-a-day program that can raise your baby's IQ as much as 27 to 30 points . . . and increase his or her attention span by as much 10 to 45 minutes." Although the book's authors would later try to backpedal on that extraordinary — and, ultimately, specious — claim, the word was out. For truly time-squeezed superwomen unable to enroll in fetal classes, technology had a solution. Newspaper and television stories reported seeing pregnant women on the way to work with a Sony Walkman stretched across the belly, piping in recordings of Laurence Olivier reading sonnets. Gadgets such as the Pregaphone, which resembled an oversize stethoscope, claimed to be able to do that job better than a home-jiggered Walkman. Making its debut at the 1986 consumer trade show Babyfair — its third annual show of the latest in infant and toddler products — the Pregaphone was launched while Susan K. Golant, coauthor of *How to Have a Smarter Baby,* spoke on a Babyfair panel, emphasizing that the point of her book was not "creating superbabies . . . the point is having well-loved babies."

PLAYLAB

Companies that make educational or "learning" toys for very young children today still cleave to some of the corporate traditions of their predecessors. For example, in the 1940s Playskool and Fisher-Price put experts on the payroll and later built product-testing facilities where local children were invited to put prototype toys through their paces. The companies gave these facilities scientific-sounding names such as the Playskool Institute and Fisher-Price's PlayLab, and asked child development experts to assist in product research. It was a maneuver of marketing genius. These testing facilities acquired the patina of respected institutions, which lent the toys educational legitimacy and allowed the toy companies to take advantage of children's curiosity and parents' status seeking to conduct usability studies and market research for free. Today, instead of inviting experts with advanced degrees to visit the lab, companies hire them to run the labs full-time.

Kathleen Alfano, who holds a Ph.D. in elementary education, has headed Fisher-Price's PlayLab for more than twenty years. Her assistants are all certified in early childhood education. LeapFrog's lab staff is even more academically distinguished. It is headed by Jim Gray, who earned a Ph.D. in early childhood development from the Harvard

Graduate School of Education, where he was a protégé of Howard Gardner, the celebrated author of *Multiple Intelligences*. Gray manages two full-time assistants, one of whom holds a doctorate in developmental psychology; the other earned a degree from the Massachusetts Institute of Technology's renowned Media Lab, where cutting-edge robotics and learning technologies are researched. Both PlayLab and the Leap-Frog Lab are state-of-the-art facilities, equipped with one-way-mirrored observation rooms and professional video resources. PlayLab is set up as a preschool, with areas for imaginative play, outdoor activities, and snack. In western New York State, gaining admission to PlayLab has an elite aura comparable to that of enrolling in a private Manhattan preschool. Many parents reportedly sign up their babies at birth, and many of those parents are PlayLab graduates themselves; according to Alfano, PlayLab is now seeing its third generation of participants. The waiting time to become a child tester at PlayLab is often more than two years. To prepare families for their visit to the lab, Fisher-Price issues a professionally produced videotape detailing the experience in store for them. The children who participate in product research at PlayLab are not paid. Company spokespeople say that the excitement of being part of the development process is reward enough for the children and their families. Some PlayLab graduates are selected as unpaid models for photo shoots for Fisher-Price's toy packaging. "That's our way of giving back to our community," according to a public relations assistant.

The Leapfrog Lab generates a similarly exclusive atmosphere. With a database of thousands of families in the Bay Area who have volunteered their children, Gray estimates that roughly three thousand children pass through the LeapFrog Lab every year. As payment, they may receive a gift certificate or a toy, but, as at PlayLab, the chief reward is getting to come at all. Even the most enthusiastic participants are not invited to return, however. Once they grow savvy about answering marketers' and product designers' questions they are no longer considered "fresh blood": children whose perspective is untainted by the market research process. Gray surmises that LeapFrog Lab volunteers — or their parents

— may feel that the testing conveys on them some of the distinction of junior inventors or scientists.

LeapFrog Baby also cultivates an air of scientific inquiry, insisting that the toys developed by the Infant and Toddler Division be tied to academic research on very young children, which has boomed in the past decade. In the baby division, learning has more or less been codified by a special document, about which people speak with hushed pride. This document is known as the S&S, short for Scope and Sequence.

Scope and Sequence, a term borrowed from academia, refers to a curriculum plan in which educational objectives and skills are mapped out according to the stages at which they will be taught. At LeapFrog, however, the S&S is jokingly referred to as "the secret weapon": It is the basis on which the division's toys are designed. As such, the S&S is guarded with extreme care. Only producers who are given clearance to work on it can access the document on the company's computer network. Only one hard copy is permitted to circulate internally at any given time; additional printouts are strictly prohibited. When analysts or journalists meet with the Infant and Toddler Division to learn about how LeapFrog applies its distinctive brand of "learning" to toy design for this age group, the producers clutch the well-worn S&S and refer to it by opening the pages gingerly, cupping their hands to keep outsiders from stealing a glance. Producers say that the S&S is kept secret because it contains the key to LeapFrog's unique competitive advantage in the zero-to-three market. They explain that the S&S is the product of years of data compiled from books, academic journals, and parenting magazines on infant and toddler development, as well as discussions with experts, and thus is grounded in serious research. While competitors may incorporate a general learning lesson into their toys in order to market them effectively to mothers and retail buyers, LeapFrog is able, thanks to the S&S, to design toys that pinpoint specific areas of learning targeted to precise ages.

After assuring themselves that I am not spying for a competitor, the producers grant me a brief chance to examine the S&S. The document, which is constantly being updated is between fifty and one hundred pages in length. Essentially, it is an enormous chart with correspondingly enormous ambition: to catalog every developmental skill from birth to two years. One axis lists a specific age or range (such as six months or six to twelve months); the other axis itemizes the developmental skills associated with that age or range. For example, under the subheading "Memory," one finds the entry "cognitive mapping" — basically, the ability to remember where things are located — listed as a skill correlating with the age of six months. If these terms sound as though they were lifted from a textbook on early developmental psychology, it is because most of them were. Although most LeapFrog producers are not academics, there is nothing inappropriate about adopting academic terminology to identify developmental milestones to clarify specific phenomena and behavior.

But in many cases the terms used to categorize developmental milestones suggest that little children will be learning academic subjects. For example, according to LeapFrog's S&S, the twelve-month-old developmental milestones of shape recognition and perception of spatial relations fall under the heading "Geometry." Also, a single developmental milestone often appears under several headings. Shape recognition, for example, turns up under "Early Reading" as well as "Geometry." This semantic shift is striking. There is a substantial difference between using academic language for the sake of precision and using it to convey an academic objective. When asked about the rationale behind their choice of language, producers contend that the reasoning is not flawed in any fundamental way. Although it may not be literally accurate to characterize shape recognition as an example of the ability to formulate geometric proofs, they argue, it is legitimate to suggest that by mastering these developmental skills, infants and toddlers are building the foundation for grasping advanced mathematics later on. It seems odd, however, that after identifying developmental skills with such precise academic terms, producers would then shift to loose, bendy language in categorizing them. What's going on?

The "Learning" Line

Producers admit that one of the larger purposes of the S&S is to establish a curriculum for infants and toddlers, one that LeapFrog hopes might ultimately serve as a government-sanctioned standard. Since President Bush's No Child Left Behind Act of 2001, which compels public schools to comply with specified academic standards, even state pre-K programs have been obliged to conform to standards published by the states' departments of education. Teachers and heads of schools must painstakingly comb through book-length guidelines and cross-reference them with their teaching plans to make certain they are in compliance.

At the 2004 annual conference of the National Association for the Education of Young Children (NAEYC), in Anaheim, California, an entire track of speeches and seminars was devoted to complying with standards without sacrificing young children's developmental need for play. But even as such seminars were under way in the conference rooms, the main exhibit hall was lined with booths of companies marketing prepackaged preschool curricula, reflecting the big business that has bubbled up since passage of the No Child Left Behind Act. Now the standards-based trend is beginning to trickle down to even lower ages. Over the past few years, the daycare industry has begun to feel pressure to offer parents some assurance that their infants and toddlers will be prepared for preschool. LeapFrog spokespeople explain that this situation offers the company a strategic opportunity. Through its Schoolhouse Division, LeapFrog already sells LeapPads and other products to kindergartens and elementary schools. If LeapFrog can create and standardize a curriculum for babies and toddlers, the company will be in an excellent position to market products in large volume directly to daycare centers. LeapFrog already has a substantial foothold in the daycare business. Its parent company, Knowledge Learning Corporation — owned by the erstwhile junk-bond trader Michael Milken — completed mergers with the nation's two largest daycare chains, Children's World and KinderCare, in 2005. Today the company operates in thirty-eight states and the District of Columbia, with nearly 2,000 daycare centers, over 500 school partnership sites, and more than 120 corporate daycare centers.

The S&S also serves several other functions. Every time a new product goes into prototype, producers check off the skills it supports on the S&S grid. They consult the S&S during brainstorming to see what has been checked off and where the holes are; holes represent opportunities for new products. But before moving forward with a concept based on these holes, producers consult with LeapFrog's focus-group researchers to find out what mothers have been saying. In the world of the zero- to three-year-old, mom is the primary consumer, and today's mom is well aware that very young children are far from blank slates, that they are capable of learning a great deal.

However, today's mom is also wary of fast-tracking her little ones. For example, LeapFrog's market research department noted that many mothers wanted to start a comforting, nurturing bedtime reading routine with their infants and toddlers. Producers consulted the S&S, and the ensuing marriage of these two varieties of research resulted in the Touch and Tug Discovery Book, an electronic toy that straps on to the side of a crib and can also be detached and used as an "interactive book"; a recorded voice reads stories and, according to the enclosed pamphlet, "When playtime is over, the included soothing music and lullabies are an excellent way to calm baby as he drifts to sleep."

Mothers also told researchers that they wanted to introduce their children to music, which they knew was important developmentally. But any product linked with classical music — particularly Mozart — would make them feel that they were trying too hard to turn their babies into geniuses. It wouldn't make learning feel like fun. After consulting the S&S, producers came up with the Learn & Groove Activity Station, which features a rotating plastic disco ball and a toy version of a rap-era turntable — both artifacts of Mom's own early childhood, when the Bee Gees ruled on radio, and, later, of a Grandmaster Flash–era adolescence.

LeapFrog has learned that "learning" must feel like fun. The company identifies itself as a maker not of "educational" or "developmental" toys but of "learning" toys. While there is only a shade of semantic difference in that distinction, it is a significant difference in marketing terms. Producers and executives at LeapFrog, like their competitors, say that the term "educational" harkens back to the achievement-driven yuppie era of the 1980s, when a child's every moment was pegged to education as insurance for present and future success. Then children were treated as glum receptacles into which "education" was poured. The present generation of parents responds much more favorably to the term "learning," which suggests that the child brings her own active agency to the experience rather than having it foisted upon her. To this generation of mothers, "learning" connotes an enjoyable, nurturing, or natural experience unobtrusively infused with some underlying lesson.

Steering clear of the stigma of the '80s and early '90s parenting style — that of the Baby Boomers — is very important to LeapFrog. Today's mothers are put off by anything that overtly smacks of academic fast-tracking. So the S&S has yet another function: mapping the mind of the Generation-X mom. In that capacity the S&S may be one of the company's most valuable assets.

2

"There's a New Mom in Town"

A S DAVE SIEGEL, the president of WonderGroup, a marketing firm, steps onto the stage, the lights dim inside Ballroom A at the Disney Yacht Club Resort's conference center in Orlando. With the click of his laptop keypad, Siegel activates a PowerPoint presentation. On the giant screen to his left, a photograph appears: a grimacing, gun-slinging woman, a cowboy hat cocked back on her head. Underneath her picture is the legend THERE'S A NEW MOM IN TOWN. The room echoes with the whistling theme song of *The Good, the Bad and the Ugly*. The audience shudders with nervous laughter.

It is May 2004, and Siegel is giving the keynote talk at Kid Power Xchange, the country's foremost kids' marketing conference, which is held annually in Disney World's capital city. Every year hundreds of marketing executives from companies ranging from Benjamin Moore Paints to PepsiCo to Disney itself — as well as Strottman International, Logistix Kids, KidShop, the Geppetto Group, S.T.A.R.S. for Kidz, the Kaleidoscope Group, and Eventive Marketing — gather here to network with peers and potential clients and learn about new strategies for marketing to children. One of their perennial challenges is working with the mothers of those children — or "getting around the gatekeeper." Until recently, many marketers say they enjoyed an all but industry-wide field day with Baby Boomer moms. These mothers felt so guilty about being career-focused that they often did not have the emotional wherewithal to say no to their kids; as a result, marketing practices went largely unchecked. But the Boomers are now becoming grandparents, and as Siegel's presentation confirms, there is a new mom in town who categorically rejects the Boomer mom's MO. To illustrate this contrast, Siegel projects In and Out lists on the screen, to scattered groans from the floor. As he clicks through his slides, the following phrases materialize: "Super Mom" is Out and "Good Mom" is In; "Indulgence relieves guilt" is Out and "Happy and involved with family" is In; "Achievement" is Out and "Enrichment" is In. Meet the Generation-X mother, he says.

THE LEAST NURTURED GENERATION

Generation X comprises 48 million Americans, the oldest born in 1965 and the youngest in 1978 (some research firms put the end year at 1981). This group was famously characterized as "the 20-something generation" in a 1990 *Time* cover article:

> They have trouble making decisions. They would rather hike in the Himalayas than climb a corporate ladder. They have few heroes, no anthems, no style to call their own. They crave entertainment, but their attention span is as short as one zap of a TV dial. They hate yuppies, hippies and druggies. They postpone marriage because they dread divorce. They sneer at Range Rovers, Rolexes and red suspenders.

They also, by all accounts, still hate to be called Generation X. The name originated with the British punk-pop band that launched Billy Idol to 1980s MTV video stardom, but it was adopted as *the* slacker identifier after the publication of Douglas Coupland's 1991 novel, *Generation X: Tales for an Accelerated Culture*, which chronicled the wanderings of a group of "underemployed, overeducated, intensely private and unpredictable" twenty-somethings with "nowhere to direct their anger, no one to assuage their fears and no culture to replace their anomie."

The slacker generation has finally matured into bona fide adulthood (the oldest turned forty in 2005). In spite of having spent its youth reviling commercial culture, Gen-X has ripened into a desirable demographic for marketers. Today two-thirds of mothers with children under twelve are Gen-Xers (Boomers account for 26 percent), and their ascent into motherhood has paralleled the ascent of the zero-to-three market.

To understand the way a Gen-X mom thinks, marketers assemble a composite picture, based on articles, sociological studies, and survey and focus-group research. They also rely increasingly on ethnographic research, since many people with advanced degrees in anthropology are entering the field of marketing. First, marketers paint a portrait of childhood for that group, the first in which large numbers were raised in daycare. Forty percent were latchkey kids: those who were not in daycare brought house keys to school so they could open the doors to their empty homes while their parents were at work. And by 1980 one American child in six lived with a single parent — the mother in most cases. Some observers estimate that up to half of the families of Gen-X children divorced. The society in which Gen-X came of age didn't inspire much hope, for as the *Time* cover story said, it was filled with "racial strife, homelessness, AIDS, fractured families and federal deficits." As a 2004 study of generational differences concluded, "Generation X went through its all-important, formative years as one of the least parented, least nurtured generations in U.S. history."

HOME ALONE

The one activity that united Gen-X children was watching TV. According to a report issued by the Carnegie Council on Children titled *All Our Children: The American Family Under Pressure*, in 1980, by the time the average American teenager graduated from high school, she had spent more time watching TV than attending school or being with her parents. With mothers at work and children alone at home, the latchkey phenomenon did not go unexploited by marketers. Indeed, the 1980s marked the first time in American history that advertisers and marketers had unchaperoned access to children, an unprecedented opportunity to sell to young customers while they were alone. While the sponsors of the television shows that Baby Boomers had grown up watching — *The Howdy Doody Show, The Mickey Mouse Club* — had targeted children directly, they did so with the knowledge that parents were watching alongside their children, acting as gatekeepers. With no parents watching, however, there were no gatekeepers. Concern that advertisers might mine this vulnerability motivated children's rights groups to push the Federal Trade Commission (FTC) to investigate TV ads aimed at kids. In 1978 the FTC issued a report contending that commercials targeting children under the age of eight were intrinsically unethical, since children of that age were developmentally unable to discern the subtle differences between fact and fantasy. The report further asserted that babies and children were typically exposed to 20,000 commercials a year. The investigation and the report were quashed by lobbying efforts on behalf of the advertising industry.

By the 1980s toy companies began producing program-length commercials — called PLCs in the industry — by wrapping story lines around product marketing. PLCs became integral to the launch of mass-market toy lines. Programs such as *He-Man and Masters of the Universe* (Mattel), *G.I. Joe: A Real American Hero, Care Bears,* and *Strawberry Shortcake* were all created with the explicit purpose of selling the eponymous toys to children. By 1985 all of the top ten best-selling toys had their own television shows. By 1987 about 60 percent of all toys sold in the United States were based on licensed characters, a dramatic increase from about 10 percent in 1980.

The other major turning point in Gen-X's childhood was the release in 1977 of *Star Wars,* a movie that transformed toy boxes forever. Disney had always timed the promotion of licensed merchandise to coincide with its animated feature films; it had originated the practice in 1937 by licensing the cartoon stars of *Snow White and the Seven Dwarfs* to several toy companies months in advance of the release. But the success of the *Star Wars* action figures and toys blew away all previous licensing statistics. As movies alone, *Star Wars* and *The Empire Strikes Back* earned a phenomenal $870 million in box office sales by 1983 (the year *Return of the Jedi* was released). But that sum looked puny compared to what the merchandise pulled in: licensed *Star Wars* products had grossed $2 billion by then. These numbers were so staggering that they changed the toy business: in the post–*Star Wars* era, entertainment media drove toys' success.

As a result, Generation X's very sense of play became different from that of any generation before it.

SECURITY AND AFFECTION

In *Kids' Stuff: Toys and the Changing World of American Childhood,* the historian Gary Cross chronicles the story of American toys, material culture, and their impact on families during the twentieth century. He observes that beginning in Teddy Roosevelt's era, "scientific childhood" and toy advertising, commercials — and toys themselves — were aimed at both parents and children. Exploiting nostalgia was the advertisers' chief ploy. The toys were not all that different from those the parents had grown up with; the toy industry understood the draw for parents of revisiting their own youth through their children. From the start of the twentieth century, advertisers also played on children's, especially boys', longing to forge a relationship with their otherwise remote, authoritarian fathers. A 1918 advertisement for Lionel model trains was directed at boys, to be sure, but the real lure was that the toy would hook fathers into playing with them: "Take Dad into your partnership . . . Make him your pal." Even fad toys were historically pegged to a character in popular culture that children and their parents enjoyed as a family. In the

1930s, for example, movie characters such as Buck Rogers and stars like Shirley Temple became so popular that their licensed likenesses sparked massive toy crazes. But these toys were calculated to appeal to children and parents alike. To parents, these items either conformed to their idealized notions of children and childhood (Mickey Mouse and Shirley Temple, for example) or inspired excitement about the future, technological innovation, or American heroism (Buck Rogers and Roy Rogers).

But in the late 1970s and early 1980s, the convergence of the *Star Wars* licensing phenomenon, the rise of PLCs, and cultural shifts in work and family life — characterized by single working parents and latchkey children — marked the start of a permanent change in kids' marketing. For the first time, Cross notes, advertisers actively strove to separate parent and child, aiming to divide and conquer. To marketers it was the birth of the "nag factor." But in the broader social context, the chief point of connection between parents, children, and toys was no longer in playing together: it was in buying something.

The toys of the late 1970s and 1980s were the first to be completely foreign to parents. Rather than exploiting nostalgia as an advertising ploy, toy makers and marketers joined forces to sharpen the line sepa rating the world of working parents and the rapidly evolving youth culture brought about by latchkey children and the rise of TV as babysitter. The toys of this period — and the play they dictated — were tied to a consumer culture that was itself tied to television shows and movies that parents were too busy to watch. Many of these new toys were action figures that adults could not relate to. Many of the characters on which these figures were based were not even human. They were monsters or androids or alien life forms that were far removed from Eisenhower-era values such as courage or a better future through technology. These toys came with prepackaged characteristics, as defined by their role in the television show or movie from which they had emerged. Any American child of that era knew that a *Star Wars* Land Cruiser could not *fly;* it *hovered.* A parent who unwittingly broke these rules while trying to play with his child revealed himself to be a rube — not the partner that Lionel Trains had promised sixty years before as the ultimate reward for playing with its toy.

Toy makers, wanting to capitalize on the action-figure formula for girls, began to create little girls' characters that were intended as licensing properties from the start. A studio called Those Characters from Cleveland, part of the American Greetings card company, was the first to do this, with a character named Strawberry Shortcake. Her curly-headed, freckle-faced, old-fashioned cute look was in fact a product of sophisticated marketing. Strawberry Shortcake's diminutive appearance and rather superficial message of "friendship" appealed to overworked Boomer parents who, too overwhelmed to vet toys carefully, would gravitate on impulse to anything that seemed innocuous. But the Strawberry Shortcake character was designed to attract Gen-X girls, whose notoriously unstable upbringing made them feel vulnerable and insecure. Those Characters from Cleveland chose the strawberry theme after market surveys showed that little girls connected emotionally with strawberries and felt "security and affection" in relation to them.

Would Prefer to Stay at Home

Given the bleak portrait of their childhoods, one might expect Gen-X women to be numb and emotionally unavailable as mothers. In fact, the opposite is true. Because they did not have stability as children, marketers observe, stability means a great deal more to Gen-X mothers now that they have their own families. Indeed, as a group, they do appear to be more stable than their mothers were: 70 percent are married. But a Gen-X mother is not a true traditionalist. According to market research, getting married is not as important to her as providing a stable household for her children; if she doesn't meet the right person, she will either defer marriage or will choose to have children on her own. According to 2004 census data, the number of college-educated mothers who have never been married and have children under eighteen has tripled since 1990. Many of these women, sociologists say, have chosen single motherhood. Indeed, the national support group Single Mothers by Choice can point to Gen-X women's sensibilities as a factor contributing to the doubling of its membership in just three years; though the group is twenty-five years old, it grew from twelve chapters in 2002 to twenty-four nationwide by the end of 2005. The average age of the Single Mothers by Choice is thirty-five, and nearly all have completed college. About 52 percent of the mothers conceived a child by donor insemination, and approximately 25 percent adopted. About 20 percent became pregnant with a "known donor" or sex partner but are raising their children alone.

Marketers have also learned that Gen-X mothers' top priority is spending as much time as possible with their kids. The 2005 National Study of Employers, conducted by the Families and Work Institute, revealed striking shifts in work patterns that can be attributed to Gen-X parents' insistence on maintaining an acceptable balance between work and family. Small businesses, the study showed, are increasingly offering employees flexible hours, while large organizations provide benefits that have direct costs, such as retirement funds and on-site daycare programs. Small companies seem to believe that without flexible work hours, Gen-X mothers might simply quit, if they have the financial freedom to do so. "Of the 92% of employers that offered at least eight work-life initiatives, including flexible work schedules, family leave and child care, nearly half, 47%, reported they provide these initiatives to recruit and retain employees," said the study; 25 percent reported that they provide these choices to enhance productivity and commitment.

Gen-X mothers do not share with Baby Boomer mothers the imperative to drive hard on the career track. According to WonderGroup's survey research, 87 percent of Gen-X moms with kids of twelve and under said they would rather stay at home to raise their children than work at an office. If they can afford to, many do just that.

Stories of the "Old Days"

Gen-Xers are famous for their hard-won self-sufficiency. Some speculate that their resourcefulness and flexibility in adulthood result from a childhood in which adults were often scarce or frazzled. However, having grown up with shaky role models, Gen-X continues to nurture a guarded view of authority and a deep attachment to individuality (32 percent of Gen-X women have tattoos). Gen-X mothers are less likely to rely on their own mothers' parenting advice than previous generations have done. Take, for example, a typical Gen-X mother deciding which brand of baby food to buy for her first child, as outlined by marketers Maria T. Bailey and Bonnie W. Ulman in *Trillion-Dollar Moms: Marketing to a New Generation of Mothers*. "Not surprisingly, the Baby Boomer grandmother will tell her how things were when she was a child and what brands she used to feed her babies as a young mother," they write. "The Generation X mom will discount stories of the 'old days' in an attempt to forget her own unstable childhood and avoid recreating it for her child." The authors also observe, however, that the Gen-X mother generally regards her own mother as a peer — perhaps an outcome of being raised in a single-mother household — and will listen to her advice as she would to that of a friend.

Friends are extremely important to Gen-X mothers, perhaps even more important than their family of origin. Gen-X mothers depend on friends for everything from emotional support to shopping tips. Market researchers explain that as children, Gen-Xers were often compelled to rely more heavily on their peer groups than on parents for support, and they continue to do so as mothers. The rise of mother-and-baby play groups and online parenting communities such as BabyCenter.com and iVillage reflect the Gen-X mom's need to connect with other women going through the same life stage to compare notes, commiserate, and offer advice. It also explains at least part of the runaway success of Baby Einstein: Gen-X moms love Julie Aigner-Clark.

A MOM LIKE YOU

Each video or DVD in the Baby Einstein series ends with a segment in which Julie Aigner-Clark introduces herself as the series creator — and as a mom. Gen-X mothers, according to Disney's market research, watch this segment repeatedly. One reason seems to be that Aigner-Clark is exceptionally ordinary — but not in the conventional way. Nearly every demographic and psychographic group in the United States sees her as one of their own. She has a broadcaster's nonaccent, and, in the American transient tradition, she is from a middle-class everywhere. She grew up in Grosse Pointe, Michigan, was living in suburban Atlanta when she made the first Baby Einstein video, and now lives outside of Denver. Her demeanor and sensibility bridge major culture gaps. On the one hand, she is cheerful and unpretentious, projecting an image of a suburban heartland stay-at-home mom who always has cupcakes and neat crafts projects waiting for the neighborhood gang. On the other hand, she has the hyphenated last name, cultural values, and educational pedigree of an upper-class urban career mother who schedules play dates for her toddler at the Metropolitan Museum of Art. Born in the mid-1960s, she sits astride the cusp of the Baby Boom generation and Generation X. She appears to be Every-Mom.

Disney focus groups have revealed that Gen-X mothers see that in the final segment Aigner-Clark is talking to them as a mom herself. Mothers connect with her as if she were a friend. Thus they support her and promote her work to other friends. First-time mothers rave about Baby Einstein videos to other first-timers. The network of Baby Einstein devotees grew quickly, in part because of the rise of e-mail and the Web in the 1990s, but also because of the growing number of mother-and-baby groups flourishing at the time. The company was able to establish immediate credibility with mothers and, soon afterward, with parenting magazines, which conferred awards on the company during its first few years. Viral marketing through new moms was so powerful that until 2003 — when Disney had owned the company for two years — there was no formal advertising for Baby Einstein products. None was needed. All promotion was by word of mouth, from one mother to the next.

Moms' viral marketing is still the keystone of Disney's promotional plan. The Baby Einstein Web site highlights a section called Family to Family, in which parents (mostly mothers) can share their product experiences for others to read. They invoke the same themes today as they did when the videos first hit the market. They rave about how much babies love it ("We started playing *Baby Mozart* and *Baby Bach* videos when our daughter was 5 weeks old . . . As soon as that Disney logo and jingle starts and the Baby Einstein caterpillar appears, she is hooked!"). Mothers appreciate being able to have a few moments to themselves, and they believe that the baby is learning something in the process ("My 9 month old has loved the videos and DVD's since he was 2 months old. Not only have they bought me precious minutes (and hours) of time to do things like 'take a shower,' BUT ALSO I have actually seen his recognition skills develop," swears another mother). Many of the mothers thank Aigner-Clark personally, addressing her warmly by her first name, as if she were a member of their mothers' group.

Gen-X mothers are also inspired by Aigner-Clark's ability to balance family with work. They like that she made the first video herself and that her business was inspired by wanting to spend as much time with her baby as possible rather than by the ambition to launch a multimillion-dollar company that would become a profitable division of Disney. Aigner-Clark is the archetypically resourceful, self-reliant Gen-X adult. To shoot the first video, she and her husband borrowed a friend's video camera and set up an improvised production studio in the basement of their home in Alpharetta, Georgia. Between learning how to use a computer-based video-editing program and raising their toddler, it took the couple about a year to complete the inaugural video. When they were finished, Aigner-Clark began distributing the tape at local mothers' groups. Moms loved it immediately. Within about a year she had sold 40,000 *Baby Einstein* videotapes. The next title, *Baby Mozart,* came out the following year and sold 60,000 copies within eight months. After being in business a little more than a year, the Baby Einstein Company posted more than $1 million in gross sales; by 1999, Aigner-Clark had sold her one millionth video and had rung up $4.5 million.

What started with a single video advertised by word of mouth and distributed to local mommy-and-me groups is now a major division at Disney, featuring sixteen videos, fifty books, sets of flash cards for infants (marketed as Discovery Cards), puppets, mobiles, bouncy seats, shape sorters, stackers, teething rings, and other products emblazoned with the video's signature animal-puppet characters. But Disney has tried to downplay its ownership of Baby Einstein, because mothers' loyalty to the brand is dependent on the illusion that they are connected to Aigner-Clark through a grass-roots network.

Gen-X mothers also like Aigner-Clark's statement that she was motivated by a desire to share her passion for art and literature with her daughter, not to make her a genius. They like her humility. In interviews and talks, Aigner-Clark appears as astonished by her success as someone who has won the lottery. In a down-to-earth tone — and a voice that is naturally infant-soothing — Aigner-Clark told me the story of deciding to stay at home after the birth of her first child, Aspen, in 1994. A former English and art teacher, she wanted to expose her child to things she felt were of artistic value — classical music, seminal artworks, canonical poetry — but the schlep from the suburbs to museums in the city was not easy and, frankly, not much fun for mother or baby. Books were often a nuisance, since her daughter seemed more interested in chewing them than in appreciating their artistic qualities. Aigner-Clark recalls thinking, "Am I the only mom who wants to develop the love of humanities and fine arts in her children?" Probably not, she decided.

And she surely was not the only mom looking for a decent video for her baby to watch. The options for preschoolers were growing — *Elmo's World* videos were very popular by that point — but there seemed to be virtually nothing educational for babies or toddlers. Aigner-Clark had read in magazine articles that babies can absorb foreign languages before they are one year old. She wondered if she could produce what she thought of as a video board book, using artful shots of playthings that would capture babies' attention combined with words in different languages and classical music in the background. But, as she admits, she is no expert.

UNIQUE GIFTS

Experts occupy a precarious position in the heart and mind of the Gen-X mother. Since she does not consider her own mother an expert on child-rearing, she is likely to compare notes with friends. If she wants a more authoritative source, she tends to rely on books by noted pediatricians, such as T. Berry Brazelton, William and Martha Sears, Penelope Leach, and Richard Ferber. But unlike previous generations of mothers, who religiously followed the advice of the celebrity pediatrician of the day, the Gen-X mother may not adhere to any one orthodoxy if it doesn't suit her own assessment of her family's needs. Most Gen-X mothers practice some form of "attachment parenting," which advocates a high level of closeness and connection between parents and children. Although Baby Boomers tend to see this practice as impractical and even indulgent, Gen-X parents embrace it to varying degrees.

Market research suggests that Gen-X mothers would rather err on the side of being too close, too involved, too loving. They hold themselves accountable for providing a happy and, above all, *secure* home life. As the marketers Maria Bailey and Bonnie Ulman point out, "While Baby Boomer moms believed it took a village to raise a child, Gen-X moms believe it takes a family." It is not that they necessarily expect life to be perfect; their own childhood experiences in many ways compelled them to adopt a self-reliant and clear-eyed view of life. And they do not expect their children to be perfect.

Gen-X mom says she does not care if her child is a genius. She believes that her child has "unique gifts" that make him special. Above all, she wants him to have fun, to make friends, and to be happy. Companies that failed to take note of Gen-X mom's sensitivities suffered in the early years of this century. The neurotically named toy company Neurosmith went out of business in 2003, as did the toy-store chain Zany Brainy. To steer away from the Boomer "education" stigma, Fisher-Price phased out its Baby Smartronics line of infant toys and changed its tag line to "Laugh, Learn, Grow" to reflect Generation X's preference for emotional stability over intellectual prowess.

Interestingly, however, "learn" still has to be there in some form. Though the Gen-X mother may *say* she doesn't care how smart her children are, her spending patterns tell a different story. Many marketers have contended that although she views her concern as a rejection of the Boomer value of prizing achievement over support, she is still a product of that value herself. That is, Gen-X mothers are not just members of the first generation to have been raised in daycare. They are also the first to have come of age during the baby genius phenomenon. Gen-X moms say they don't like toys that are aggressively marketed as educational, but they buy them anyway.

One marketing study revealed that Gen-X moms will even lie about fast-tracking their babies. When new moms were asked if they regularly observed other mothers pushing their babies to learn academic skills at an age earlier than what is expected, more than 85 percent said they had, but only 33 percent admitted to doing so themselves. In marketing surveys, such a discrepancy usually indicates that interviewees are underreporting participation in activities they disapprove of. They don't want to be, or to see themselves as being, aggressive Boomers, fast-tracking their infants' education; they would prefer that educational products do the fast-tracking for them, albeit tacitly. Interestingly, this paradox has allowed companies to attract both Boomers *and* Generation X as customers. Market research shows that while the Gen-Xers are drawn in by the "learning is fun" line, Boomer grandparents are taken by the academic undertone. This is a coup, because grandparents are big spenders. According to the U.S. Bureau of Labor Statistics' Consumer Expenditure Survey, the fifty-five to sixty-four age group spends more per capita on toys than the twenty-five to forty-four age group.

BEFORE AND AFTER

Marketers have also learned to play on Gen-X parents' abiding childhood fear of being left alone — a fear they go out of their way to avoid re-creating in their own children. Fisher-Price learned this the hard way in the early 1990s, when the first Gen-X women were becoming mothers. Marketers knew very little about their behavior and, frankly, did not register the significance of this emerging demographic. They did, however, know a great deal about Boomer moms, and most marketing efforts were concentrated on developing relationships with that group. Recent research had revealed that new mothers and fathers often clashed over who would attend to the crying baby in the middle of the night. Boomer mothers had complained of a fundamental inequity in parenting responsibilities. They were under enormous pressure to compete with men in the workplace, and to have to endure the lash of sexism at home seemed intolerable. The friction was stressing their self-esteem, their marriages, and their quality of life. If a company offered a product that would help solve this problem, mothers said they would buy it — and if it had some educational value, all the better.

These findings inspired Fisher-Price to develop a musical electronic mobile that could be activated by remote control. The TV ad created for the launch of the mobile was designed to dramatize the conflict and, of course, to portray the mobile as the solution. The spot opened with a husband and wife in bed, asleep. Then a baby's wail is heard. The husband and wife awaken under a cloud of dark resentment and bicker groggily about who is going to attend to the baby. That marked the "Before" scenario. The "After" scenario returned to the same peacefully sleeping couple, but this time, when the baby wails, a hand reaches for the remote control and pushes a button. Without either parent having to rally to full consciousness, the mobile is activated, and the baby is shown cooing contentedly as a soothing lullaby calms her back to sleep. Husband and wife snuggle, blissfully dead to the world. Fisher-Price was pleased with the ad. The research was solid, the mobile was charming and practical, and the ad was funny and engaging. Before running it live, however, the marketing department presented it to a test market of new mothers.

The mothers did not like it — in fact, they couldn't stand it. They were offended that a mother would be portrayed as so unfeeling. What kind of self-centered princess would lie in bed dickering over domestic duties when her baby was in distress? Was a little sleep so important to this woman that she would endanger her child's sense of security? No, these mothers would not buy this electronic mobile. What could be more obnoxiously yuppie-ish than buying a gadget that would swap a mother's love for convenience?

Fisher-Price marketing executives were astonished. Had they misinterpreted the findings of the market research? Where were all those women who had said they wanted an easy way out of power struggles with their husbands at two o'clock in the morning? The researchers retraced their steps, conducted additional interviews, and updated their files. Ultimately, they realized that their target mother had disappeared. In the interval between the initial research and the final ad, a massive demographic shift had occurred. Fisher-Price was meeting the *new* target mother, a member of Generation X, for the first time.

The market researchers changed course. They talked with this new mother about her life, her approach to parenting, her hopes for her children. Although they were not able to uncover the degree of detail that a firm such as WonderGroup could in 2004 (largely because in the early 1990s the image of Gen-X mom hadn't solidified yet), they did see many of the same broad brush strokes. The Gen-X mom was certainly much more hands-on than her Boomer predecessor and also far less interested in pushing up against the glass ceiling. She was willing to ask her boss for reduced hours with reduced pay or even to drop out of the workforce entirely if she felt it was best for her child. She wanted to spend whatever downtime she had with her baby — even in the dead of the night.

But perhaps the most important marketing insight into the psyche of the Gen-X mother was that when she did have to be away from her child, *she wanted her presence felt.* This was an extraordinary finding, and it took the marketers some time to understand its nuances. They ultimately realized that this wasn't about mom tucking a snapshot of herself into her toddler's pocket before waving goodbye to him at the daycare center's drop-off area. She wanted her child to feel that she was there *no matter how briefly she was gone.* Whether she needed to take a shower, make a phone call, or even pay bills in the same room, the Gen-X mother needed to be assured that the toy, musical selection, or gadget she offered her baby would *feel to her child like an extension of herself.* A rather poignant psychological trend was emerging in this generation of new moms. Perhaps because of their own painful memories of latchkey childhoods, they felt separation anxiety from their children almost as acutely as their kids did from them. They could not tolerate the thought that their own children might feel abandoned. Even for a second.

Fisher-Price was left with the question, How can we use this information to get the Gen-X mom to buy the mobile? Whether she wanted to admit it or not, the marketers reasoned, she *did* need to take a shower, make a phone call, pay the bills. She needed to get *some* sleep. What she was looking for, they concluded, was a product that would let her off the hook without forcing her to confront her own ambivalence. They would have to convince her that their product *was* her surrogate. From a marketing standpoint, the message was based on pure irony. They went back to the advertising team with the new findings, and the team reconceived and reshot the commercial for the Slumber Time Soother.

This time mother and father were shown relaxing together in the kitchen over a cup of tea. Now, on hearing the baby cry, both parents willingly rise to go to him, but the mother says, Don't worry, she is happy to handle it. As we see her activate the remote control, the voice-over assures viewers that mother can be there for her baby without having to disturb him, giving her child the precious gift of learning how to "self-soothe," a baby-expert buzzword of the day. Fisher-Price even changed the packaging. Now the box showed a smiling mother standing in the doorway holding the remote control, while her baby gazed contentedly at the mobile — apparently feeling his mother's presence but not interrupted by it.

The marketing team then retested the commercial with a different focus group of Gen-X mothers. They loved it. They identified completely with the mother and the entire scenario. Not one of them pointed out that the mother did not personally comfort her baby but instead used an electronic device to distract him. On the contrary, they all approved of the mother's attentiveness and her demonstration of attachment to her baby. Marketers were also surprised that none of the Gen-X moms noted the irony inherent in the claim that a machine could help a baby "self-soothe," since the term refers to the baby's ability to soothe herself. Instead, the moms agreed that self-soothing was an important skill for babies to learn and that this mobile could play a gentle, supportive role in helping them master it. When Fisher-Price brought the mobile to market with the new advertisement and marketing campaign targeting Generation X, the product sold very well. At the time electronic, remote-control mobiles were rare; today they are extremely common.

TELEVISION IS GOD AND GUARDIAN

This experience taught Fisher-Price and many others in the industry that marketing infant and toddler products to the Gen-X mom requires playing to her blind spots. Marketers must deftly disguise her absence not as a chance for a break but as a learning opportunity for her young child. The evidence of this marketing strategy can be seen in any toy store or baby-gear emporium. Look at the photograph featured on the package of just about any infant or toddler toy. Chances are it depicts a smiling mother looking on as her baby happily investigates the features of the bouncy seat, exersaucer, or electronic "book" inside the box. This photograph has become an archetype in baby-toy packaging because it capitalizes on the Gen-X paradox. Go ahead, leave the baby alone for a moment, the photograph urges wordlessly; this toy is making learning fun for him, an experience you shouldn't interfere with. Furthermore, the picture suggests that the reason he looks so happy and secure is because this toy embodies the same hopes and values you have: he can *feel* you there, even if you're not right by his side when he plays with it.

This marketing tactic probably would not have worked on stressed, pragmatic Boomer mothers. But then, Boomers growing up did not have to depend on surrogates as constantly as Gen-Xers did. As babies in daycare, cleaving to their favorite stuffed animal or security blanket from home, Generation X attached to surrogates from the start. And as marketers point out, there was really only one consistent surrogate in Generation X's childhood: TV. And specifically, *Sesame Street*.

3

"It's Like Preschool on TV"

I N 1968 AN ICON OF Generation X's childhood was born. The Children's Television Workshop (CTW), a federally funded program folded into the Head Start initiative, was founded in March of that year, with $8 million in grant funds and a mandate to "create, broadcast, promote, and evaluate an experimental television series of 130 hour-long programs that would seek to advance the school readiness of 3- to 5-year-old children, with special emphasis on the needs of youngsters from low-income and minority backgrounds." The series was called *Sesame Street*.

Sesame Street's roots were embedded in the idealism of the late 1960s. The Head Start initiatives themselves were part of the sociopolitical aims of Lyndon Johnson's vision for the Great Society. Civil rights activists, along with child development researchers, were making the case that young children from underprivileged backgrounds were at a great disadvantage by the time they arrived at school. Through no fault of their own, advocates argued, children who had not been taught self-control at home were quickly labeled as behavioral problems and treated differently by teachers from children whose caregivers were able to devote more attention to thoughtful child-rearing. Since this disparity could have far-reaching consequences, supporters argued that the playing field had to be evened out as much as possible if the United States was to achieve socioeconomic and racial equality. Some believed that a television show like *Sesame Street* might help. The creators of the show thought that developmental psychologists could help them by applying the principles of early childhood, which were grounded in the theories of Jean Piaget and Lev Vygotsky.

A PARTICULAR KIND OF THINKER

By the 1960s Piaget's theories were gospel. In the 1930s Piaget had become the first researcher to base his theories on scientifically rigorous studies of babies and toddlers rather than on preconception, conjecture, or behaviorist experiments designed to produce certain outcomes. Famous for his relentlessly exact observations of his own infant children's every move, Piaget demonstrated that babies are not blank slates but rather assemble their own picture of the world by building on their immediate prior experience. Like scientists, they develop theories based on the available empirical evidence and are constantly testing those theories. Because they are constantly in a state of revelation, babies and toddlers view the world in very different ways from adults. In fact, when adults believe they are on the same page as their young child, they are very often not even in the same room. That sentence is a Piagetian case in point. An adult would grasp the metaphor without much thought. A two-year-old, however, might puzzle over the meaning of a sentence that seems to ask her to imagine herself and her mother standing on a page in a book and then being transported into two separate rooms. Babies, especially, and very young children are concrete thinkers. The classic separation anxiety that an eight-month-old baby feels when his primary caregiver leaves the room is rooted in the absolute certainty that she is really *gone*. It is only after years of experience and practice that people are able to comprehend symbols and abstractions, to build the connective tissue to join two apparently dissimilar things, to understand the difference between permanent and temporary.

Also central to Piaget's thinking was that the very young are not products of their culture. All babies, according to him, make their way through the same developmental milestones in the same order. One could travel the globe and observe a four-month-old in Moscow busy with the work of sucking her toes, just the way an infant of the same age in Muncie is. The evidence to support Piaget's view is persuasive. The archaeological record shows that toys for infants have been fairly uniform throughout history and across cultures. For example, hand-held rattles and teething toys seem to have been used by ancient Mesopotamian babies as much as by infants in present-day Manhattan, indicating that babies have progressed through the same developmental milestones, in the same order, from time immemorial. In Piagetian terms, even though the culture around babies varies widely, the culture they themselves experience appears to be static.

Certainly, the Piagetian view of babies working to master one milestone after another appealed to goal-oriented Americans (hence his famous remark about Americans' "big hurry" to push their infants through developmental stages). Browse through any American parenting magazine or baby-rearing book, and you immediately see evidence of the Piagetian emphasis on milestones. Most such articles and books are organized by age increments and corresponding highlights in behavior and physical capabilities. From birth to three months, expect small periods of quiet alertness sandwiched in between long stretches of slumber; smiling may be observed by six weeks, laughing by twelve weeks. By six months, most babies are beginning to sit up unassisted; by eight months, most start to crawl. Between nine and fourteen months, most advance to toddlerhood by moving from "cruising" between armchair and coffee table to walking. And so on.

But not everyone agreed that the Piagetian portrait of infant development told the whole story. It seemed improbable that the quality of human interaction — as well as the larger culture — played no role in the way babies and toddlers learned about life. As historians and developmental psychologists have emphasized, Piaget's milestones were so neat, so clockwork — so Swiss. They have also pointed to the Marxist leanings of Piaget's foremost challenger, Lev Vygotsky. Younger but still a contemporary of Piaget, Vygotsky was a doctor and a Russian socialist; not surprisingly, he believed that learning was the product of culture. By the 1980s, Vygotsky's theories were considered to be as important as Piaget's, and complementary to them.

Vygotsky countered Piagetian, and American, beliefs in maintaining that *all* logical processes are rooted in cultural context. Children do not all learn to think, perceive, and communicate in the same way. The kind of learner each one becomes depends on the nature of his social interactions with parents, family members, caregivers, teachers, and other children. Vygotsky further argued that only in a social context do young children develop what he called "mental tools," the thought processes that allow them to master their physical, cognitive, and emotional behaviors. When a child learns how to do something, she is creating that knowledge with another person in a way that is specific to their interaction at that moment. Only by repeatedly practicing the application of that knowledge with another person can a young child begin to develop her own mental tools, which she can then use when she encounters a similar situation later. Vygotsky called this process "scaffolding," comparing an adult caregiver's support of the child's learning with the scaffolding that supports a building during construction.

Vygotsky theorized that in any learning environment some of the child's peers are slightly ahead, or the child may be cognitively out of his depth, and he is thus continually motivated to use his mental tools to learn more. He called this state the "zone of proximal development." But if the adult pushes the child too strenuously, he will shut down or will appear to have learned a lesson when he is simply parroting back what he has heard, without truly understanding the content. Vygotsky believed that relationships between children and the people around them are shaped by the larger culture and its values. While generalizations are invariably sloppy, one could paint a rough portrait of a Russian mother whose approach to child-rearing was distinct from that of, say, an Italian mother. Naturally, the more one telescopes in — through region, socioeconomic status, ethnic background, family structure, and so forth — the more nuanced the cultural portrait becomes. In this way, the culture in which a child lives, from the societal level down to the interpersonal, is tremendously influential in the development of her mental tools.

97 PERCENT OF AMERICAN HOUSEHOLDS

The influence of both Piaget and Vygotsky increased in the mid- to late 1960s for several reasons, the first being that more academics were studying early childhood development. Also, these theorists fit with the social thinking of the day. As Piaget had shown, babies are wired to master certain milestones in a certain order, but if that progress is not supported by a consistent caregiver, there can be developmental difficulties. And as Vygotsky argued, culture is a determining factor in the type of learner, communicator, and citizen a child will become. With these ideas in mind, the federal government allocated unprecedented funds for programs to support preschoolers' healthy development and for research into the behavioral and developmental patterns of children under six.

The creators of *Sesame Street* realized that the lives of most preschool children (then defined as three- to five-year-olds) were increasingly shaped by television. By 1968 research by Nielsen reported that 97 percent of American households had television sets. With the creation of the first nationwide public television network in 1969, *Sesame Street* was able to reach as many as 8 million of the country's 12 million preschoolers. CTW's mission statement was remarkable for a number of reasons, notably its adaptation of Vygotsky's argument that parents, teachers, caregivers, and others were the agents steering the social context in which young children learned. *Sesame Street*'s creators argued that if a young child was living in an at-risk home, the people surrounding him might not be able to support his development, and television could stand in as a guiding social agent. Where Vygotsky stressed that the family is its own microculture and that its values and traditions tended to reflect those of the larger culture, *Sesame Street* was predicated on the frank acknowledgment that its characters might appear as regularly in its young viewers' lives as key family members would — and that American culture, whether we liked it or not, was more and more defined by television.

When the initial *Sesame Street* proposal suggested that the television series could help narrow the academic achievement gap between middle-class white children and low-income minority children, the responses from the press and academia were ecstatic. Although CTW staffers subsequently, and repeatedly, retracted that suggestion and admitted to its unfeasibility, it had become lodged in mass consciousness. From the start, CTW producers and researchers made clear that children would learn more if caregivers watched *Sesame Street* alongside them, asking questions and talking about the issues presented on the show; indeed, the main reason the characters were given so many clever lines was to hook adults into viewing. CTW never offered evidence or claimed that watching *Sesame Street* would offer a child a richer experience than direct contact with a loving, interested caregiver. While stating that the program could offer the child who had little to enrich her life measurably important lessons she might not receive otherwise, CTW never argued that it could offer anything extra to a child who already had such advantages. *Sesame Street* could not close the gap between the haves and the have-lesses. For years after the program's debut, however, academics continued to ask the production and research staff to prove that the show could bump at-risk children's performances up to the same levels as those of their middle-class peers.

The suggestion that preschool education could be outsourced to a television show was irresistibly compelling to many in academia and politics. As some observed at the time (including several of the show's founders), launching a television show — even one as well funded as *Sesame Street* — was far less costly for the government than funding more Head Start centers.

No Connection

Around this time, in the early 1970s, Daniel R. Anderson had recently received his Ph.D. in developmental psychology from Brown University and had landed a tenure-track job at the University of Massachusetts at Amherst. Anderson didn't think much of *Sesame Street*. Standing in opposition to the show's cheerleaders was also the school of thought that TV turned kids' brains to mush; Anderson agreed with that view. One day, however, a student in one of his child development courses asked why, if it was true that young children had short attention spans, so many of them were able to sit through an entire hour of *Sesame Street*. It was an excellent question. If as CTW contended, 1970s children, presumably reared on television, could tolerate only "commercial-length" segments of a few minutes or less, how could so many of them stay still through the entire sixty-minute program? Anderson had no idea.

He enlisted several graduate students to observe preschoolers as they watched *Sesame Street*. Anderson did not know specifically what they might find, but he had a few hunches. One was that the children weren't actually learning anything of measurable cognitive value from the show but were, rather, in a sort of spellbound state as their brains worked overtime to keep up with the show's quick-moving camera cuts. More specifically, Anderson speculated that while young children appeared to be "watching" television, their brains were actually jammed in the "orienting reflex." This neural function kicks in as the first response to unfamiliar sensory input, allowing the brain to make sense of it. When we hear a loud noise, for example, we automatically startle, and then our brains scurry to figure out where the noise came from, what made it, when we have heard a similar noise before, and whether it is associated with a condition requiring a fight-or-flight response. The whole sequence happens in an instant. It also happens quite a lot when we watch television, though we don't register it the way young children do, largely because our prior experience of television has provided the orientation we need to make sense of it. That is, *Sesame Street* may not seem to cut so quickly from camera shot to camera shot compared to *NYPD Blue*, for example, because most adults have many years of TV-watching, as well as life experience, under their belts. Fast changes in camera perspective — or cuts — do not seem jarring to adults because our brains have learned to fill in the blanks when the point of view on the screen shifts from one object, person, or scene to another. When adults see the cone-headed Bert walk through a doorway, followed by a shot of him in another room, our media-trained adult brains formulate the necessary connective tissue not supplied by the camera: Bert walked out of the first room into this new room.

But piecing together even this rudimentary sequence turns out to be a pretty sophisticated job, cognitively speaking. Brain scans of adults watching TV have shown that seventeen different neural areas are used; synapses connecting these areas are built over time. Young children, and even adults who have never watched TV, do not yet have such connections. To them, the two cuts may represent two completely different stories. After all, a camera cut does not have an analogue in real life. People do not zip instantly from one place to the next; they must take steps, literal and figurative, to get there. We live in reality, and our understanding of how a person gets from one place to another is inextricably linked to the literal experience of taking those steps. Over time, watching television and movies teaches us to read the visual shorthand taught by the creators of such entertainment, so that they (and we) won't have to laboriously track the characters' every movement. We have undergone this training not only as individuals but also as a culture. Watch a scene in a 1940s movie depicting a model plane trailing its flight pattern over a map to show us that the protagonists are traveling from New York to Cairo, and you get a glimpse at how far we as a culture have come in understanding symbols in media. But for very young children, this is not a cultural issue; it's a cognitive one. Until they reach the age of four or so, their brains are simply unable to make the mental jump with the cuts. They may grasp something, but not what adults do — and invariably not what the writer intended.

BROKEN SHOW

Anderson was considering these ideas as he began reviewing the results of his *Sesame Street* experiment. Instead of finding what he expected, that children between four and five years old were jammed in the orienting reflex, he discovered that their attention was focused and alert during segments that contained coherent, unbroken plot lines and narration. But they became disoriented and lost interest when transitions were too abrupt, dialogue became too complex, or plot lines bifurcated into subplots, as often happened on *Sesame Street*. It was clearly a testament to the show's ingenious puppeteers, and to the charming Muppets themselves, that young children stayed to watch the show at all, since according to Anderson's evidence, much of it was far too jarring and disjointed for them to grasp. He wondered if very young children would better understand content in the form of single stories embedded in longer segments or, to use the industry term, a "single-premise" show. What if all they wanted was one easy-to-follow story with very few cuts?

To find out, Anderson scrambled *Sesame Street* segments to make the sequence incomprehensible, at least by adult standards. Observing young children's reaction would tell him for certain whether they were able to grasp longer, uncut narratives or whether the narrative was inconsequential and they were watching because they were riveted by the characters. The answer was clear right away: preschoolers understood stories. When the scrambled segments appeared, they rebelled immediately. Some knocked on the TV screen, as if jiggling it would somehow take care of the problem. Some hollered to their mothers to fix the "broken" show. Not only was the premise of *Sesame Street* — that kids had a TV-ad-length attention span — apparently wrong for preschoolers, but the act of watching television was not nearly as passive as had been previously imagined.

THE COMPREHENSIBILITY EFFECT

Anderson then set about debunking another popular TV myth: that television was a "plug-in drug" (as Marie Winn's 1977 book of that title claimed). After extensive research, Anderson observed that preschoolers would, if invited via the show's script, respond to cartoon characters, puppets, and people on TV. Anderson then began to believe that TV was not an inherently passive medium, that the writers and producers made it so. As psychological research has long shown, most adults remember little or nothing of the first five years of their lives, though they may have a few vivid flashes from their early years. But adults do not remember how they constructed thoughts, tested theories, and felt: how the world really looked through preschool eyes. Therefore, Anderson believed, since even the best writers for kids' television could access their childhood imaginations only after the age of five, they were unwittingly promoting what marketers call "age compression," the imposition of older children's cognitive, emotional, and cultural issues onto younger ones. Because of age compression, little kids often feel compelled to mimic older ones' behavior without fully understanding what they are doing. To create a verifiably educational TV show for preschoolers, Anderson argued, writers had to work closely with research psychologists, because to rely on creative intuition alone would often be to get it wrong. Even an issue as seemingly straightforward as program scheduling could have a significant impact on comprehension. A program director who insists on a fresh, new episode every day is bringing an uninformed adult sensibility to her job that detracts from a show's educational value. Preschoolers, Anderson insisted, need repetition to strengthen thinking and problem-solving skills. A single episode should run every day for a full week.

Anderson's findings formed the basis for several academic articles that he wrote in the 1970s and 1980s, in which he termed the phenomenon identified by his research the "comprehensibility effect," by which he meant that very young children *could* learn from television shows, provided they were written to be comprehensible to their specific developmental stage. As it happened, a Columbia University graduate student named Angela Santomero read Anderson's articles just as she was thinking about how to develop a TV show that would actively engage young children. Santomero went on to work at Nickelodeon as the creator of *Blue's Clues,* and in 1993, remembering Anderson's work, she asked him to consult for the program. During the show's first two years, he reviewed every script for developmental appropriateness. *Blue's Clues* was the first single-premise, interactive television show for preschool children with a demonstrably educational curriculum. From the start, each episode ran for five consecutive days. The show's producers heavily publicized this schedule and educated parents about the concept behind it.

MULTIPLE INTELLIGENCES

Over the next several years, preschool TV took off, in part because of Anderson's work and insights. His research challenged academic beliefs about TV and child development and transformed the way programs are produced for preschool-age children. His studies documenting how children between the ages of three and five watch television formed the basis of what became major cultural institutions for many young American children: *Blue's Clues, Dora the Explorer,* and the Elmo-driven overhaul of *Sesame Street.* By adopting Anderson's approach to children's programming, Viacom — Nickelodeon's parent company — gained an excellent reputation for developing educational television for preschoolers, which it spun into a multibillion-dollar business.

Promoting its shows as educational became the core of Nickelodeon's brand identity. Noggin, its preschool "educational" cable channel, adopted the tag line "It's Like Preschool on TV." Public relations executives carried the message further. PR material for *Dora the Explorer*, for example, claimed that when Dora dances to her theme song "We Did It!" she is modeling "bodily-kinesthetic intelligence." When she pulls out her map, she is demonstrating "spatial" skills. And when Dora asks kids for help building a bridge, she is establishing "interpersonal intelligence." Such argot was lifted directly from Howard Gardner's famous 1983 treatise on education, *Multiple Intelligences*. Gardner argues that children cannot be assessed on the basis of standardized test scores alone, since such exams can't evaluate many valid forms of intelligence, including artistic and athletic ability. Gardner himself, who had not seen *Dora* at the time Nickelodeon issued this press release, was leery of the claims.

But marketing television as educational for preschoolers had become big business, and all the major companies were working this pitch. Viacom and Disney knew that many parents were wary of having their young children watch anything except PBS, whose image is inextricably linked with the idea of educational value. That's why Nickelodeon stressed the multiple-intelligence line. Similarly Disney, in launching its preschool channel Playhouse Disney, claimed that programs were based on a "whole-child curriculum" promoting emotional, social, and cognitive development. "Playhouse Disney's programs teach preschoolers a variety of skills that will help them become well-rounded," according to the network's Web site. The site went on to enumerate these abilities: "Social Skills: Understanding feelings and emotions, and learning to cooperate with others"; "Thinking Skills: Learning to work through and solve everyday problems"; "Early Academics: Learning to grasp concepts — such as shapes, numbers, language, and patterns — as well as facts about our world"; "Imagination and Self Expression: Creatively expressing ideas and emotions through art, dance, music, language, role-playing, and storytelling"; "Ethical Development: Learning to think about right and wrong, and the consequences of words and actions"; "Daily Living Skills: Learning the importance of safety, healthy eating and good hygiene"; and "Motor Skills: Developing coordination and control of movement, through activities associated with the skill sets above." The only way to receive the full benefit of this "whole-child curriculum" was to sit your preschooler down in front of Playhouse Disney for an entire programming block — several hours.

To verify such educational claims, television studios would either call on in-house research staff members, whose academic backgrounds were comparable to Anderson's, or contract with private firms whose principals had impressive academic pedigrees. Preschool television divisions, including Playhouse Disney, Nick Jr., and PBS Kids, hired such firms to conduct tests that the studios lacked the time or resources to carry out in-house.

ACTIVE PARTICIPATION

One such company is the Hypothesis Group. A market research and consulting firm with offices in New York and Los Angeles, Hypothesis has done work for all the major studios. Its New York office is headed by Iris Sroka, a striking and articulate woman in her fifties with a Ph.D. in developmental psychology; her dissertation explored children's representational thinking. A great deal of what distinguishes Hypothesis from its competitors in the field is Sroka's and her staff members' academic bona fides and years of work in the field. One holds a Ph.D. in educational psychology from UCLA (and a B.S. in human development from Cornell); another majored in psychology as an undergraduate at Stanford and has a Ph.D. in developmental psychology from the University of Michigan.

To conduct research on the educational value of a client's preschool

TV show, Sroka and her team usually observe one of the preschool programs in Jackson Heights, Queens, with which the company had established a working relationship. Jackson Heights offers perhaps the most
astonishingly diverse cultural, ethnic, and socioeconomic population in
the Northeast, if not in the country. There her team can observe and interview children from a range of households, from those headed by
single Puerto Rican women in their early twenties whose education
stopped in high school, to Chinese immigrants speaking little or no
English but pushing their children academically, to Caucasian parents
with Ph.D.s who had children relatively late in life. Sroka and her team
generally come to the preschool with a videotape of the show that
the client company wanted to test. In return for a small honorarium
(and with consent forms signed by parents), the preschool's director allows children to watch the show and then submit to the Hypothesis
team's questions and observation. One of the most important discover-
ies Sroka has made, she said in an interview at her Jackson Heights office, is that to get the most nuanced picture of what young children are
actually learning from a show, researchers must observe them very carefully and ask the right questions. If they are not careful, they may miss
something very important — something that may qualify as learning.

Sroka discovered the need for close observation early on in her work
for Playhouse Disney, which had asked Hypothesis to evaluate a preschool TV show intended to get children up and moving; in terms of
Playhouse Disney's "whole-child curriculum," the program would fit
under the rubric of "Motor Skills: Developing coordination and control
of movement, through activities." When Sroka and her team showed
the video to children at the preschool, however, no one moved. The kids
simply sat on the floor, eyes glued to the screen. As Sroka and her colleagues reviewed the videotapes of the children watching the show, they
felt discouraged. Considering the plain evidence of inertia, it would be
difficult, if not outright dishonest, to publicize this show as capable of
inspiring young children to engage in physical activity. Then Sroka noticed something interesting: one of the kids started moving his index

and middle fingers in a sort of Rockettes-style kicking pattern. They rewound the tape and looked at the movement again. Sure enough, says Sroka, the child was miniaturizing the kicking movements he had seen characters perform on the television show. He was mimicking the movements with his fingers. When Sroka reported these results to the client, Playhouse Disney producers were unimpressed; they had expected the children to be literally jumping up and down. But Sroka and her team argued that this transforming activity was very important, for it clearly showed that the children were internalizing what they saw. "We considered this active participation," said Sroka. The show, consequently, got credit for "developing coordination and control of movement, through activities."

A BABY'S POINT OF VIEW

By 1999 Anderson began to be concerned about the way TV and videos for very young children were being marketed. It wasn't the business aspect of educational TV for preschoolers that disturbed Anderson; business was not the professor's bailiwick. And at least the publicists at Noggin were promoting shows that he personally had approved as containing actual educational content — for three-and-a-half-, four-, and five-year-olds. But babies and toddlers were watching these shows, and nobody could legitimately claim that there was such a thing as educational television or videos for that age group. Even *Sesame Street* was never intended for children under three. Over its thirty-six-year history, research by CTW has shown that three- to five-year-olds can learn certain lessons via television, though their greatest successes have been in learning letters and numbers rather than — to researchers' and producers' disappointment — in working through the important and complex socioemotional issues it has always tried to present. But *Sesame Street* was never designed for babies or toddlers. There was no research on the effects of broadcast or cable television or videos on that age group.

By their own admission, all the top executives who oversaw the production of popular shows and videos for preschool children — including Brown Johnson at Nickelodeon, Lewis Bernstein at Sesame Workshop, and Nancy Kanter at Playhouse Disney — knew that infants and toddlers were watching their programs. Although these studios conducted extensive tests of the educational efficacy of each show with preschool children, they did not test toddlers and babies. Most said it was impractical. Since babies and toddlers can't verbalize clearly, and their attention spans are limited, it is too difficult to test them. Even the producers of *Baby Einstein* didn't conduct or commission tests to see what babies might be learning from their videos and DVDs. When asked, as late as 2004, what guiding principles its producers used to design developmentally appropriate TV for infants, a spokeswoman for Baby Einstein replied, "We're just really good at seeing the world from a baby's point of view."

Babies and toddlers were watching preschool shows in record numbers by the turn of the twenty-first century. Market research revealed that mothers of toddlers considered *Blue's Clues* an appropriate educational show for youngsters of eighteen months to two years, even though its intended viewer was a four-year-old, *maybe* an older three. The cognitive, socioemotional, and physical leap from eighteen months to four years is about as wide a chasm as exists in human development. (Recall that a fifteen-year-old girl has more in common, cognitively, with a fifty-five-year-old man than a toddler has with a four-year-old.) A toddler could not possibly experience preschool television the same way a four-year-old would. And by 1999 it wasn't just that babies and toddlers were watching preschool shows; so-called educational television and videos were being created specifically *for* infants and toddlers — or, at least, were being marketed that way.

What's So Sacrosanct about One-Year-Olds?

Teletubbies had a lot to do with this trend. The program's American debut, in April 1998, just six months after the White House brain conference, was controversial from the start; indeed, among people in early childhood care and education, the show had sparked incendiary debates months before it was broadcast. The show's producers promised in advance press interviews that each episode would work with the concepts of early childhood development and that even babies old enough to play peek-a-boo would get something of value from it. Kenn Viselman, president of the itsy bitsy Entertainment Company (now defunct), which initially secured the U.S. licensing rights, admitted that the show was entirely about entertainment. "But," he added, "when you're dealing with a child this young, anything is a learning experience for them."

Many experts in pediatrics and education contended that his statement was meaningless and was deliberately intended to confuse the public, that even child abuse could be said to be a "learning experience." The American Association of Pediatrics (AAP), in particular, was outraged. "The AAP is concerned about the language and developmental impact of television programming intended for children younger than age two," the group said in a news release. "The AAP strongly opposes programming that targets children younger than age two, which also may be designed to market products." Victor Strasburger, a professor of pediatrics and a member of AAP's communications committee, declared, "There is no excuse for targeting children under two. They should not be watching television, and to target them with a show is immoral."

Alice Cahn, the director of PBS Kids at the time, was undeterred. Just because this is a new medium for very young children, she argued, that doesn't mean it can't be used in appropriate, wholesome ways. The show encourages very young children to interact with the television screen in ways that are "very healthy," she maintained in an interview with *Current*, which reports on public TV and radio. Young children watching *Teletubbies* would not be "mesmerized" by television "washing over them." Cahn assured parents and the press that all the Teletubbies' activities — singing, dancing, naming objects they encountered

— were those that parents did with their own little ones. As for the concern that the show's characters modeled poor language, the series' cocreator was a trained speech therapist. To counter academic critics from Yale and the University of Massachusetts, Cahn called on Ellen Wartella, then the dean of the College of Communications at the University of Texas at Austin and one of the country's leading researchers on media and children, to make the point that the series was appropriate, even essential, fare for children growing up in a digital age. Wartella declared, "Television is a part of our children's lives just as other technology are [sic], and this is a program that's at least acknowledging that and trying to help children come to understand that technology from their perspective." (Five years later, however, as coauthor of the Kaiser Family Foundation's landmark census on the use of screened media among American children under the age of six, Wartella, along with her colleagues, expressed concern about the lack of research on the effects of screened media on very young children.) Cahn answered the critics of *Teletubbies* by saying, "What's so sacrosanct about one-year-olds? Whether we as a society like it or not, kids watch TV. We're lucky if they watch public TV."

It would be unfair to say that Cahn then simply sat back and watched as public opinion slowly turned in her favor. But it did turn. For all the Sturm und Drang surrounding its launch, *Teletubbies* became a fixture in American media culture. Like *Baby Einstein* before it, *Teletubbies* flattened another cultural barrier: the one that kept infants and toddlers from being deliberately planted in front of television. Through Cahn's efforts with the press and the glow cast by PBS's halo of enlightenment, Americans came to believe that there could be PBS-approved, educational TV for babies. That message stayed strong well after *Teletubbies* was canceled. Even parents who don't see the series as exactly educational probably believe that it is cognitively appropriate for babies and toddlers. A significant portion of the medical community agrees that the series moves at the right pace for children six months to three years old. Even a provocative 2004 study published in the medical journal *Pediatrics*, which found that television viewing by children aged one to three can lead to a constellation of attention-deficit problems by age seven, conceded that some of its conclusions might be flawed because shows such as *Teletubbies* did not exist when the data were collected, and thus the toddlers studied were not watching programs tailored to their developmental level. (The most serious charge levied at *Teletubbies* in recent years is that it is either simply dopey or its psychedelic features make it best enjoyed by adults under the influence of dope.)

No legitimate academic research ever showed that *Teletubbies* was developmentally sound for babies or toddlers. Indeed, it would have been virtually impossible to design such a television program because, while there was plenty of speculation, nothing substantial was known about the responses of children under two to TV.

THEY ONLY WATCH VIDEOS

Cahn was not solely responsible for spreading the idea that there was such a thing as educational TV for babies and toddlers. Anderson figured that some of the confusion about this issue could be traced to the marketing industry's exaggerated take on the White House brain conference and the so-called Mozart Effect. The baby genius zeitgeist had somehow made it acceptable, if not essential, to consider infants and toddlers as "preschoolers" — a term that prior to the 1990s had been used to describe four- and five-year-olds. In today's society Noggin's tag line, "It's Like Preschool on TV!" seemed to signify that the shows were designed for *any* child under kindergarten age. Part of that widespread misconception, Anderson believed, had to do with this generation of parents. As latchkey kids, Generation Xers had grown up with TV, so they were more comfortable letting their little children watch it, too. But what they were forgetting, or were simply not conscious of, was that they had probably not watched television as babies, though many had watched *Sesame Street* as four-year-olds (and a great deal of decidedly uneducational TV as they grew older). They didn't seem to grasp that point, however. During the early stages of the creation of *Blue's Clues,* Anderson confronted television writers who claimed to remember their childhoods perfectly, and he had to convince them they couldn't recall much before the age of five. When Gen-X parents said they had grown up on TV as kids, they were right, but what they weren't remembering accurately was that they were much older, developmentally speaking, than their babies and toddlers were now.

What also seemed odd to Anderson was that these parents seemed to make a distinction between videos and television. Showing infants and toddlers a supposedly educational video was somehow different from letting them watch an educational show on broadcast television. Parents seemed to make this distinction all the time, saying, for example, "Our children don't watch television — they only watch videos." Obviously, to an infant or toddler, the delivery mechanism is completely beside the point: a TV show, whether transmitted via a VCR, DVD player, satellite, or cable provider, is still a TV show. But parents had gotten the idea that a video for a baby was not just a form of TV but an educational tool.

A final, and damning, contribution to the misguided belief in educational TV or videos for babies and toddlers was, ironically, that no research had *disproved* it. This glaring lack pointed to what Anderson considered a longtime scandal: the dearth of public funding to study the effect of television on very young children. He had been grappling with this quandary his entire career. The Department of Education routinely rejected proposals for such studies because, it said, very young children should not watch TV; they should be playing or being read to. The National Institutes of Health had limited funds for such research, and it was often difficult to win grants from the National Science Foundation because the field was inherently multidisciplinary and was therefore viewed by many academic screeners as impure science. The scarcity of funding made it difficult to persuade young academics to go into research on media and young children, especially when they could make more money working for the television studios. Several of

Anderson's former students were now working as researchers at Sesame Workshop, Viacom, and Disney. Roughly half of his graduate students went on to work in the private sector instead of academia. From the studios' point of view, one advantage of hiring developmental psychologists as in-house researchers was to ensure a high level of educational programming. Another reason, however, was that by keeping the research in-house, corporations maintained ownership of the information; negative results would not be released to the public. Another way the studios could control test information was to hire cash-strapped graduate students to conduct studies independent of their academic work. The students were required to sign confidentiality forms; if they turned up any negative information, they would be legally bound to keep quiet about it.

Symbolic Functioning

One of the few significant publicly funded studies on how infants and toddlers process television was a 1997 study funded by the National Institute of Child Health and Human Development, which explored toddlers' perceptions of video representations versus reality. The chief researcher was a well-known psychology professor at the University of Virginia, Judy S. DeLoache. Her specialty is early cognitive development, especially infants' and toddlers' development of mastery of symbols and symbol systems used for communication. Over the course of her career, DeLoache has contended that to use and understand symbolic objects (including everything from picture books to dollhouses to TV), a person must perceive what she called its "dual representation." That is, one must acknowledge the object itself as well as what it stands for. DeLoache's work showed that grasping dual representation was an extremely complex task for infants and toddlers. While Piaget had theorized that very young children are concrete thinkers, DeLoache was able to demonstrate that this is the case through a number of experiments, often with surprising and intriguing results.

One experiment showed how difficult it is for toddlers to negotiate scale models. A group of two-and-a-half-year-olds watched an experimenter hide a small toy in a model of a room and were told that the experimenter would then hide a larger version of the toy in the "same place" in the room itself. When they were led into this room and asked to find the toy, the toddlers had no idea where to look. To the toddlers, the large toy was not simply a bigger version of the toy they had seen; it was a different animal entirely. In another experiment testing understanding of scale, the toddlers consistently tried to treat miniatures — replica objects — as if they were the larger counterparts. They tried to sit on tiny chairs and jam their feet into toy cars. In an experiment involving infants' perception of pictures, nine-month-olds continually tried to grasp pictures of objects printed in books as if they were real — as if, like Willy Wonka, they could pluck an actual blueberry from a page on which it was pictured. "Symbol-referent relations that seem simple and obvious to adults are neither simple nor obvious to young children, in large part because they focus too much on the object itself to the neglect of its relation to its referent," wrote DeLoache in a summary of her research.

In 1997 DeLoache tested toddlers' understanding of the relationship between action they watched on television versus live action. A group of two-year-olds watching a video monitor saw a researcher hide a toy in an adjoining room. The toddlers were then asked to go into the room and find the toy. Most of the toddlers could not do so — even when the adult modeled finding the toy on the videotape. However, when the same two-year-olds were led to believe that they were watching a live demonstration of the adult hiding the toy *through a window* (even though the "window" was actually a video monitor), the majority were able to find the toy. This showed researchers that the toddlers were able to learn from events easily through live demonstrations, or what they *believed* were live demonstrations, but not when they knowingly viewed the same event via a symbolic medium, such as television. DeLoache concluded that toddlers had an extremely difficult time translating what they saw on television into actual life in a meaningful way. She pointed out that mimicry — repetition of phrases from a program or recognition of characters — should not be mistaken for an "educational experience." It did not mean that the toddlers could apply what they had learned in another context — which is the most basic way of measuring learning.

DeLoache's research showed that symbolic thinking (which one must use to understand anything on television) is an extraordinarily complex cognitive process for toddlers. But her study did not look at any television show or video marketed as appropriate for infants or toddlers. And in Anderson's view, there was the rub.

CRITICAL NEED

In 1999 Anderson read an editorial in the journal *Pediatrics* that left him open-mouthed. The article announced the American Academy of Pediatrics' new position on children's media consumption: children under the age of two should not watch TV, period. "While certain television programs may be promoted to this age group," said the new policy, "research on early brain development shows that babies and toddlers have a critical need for direct interactions with parents and other significant care givers for healthy brain growth and the development of appropriate social, emotional, and cognitive skills."

To Anderson the AAP's announcement was galling. It wasn't just bad science; it wasn't science at all. On the one hand, the warning seemed premature and conservative, considering that very little research had been done on how infants and toddlers respond to television. Where was the evidence that TV-watching by children under two was so awful?

He was about to find out.

4

A Vast and Uncontrolled Experiment

IN 2003 ANDERSON and his students set up a series of experiments. To distinguish between baby shows or videos and all other TV shows they coined the terms "foreground" and "background" television. "Foreground television" was defined as any show or video intended to capture babies' and toddlers' attention, which would therefore occupy the foreground of a very young child's awareness. "Background television" was, essentially, everything else. Programming aimed at teenagers or adults that happened to be on in the young child's immediate environment (parents watching the evening news in the living room, for example) would be so far out of the child's cognitive reach that it would reside in the background of her conscious attention.

For the foreground test, Anderson and his students selected *Teletubbies*. From the time it debuted, Anderson was very curious about what infants and toddlers might be getting from the show. He conceded that its bouncy, Technicolor characters and cooing sun baby would undoubtedly catch the attention of infants and toddlers, but privately he was skeptical that the show could advance an underlying curriculum — that it was designed correctly for that age group to learn something developmentally appropriate. To test the comprehensibility effect on babies and toddlers, Anderson used techniques similar to the ones he had used with preschoolers in his early *Sesame Street* research. He presented three different versions of *Teletubbies* to separate groups of six-, twelve-, eighteen-, and twenty-four-month-olds. One version was the show itself, playing as it normally would. The second version was the show cut up and scrambled into random segments. The third version displayed the video portion of the show normally but played the soundtrack backward. As in his experiments in the 1980s with preschoolers' attention to *Sesame Street,* Anderson and his team were looking for three basic signs that the infants and toddlers were grasping and engaged with the program: overt interactions (naming characters, expressing joy or recognition); length of looks at the screen (the longer the look, the greater the comprehension); and heart rate.

They found, not surprisingly, that twenty-four-month-olds were distracted by both the scrambled shows and the linguistically incomprehensible ones; this age group clearly *knew* what was awry. The eighteen-month-olds didn't look as long at the jumbled versions, though they weren't as obviously distracted as the twenty-four-month-olds; it was as if they knew something wasn't right, but they weren't quite sure what or how to react. Both toddler groups, however, gleefully identified or pointed at their favorite characters — the baby in the sun, Po, Lala, and the others — regardless of whether the show was muddled or not. The six- and twelve-month-olds reacted very differently. They showed no signs of comprehension watching *any* version of the program. They did not understand it whether it was playing normally or was jumbled. But when the babies did appear to be attending to the program, Anderson and his team noted that, in Anderson's words, they were "essentially watching it the way they would any kaleidoscopic display." It seemed quite possible that the six- and twelve-month-olds were getting lassoed by the orienting reflex, the neural response to new, startling sensory information. This would mean that the babies' brains were scrambling to cope with the visual and audio bombardment.

There it was. The target audience was *not learning anything* that the producers of *Teletubbies* intended them to learn or claimed they could learn from it. So far as babies were concerned, the show was gibberish, no matter how you sliced it — literally. So what were toddlers learning? Anderson wasn't entirely sure. But if they were gleaning any meaning from the show, it was strong character recognition.

BACKGROUND TV

Anderson had been mulling over the effects of background television on very young children since April 19, 1993. That was his daughter Emma's first birthday and also, coincidentally, the day the FBI raided the Branch Davidian compound in Waco, Texas. While Emma puttered around the room, tinkering with her toys, Anderson turned on CNN and watched as fire ravaged the building complex, burning some eighty people to death. Emma would look up from time to time, but she didn't seem to be registering anything in particular. That Emma did not pay much focused attention to the news — or any other program not specifically produced for children — did not surprise Anderson. This kind of "background" television was clearly intended for older viewers and largely incomprehensible to young children. They were, nonetheless, subjected to it as their parents or older siblings watched shows during the day or simply left the TV on. But Anderson observed that the footage was clearly disrupting Emma's attention span as she played. When she looked up, her train of thought was interrupted. She would either forget whatever project she had been working on or, because Anderson was busy watching the news, be unable to get his attention for help in completing an activity. Anderson wanted to know what the nature of the disruption was and what effect it would have on Emma in the long run.

That inquiry eventually became the basis of an ongoing study. Funded by a three-year grant from the National Science Foundation, Anderson and his graduate students began studying whether background television had any impact on children between one and three years old. As a child development psychologist, Anderson had a few hypotheses. He knew that every major figure in the history of child development research — from Montessori to Piaget to Vygotsky — believed that play was the most important work of childhood, and that it was essential for toddlers, especially, to have the space to give play what is called "focused attention."

It turns out that everything about focused attention is important. Anyone who has watched a two-year-old play, for example, has listened to the running monologue she performs as she goes about her work, describing her actions and what she sees. This monologue is termed "private speech" by child developmental psychologists, and it is actually the precursor to the inner voice we use as adults, often unconsciously, to organize our thoughts, feelings, and behavior throughout the day. Similarly, most theories of child development consider toy play to be a necessary and valuable activity for young children. Indeed, Piaget maintained that safely experimenting with objects in the physical world allows a child to proceed from one developmental milestone to the next. Vygotsky argued that parents and caregivers are essential in enriching these forms of play, which help children master physical, cognitive, and emotional behaviors. Anderson theorized that background television would disrupt all of these processes.

In the study of background TV, Anderson and his team observed the toy play of twelve-, twenty-four-, and thirty-six-month-old children with and without a television program (*Jeopardy!*) playing in the background. When the TV was switched off, parents clearly interacted with their toddlers. In the best cases, they challenged or enriched play (asking a child having trouble stabilizing a block tower if she might want to fortify it with an additional block, for example) and allowed a child clearly on the verge of learning something new to figure it out on her own. To be sure, some parents were too eager to manage their children's experience and others failed to engage meaningfully, but overall, they were doing what he considered a good job. Anderson then conducted two tests with the television on. In one he invited parents to behave the way they normally would at home when the TV was on. In the other, parents were asked to limit their interactions with their children so that the team could observe the impact of background TV on toy play independent of the parent-child interaction.

The results from the first test were unambiguous. Interactions between parents and children substantially decreased — by 22 percent — in the presence of background television. Parents either tuned out their children's requests for help and "look at what I did" calls or offered them shallow, cursory attention. The results from the second test were similarly clear: background television diminished both the length of children's play episodes and their degree of focused attention during play. Ordinarily, a one-year-old will spend up to one minute playing with a toy he is interested in before moving on to another one. But Anderson found that when the TV was on, the amount of time dropped to about 25 seconds; for two- and three-year olds, attention span plummeted from about 80 seconds to 50 seconds. Television was breaking their focus, their ability to think clearly.

LEAST LIKELY TO LEARN

In the meantime, colleagues at other universities had begun to do related research on the effects of television on infants and toddlers. In 2003 a team of psychologists at Tufts University conducted an experiment in which one-year-old babies were placed in front of a TV screen. The conclusion, published in the journal *Child Development*, was that babies respond to — and identify with — nuances of emotion not thought possible and in very short periods of time. About as long, for example, as a TV commercial.

In 2004 Deborah L. Linebarger of the University of Pennsylvania published findings that correlated infants' and toddlers' language acquisition with the regular viewing of certain foreground television programs. She and her team followed a group of babies from the age of six months to thirty months, meeting with them, their caregivers, and their families every three months. They found that about 70 percent of the group began watching television before they turned twelve months old; 30 percent started watching after their first birthday. TV-watching seemed to take off most noticeably by the time the children turned eighteen months old; by thirty months, the toddlers were watching about 9.3 hours of foreground television per week. After controlling for family characteristics (including parents' education and income, number of siblings, parental involvement, and organization of the home environment) and the child's cognitive ability, Linebarger and her team began measuring language acquisition on the basis of two variables: vocabulary size (number of words used) and use of expressive language (frequency of single- and multiple-word utterances).

They found that watching *Sesame Street* was "negatively related" to expressive language use — that is, it decreased — and unrelated to vocabulary size. Watching *Teletubbies* was negatively related to both vocabulary size and expressive language use. Watching *Barney and Friends* was positively related to expressive language use and negatively related to vocabulary size. Watching *Dragon Tales* was positively related to expressive language use and unrelated to vocabulary size. The only unequivocally positive finding was that watching *Arthur and Friends, Clifford the Big Red Dog, Dora the Explorer,* and *Blue's Clues* was positively related to both vocabulary size and expressive language use. But there were problems with the findings: Linebarger and her team could not tell if watching these programs was what caused the increase in vocabulary size and more use of expressive language. They could not rule out the possibility that children whose general language skills were more advanced than their peers might prefer programming that supported their abilities; in other words, young children who were naturally more verbal might be inclined to watch programs with more sophisticated verbal qualities and a strong storybook-style narrative. Their research did not suggest that TV would do a better job of helping toddlers learn new words than an adult would.

Another study, titled "Can Television Help Toddlers Acquire New Words?" settled the issue. The study, conducted by University of Connecticut research psychologists specializing in early speech acquisition, showed that while older toddlers (twenty-two to twenty-four months) learned more words from TV shows than younger toddlers (fifteen to twenty months), the children with larger vocabularies learned words from television characters better than children with smaller vocabularies. But none of the children learned better from television; in fact, the study's authors concluded, "Toddlers do learn the meaning of new words best when taught by an adult caregiver, and they are *least likely to learn new words presented via television programs with animated characters."*

A VAST AND UNCONTROLLED EXPERIMENT

Another question Anderson wanted to resolve was how much TV very young children in America were watching. In late 2003 the Henry J. Kaiser Family Foundation released its large, startling study on young children's media habits, which all but put the matter to rest. According to the report, more than a quarter of American children under two had a television set in their room, and on a typical day, 59 percent of children six months to two years watched TV, and 42 percent watched a videotape or DVD. The median time they spent watching some form of media on the screen was slightly more than two hours. The TV was on in the home for an average of about six hours a day, and 40 percent of parents with young children reported that the TV was on "most" or "all" of the time. Furthermore, researchers estimated that about half of the exposure was to programs not made for young children. These statistics suggest that a large percentage of America's very young children are exposed to many hours of background television at home, not to mention in daycare. By 2005, babies and toddlers were watching far more foreground and background television than they had been when Anderson began his research. (In 2005 PBS launched the twenty-four-hour cable network Sprout, specifically aimed at toddlers.)

By the middle of 2004, Anderson was ready to submit his findings. For more than thirty years he had championed the remarkable educational possibilities of TV for preschoolers, but now he found himself on the other side of the fence. In a paper titled "Television and Very Young Children," published in *American Behavioral Scientist* in 2005, a compilation of his own research and an inventory of other relevant research on the subject, Anderson wrote:

> At the time of this writing, the AAP guideline, adopted without the guidance of almost any relevant research, appears to have been prescient. With the exception of [one finding], there is very little evidence that children under two learn anything useful from television. The evidence indicates that learning from television by very young children is poor and that exposure to television is associated with relatively poor outcomes.

His conclusion, unlike the AAP's carefully worded recommendation in their 1999 policy statement, was an unequivocal call to action: "As a society, we are engaged in a vast and uncontrolled experiment with our infants and toddlers, plunging them into home environments that are saturated with electronic media. We should try to understand what we are doing and what are the consequences."

DOUBLE EXPOSURE

Rachel Barr, an assistant professor of psychology at Georgetown University, is a diminutive, birdlike New Zealander with a firm and focused manner. Like Anderson, she does not smile or scoff easily, preferring to observe and record. In her mid-thirties, Barr does not have Anderson's years of experience, but she has long admired his work and shares many of the same clinical interests. At present, she is the only developmental psychologist at a major university studying the effects of television on babies and toddlers exclusively. Barr became interested in the field about the same time Anderson did — when the AAP issued its warning — and was motivated to pursue it by many of the same questions. But she was interested in studying much younger children. She knew that babies as young as six months old, and even younger, were being propped up in bouncy seats to view videos such as *Baby Einstein*. What she wanted to focus on primarily, however, was not what very young children might be learning from the most popular videos or TV shows but what they *could* learn from television programming produced in a way that they could understand. Barr wanted to find out if increasing the number of times that toddlers watched a simple game on television would enable them to replicate the game in real life. If they were able to do so, Barr believed, it would demonstrate that TV could teach something verifiable to very young kids.

In early 2003 Barr and her students produced a short, simple TV program in which a hand puppet removes a mitten from the puppeteer's other hand and then shakes a bell. On the first day, twelve-, fifteen-, eighteen-, and twenty-one-month-olds watched either a thirty-second live demonstration or a sixty-second video demo of the game. They showed the actual toys to the twelve-month-olds later the same day and showed them to the older toddlers the next day. If toddlers who saw the video demonstration could imitate the game as effectively as those who had seen the live demo, Barr could report that imitation from television was as effective as imitation from a live demo. The researchers found that fifteen-, eighteen-, and twenty-one-month-olds were able to imitate as well from video as from a live demonstration, but only after watching the video demonstration *twice as often* as the live one. For twelve-month-olds, however, the game seemed to be too difficult; babies in both the live and the video group just didn't get the hang of it. Barr and her team surmised that twelve-month-olds needed more time to learn the game. But even after watching the live demo six times, the babies still did poorly at imitating the game.

By the end of 2003, Barr and her team were able to recommend that television studios take their conclusions under advisement when developing programs for toddlers. "As producers develop children's educational programming, it is beneficial for them to know that repetition of actions and episodes may enhance learning," Barr wrote. "This may guide them as they aim to create programs that supplement learning inside and outside of the home."

Unfortunately, there were no shows or videos even remotely like the one Barr's team had created. Their show had demonstrated a single, extremely simple game, and for the youngest toddlers to learn anything from the demonstration, it had to be simplified even further. On top of that, specific conditions had to be met for toddlers to learn something concrete. While toddlers might learn how to complete a task after seeing a live demonstration six times, they would need to watch a video demonstration *twelve* times. Moreover, children would need to have the same materials used in the show in order to solidify what they had learned from it. Real TV programming wasn't like this at all. None of the Nick Jr., PBS Kids, Playhouse Disney, or Noggin shows conformed to any of these principles, and neither did any of the baby videos on the market. In fact, Barr noted that the most popular of these, the Baby Einstein videos, actually flew in the face of her findings. She had shown that the only way toddlers could verifiably learn something from TV was through repetition; indeed, developmental psychologists from Piaget on had explained that toddlers learn virtually everything through repetition. Videos in the Baby Einstein series represented a very different approach. Although some sequences might suggest a theme to adults, to very young children they would seem like an utterly random sequence of dazzling kinetic images.

BRIGHT, SHINY CHAOS

After watching any of the Baby Einstein videos for about ten minutes, most adults will notice one of the series' stylistic hallmarks: all the images that flash on the screen relate to a central theme. It is not always clear at first what this theme will be, but as one watches the progression of shots, it emerges — sometimes obviously, sometimes obliquely. Take the *Baby Newton* video, for example. The opening shot reveals a tableau of color-coded shapes — square, circle, rectangle, triangle, and oval — against a white background. Each shape proceeds to star in its own segment, with its own theme song. During its time in the spotlight, each cartoon shape superimposes itself on various objects that share its form (a door is the shape of a rectangle, a circle the shape of a ball). To the average adult, it's obvious that the theme of *Baby Newton* is shape recognition. But consider the *Baby Mozart* video. In one segment, the opening shot is of a gyroscope twirling on its axis; then it cuts to a chrome toy teeter-totter bobbing up and down, then suddenly to a colorful disco ball reflecting a mosaic of light in the darkness, then to a bubbling riot of red globules suspended in clear liquid. By now, the average adult might surmise that the theme is kinesis, although it could just be a random stringing together of hypnotically moving objects.

Very young children learn from concrete, simple repetition; *Baby Einstein* offers bright, shiny chaos. If this is an issue for toddlers, it is an even greater one for infants. Barr speculated that babies seemed riveted by these videos because they were sucked into a loop from which they couldn't escape. Every time they tried to process what they were seeing, to make sense of an object or action, the scene would shift to something different. She suspected that they were being continually stimulated and not necessarily assimilating anything — not good. But was there a chance that babies could learn something of value from these experiences? Barr suspected that they might, if parents watched along with them.

Earlier CTW research with four- and five-year-olds had shown that they learned much more when adults watched *Sesame Street* with them and asked questions about what was happening in the show, as they would when reading a book. What was happening, CTW researchers knew, was a classic example of Vygotskian scaffolding: the adults' questions helped the children organize their impressions and ground their understanding of what they were seeing. Barr wanted to know if babies and toddlers could learn something if parents helped them decode what they were watching. Of course, it would be impossible to tell precisely what the babies were learning because they can't talk. But by comparing the quality and quantity of their responses during active co-viewing sessions and sessions when babies watched on their own, Barr felt it would be possible to make an educated guess about the conditions necessary for babies to become actively and meaningfully engaged with TV programs or videos.

Barr and her team of students showed groups of six-, twelve-, fifteen-, and eighteen-month-olds either *Baby Mozart* or *Kids' Favorite Songs 2,* an Elmo sing-along from *Sesame Street.* Half of each group had seen the program beforehand, while the other half had not. Knowing that the parents would likely be on their best, most attentive behavior in front of them, the researchers asked parents to act as they normally would while their infant was watching a video. Barr and her team would thus see how babies responded under optimal conditions. As they videotaped the session, researchers observed how the infants attended to the video. How often were they looking and for how long? Did they point, smile, imitate, vocalize? They also recorded what the parents did and said, to see if that affected the infants' attention to and interaction with the video. The classifications of parental involvement were as follows: questions ("Who is that?" or "Is that Elmo?"); labels ("Those are seals"); descriptions ("The seals are going around and around"); attention-seeking statements ("Look at that!"); corrections or confirmations ("No, that's not Elmo, it's Zoe"); and singing along with the music.

By late April 2004 the researchers were able to report that infants paid more attention to the video if they had seen it before and that those watching the Elmo video also paid more attention to the familiar characters and songs than to the animated segments, which researchers surmised were confusing. These findings seemed consistent with those from Anderson's *Teletubbies* research, suggesting that the only verifiable learning that very young children get from repeated television viewing is recognition of characters or puppets that have become familiar. The researchers also found, however, that the more parents interacted with the videos — as if they were "reading" the program to their children — the more attention the babies paid, even if they had never seen the video before. Barr concluded that parents can help babies engage more actively with foreground television programming if they offer supportive scaffolding.

A COMPLETE STRANGER

A personal observation that did not make it into Barr's published findings was that many parents did *not* regularly view these videos with their babies. Although she had wanted to keep the report's focus positive by sharing the information that parental involvement made a huge difference, Barr learned that many parents were, as she had suspected, popping in the tape and leaving to take a shower or make a phone call. Many claimed they didn't want to interrupt their babies' attention, since it might spoil a learning opportunity. All the families that participated in the study, whether upper middle class and highly educated or working class with minimal education, reported feeling confident in leaving because they believed the videos were educational; many said that they had read about the research supporting their educational value. Such comments were something of a wonder. Parents had been told explicitly via letters, e-mails, and conversations that Barr and her team were enlisting the families' help in conducting the first studies on whether babies could learn from television and videos. These parents were then saying, with no apparent awareness of contradiction, that they had read the research. *There was no existing research.*

Barr was very intrigued by how much parents trusted these videos. Their confusion over the "research" she chalked up to cultural influences, including the brain conference and the Mozart Effect, as well as to very clever marketing, which *implied* that these videos contained secret baby genius formulas. But she was fascinated that these parents treated these videos as if they were familiar, trustworthy entities, often *before* they personally viewed the programs. When she asked parents how they usually introduced their babies to new people, places, or things, they reported that they made a concerted effort to talk the infants through each new experience so as not to overwhelm them. When giving her baby a new ball, the mother would say something along the lines of "Oh, a *ball!* A *red* ball! Look at the *ball!* Mama is rolling the ball to *you!* Catch the *ball!*" A similar scenario would unfold when a baby was introduced to a new person or someone she had not seen in some time. "Look, it's *Grandma!* Say hi to *Grandma,* sweetpea! *Grandma* has come all the way from Grand Rapids to see us! Can you give *Grandma* a kiss?" And indeed, this process of introduction that most parents engage in naturally — labeling, repetition, offering a feeling of security, as well as the interaction itself — helps babies make sense of the encounter and learn from it. In short, it is the kind of behavior the parents had modeled so nicely during Barr's study. But with videos, they felt comfortable simply leaving the room, even if the baby had never encountered anything on the video before. As far as Barr knew, it was the only situation in which ordinarily involved parents would leave their babies with a complete stranger. And this stranger was either utterly confusing the baby — or was a character on his way to becoming a peculiar sort of friend.

The connection a baby or toddler was forging with a television or video character whom she saw regularly had a fundamentally different quality from that of any other beloved creature in her life. For example, a toddler who delights in having a dog will seek out opportunities to play with him, point excitedly at pictures of dogs, and feel pride when she can finally say the word "dog" and recognize other dogs as "dogs." She has a personal connection to her own dog but also works to create a "dog" category.

In a similar way she would form a bond with the *Teletubbies* characters or any appealing "foreground" character — Elmo, Clifford the Big Red Dog, Dora — who had become familiar through repeated exposure.

But there were several major differences between the relationship with a real dog and one with a cartoon character. First, the context of a toddler's connection to the characters was unclear, in contrast to the family dog, which enjoys a clear role in her life. She can see how her parents and siblings treat the dog and how the dog responds to them and to her; these experiences help her develop her own way of relating to the dog. Since Anderson's research showed that toddlers did not understand the narrative context of *Teletubbies,* what was the nature of their relationship to the characters? As Anderson's findings pointed out, it was likely that toddlers simply recognized the characters, delighting in their engaging appearance and in their own ability to recognize these creatures.

But toddlers would also encounter these characters in a context outside of TV or videos — offscreen. And in the outside world there is a substantial difference between relating to the family dog and to a familiar TV character. Babies and toddlers learn about their own dog's place in the world by comparing it to the other dogs they encounter: her neighbor's dog is brown and small and barks a lot; her dog is black and shy. The big dog at the park likes to jump up high to catch a Frisbee; her dog prefers a tennis ball rolled along the ground. Grandma's dog eats wet food; hers eats dry kibble. In the real world there could be an infinite number of ways in which she would encounter live dogs or depictions of dogs. But the offscreen environment in which toddlers encounter beloved television or video characters is almost invariably a tightly controlled retail or commercial one: on juice boxes in the supermarket, in McDonald's Happy Meals, as plush dolls lining the shelves at Wal-Mart, on Band-Aids in the drugstore, on her diapers. In this case, her relationship to the beloved character would be a purely commercial one. He would be selling her something.

5

....

Elmo's World

ANN KEARNS HAS HEADED the licensing department at the Sesame Workshop for more than thirty years, nearly since its beginnings as the Children's Television Workshop. CTW launched the licensing department as a means of providing enough revenue to cover production costs as well as its other nonprofit outreach projects. The *Sesame Street* characters would be licensed only for use on consumer products that CTW considered educational, wholesome, or healthy. The executives were aware that fulfilling this mission would be a tall order. After all, the television show was no mere Saturday morning cartoon. Many in the academic community, government, and public at large had conferred on *Sesame Street* the status of a virtual preschool classroom and nationwide neighborhood. It wasn't crass commercial TV; it was publicly funded. Big Bird wasn't just a Muppet; he was a surrogate teacher and a loyal friend. By extension, the products on which Grover, Bert, or Ernie appeared would not be considered commercial schlock; they would be perceived as educational. They would have the appeal of seeming enjoyable to very little children and educational to their mothers. And by having the characters appear in a number of different places across a variety of media, *Sesame Street* would build brand equity for itself as well as its licensees. The brands associated with *Sesame Street* and the way customers viewed the *Sesame* brand all contributed to a cultural and emotional sense of what those characters meant in a larger context. They reflected light from the halo of fun and educational value back onto each other.

Kearns, an earnest but approachable woman, recalled over lunch at a restaurant close to Sesame Workshop's offices near Lincoln Center in New York City that in the early 1970s, CTW's licensing department generally granted licenses to companies selling products to children in the same age range as *Sesame Street*'s intended target audience: three- to five-year-olds. Some of the first licensees were Playtime Colorforms, for a vinyl sticker set; Fisher-Price, for a playhouse decorated to resemble Sesame Street itself (complete with Mr. Hooper's store and Oscar's trashcan); Little Golden Books; Warner Bros. Records (including *The Official Sesame Street 2 Book-and-Record Album,* starring the original cast and songs such as "Everyone Makes Mistakes," sung by Big Bird); and CBS Records. Within several years, however, Kearns's department began to receive more and more requests to license characters for infant and toddler products. She and her staff began to realize that in many cases, the products were not only drawing more viewers to the television show, they were drawing *younger* viewers. Almost from the beginning, she says, the *Sesame* licensed products sold to younger children before the show itself targeted that group. When CTW decided to expand its licensing to publishing, the licensing team urged the creative staff to develop "secondary characters" in *Sesame* books before they were introduced on the show. By the mid-1980s, consumers were interested in introducing their babies to *Sesame* products, says Kearns, so baby characters (known as Sesame Babies) were introduced in the books before they appeared on *Sesame Street.* Licensing became a way to expand the audience via retail products, Kearns explained. "Products introduced babies to the show." But it wasn't Sesame Babies that lured babies to the screen in record numbers. It was Elmo.

BABY MAGNET

"Why? What? How?" Rosemarie T. Truglio, vice president of research and education at Sesame Workshop, chuckles that these are the questions she is most frequently asked about Elmo. What *is* it about Elmo that makes him so uniformly and instantaneously appealing to babies and toddlers? Truglio, who earned her Ph.D. in developmental and child psychology from the University of Kansas (and served as assistant professor of communication and education at Teachers College, Columbia University) before coming to the Workshop in the mid-1990s, is responsible for developing the curriculum underlying *Sesame Street* as well as for conducting research that makes clear which parts of the program young viewers grasp and learn from and which parts may be too confusing. Truglio develops and reviews the content of all Sesame Street products and programs, including publishing, interactive media, home videos and DVDs, and outreach materials. She says that Elmo's appeal is part science and part art. As Piaget observed, children six years old and younger are concrete thinkers: if something looks scary, it *is* scary. Infants and toddlers attach themselves to creatures that look like themselves, with big eyes and rounded features — creatures that are, simply, cute. Furthermore, because their visual systems are in the early stages of development, infants and toddlers are attracted to bright primary colors — such as Elmo red. They also like singsongy voices that match the lyrical cadences mothers — and many adults — intuitively use when interacting with very young children. Language development experts call this kind of intonation "Motherese." Academic research has shown that very young children attend much more closely to people speaking in Motherese than to those who use normal speech patterns, which are comparatively flat and rapid-fire. Babies are better able to comprehend language spoken in a slow, syllabically stretched-out way, and adults speaking it tend to become more happily engaged with the child when they speak in this nurturing dialect. Elmo not only speaks Motherese, he is also silly, charming, and cuddly. He giggles a lot, and children love listening to other children giggle. These characteristics, taken together, make Elmo a baby magnet.

When Elmo was introduced in 1987, babies and toddlers flocked to the show. He debuted at a time when producers and the licensing department realized that audiences younger than the target age were tuning in regularly and needed to identify with someone their own age: Elmo was that someone. "Elmo was the crossover character," said Kearns. "He was the link between babies and preschoolers." But the famously self-referential furry, red monster was not an overnight sensation. Kearns recalled that her department tried Elmo out as a licensed property in "small ways" at first. "We said, 'We'll test it. But if it doesn't work, we'll drop it.'" That nearly happened. Elmo's licensing debut as a ten-inch plush doll at specialty gift stores did not produce impressive sales. The real spike came with Tickle Me Elmo.

Elmo's stardom reached hysterical heights in 1996. The toy — a pricey ($29.99) motorized plush doll that giggled more and more uproariously when you tickled it — caused an unprecedented Christmas rush. By October the demand for Tickle Me Elmo had outpaced the company's production capacity of fifty thousand dolls a week, and the factory in China had to be pushed to overdrive to produce one million to be sold by Christmas Eve. The buying frenzy made national news. At a toy store in Camden, New Jersey, one hundred Elmos sold out within four minutes of their arrival; Target discounted them at $21.80 and was sold out nationwide in two hours. Some FAO Schwarz stores were selling them for $54 when they had them in stock. By Christmas, Elmo had pulled in more than $22 million in revenue. In the licensing business, Tickle Me Elmo catapulted the character to the big time. He went on to appear on diapers, Band-Aids, cool packs, toothbrushes, hooded towels, sleeping bags, pillows and sheets, bibs, melamine plates and bowls, sippy cups, step stools, toilet seat covers, plastic potties, child-size sunglasses, fuzzy photo albums — and more.

Toys based on Elmo drove increased viewership of *Sesame Street*, and that led to greater toy sales. Today Elmo is by far the most licensed *Sesame Street* character. This is an extremely important role, since, according to Sesame Workshop's 2004 annual report, 68 percent of its revenues are derived from licensing; funding from government and other agencies accounts for only 9 percent, while 17 percent comes from institutional giving and "support from viewers like you." Elmo's breakaway popularity confirmed that the character-licensing business in the infant and toddler market was enormous. Indeed, it inspired a line of products for zero- to two-year-olds called Sesame Beginnings, launched in 2003. Starting with a series of board books based on baby versions of Sesame characters (with titles such as *Snap! Button! Zip!, So Big!, Cookie Kisses, In My Stroller,* and *Time to Eat*), the line expanded to include crib bedding and fleece blankets, lamps, crib mobiles, bath accessories, baby shoes, layette sets, bottles, ring teethers, pacifiers and pacifier clips, and swings, walkers, and portable playpens.

The most publicized Sesame Beginnings products, brought out in April 2006 — to much controversy in the press — were two DVDs, *Beginning Together,* starring Elmo, and *Make Music Together,* featuring Cookie Monster, created by Sesame Workshop and distributed by Sony Wonder. The promotional materials for the DVDs stated that "content is designed for children 6 months and older and grownups of all ages," but everyone at the Workshop — especially Truglio — knew that this statement wasn't entirely accurate. Having consulted with Dan Anderson and Rachel Barr, the Workshop had concluded that it was not really feasible to develop a video or television series that children under twenty-four months could learn from directly. "We decided not to go the infant learning route," said Truglio when I spoke with her in May 2006. "We would have to have done extensive research to say that it was educational." The evidence did not point to infants and toddlers being able to learn anything coherently educational from any program shown on a TV screen. But adults could learn from the DVDs, said Truglio. "The aim of Sesame Beginnings is to model good, interactive parenting behavior to the adults who care for babies." But babies would recognize the Sesame Beginnings characters, and major licensing deals were being inked. They would, it was hoped, walk in Elmo's footsteps.

ROLE MODEL, SALESMAN, AND CORPORATE LOGO

Characters have been used to sell stuff to kids for nearly a century. When the Walt Disney Company began marketing Mickey Mouse in 1929, it established a model for much of today's standard marketing practices in the kids' media industry. Practically from its inception, Disney made licensing its cartoon characters to toy and children's apparel companies a pillar of its business strategy — in addition to integrating the characters' likenesses into a variety of Disney-branded merchandise. Mickey Mouse is recognized globally as one of the all-American icons; this legacy is directly related to the aggressive licensing program Disney originally devised for him.

The company's first merchandise licensing executive, Herman Kay Kamen, determined that Mickey could become a role model, salesman, and corporate logo all at once if his image was seen on alarm clocks, blankets, watches, and toys of all kinds. The first product, a spiral notebook for kids with Mickey's image on the cover, appeared in 1929, the year after *Steamboat Willie*, the first Mickey cartoon, was first shown. Within a few years, Kamen was overseeing the mass-merchandising of Mickey. Early products included everything from sweatshirts and tricycles to card games, dolls, and toothbrushes. Mickey's ubiquitous likeness generated the momentum of an exciting new fad, as well as the sense that Mickey was as omnipresent as the American flag. Indeed, because it appeared everywhere — and had the same graphic look everywhere — Mickey's image sold not only that product but other Mickey products, too: the products advertised each other. (In 2006 Disney launched efforts to make Mickey relevant again with preschoolers by giving him the lead role on a *Dora*-like TV show on Playhouse Disney.)

Walt Disney himself planned the same course for Winnie the Pooh from the character's first days at the company. Although Pooh began as Christopher Robin's diminutive, bumbling buddy in the children's story "Winnie-the-Pooh" by the British writer A. A. Milne, published in 1926, most American children came to know the honey-colored bear as a Disney movie star some forty years later. Pooh is second only to Mickey as the biggest moneymaking character in the company's history and the best earner in the infant and toddler market. Retail sales of Pooh videos, teddy bears, and a variety of other merchandise were $6.2 billion in 2005 and have been in the $5 billion to $6 billion range annually since 2002. Pooh makes more than *twice* as much annually as any other popular children's character of the past five years. According to *Forbes* magazine's yearly ranking of the top-earning fictional characters, in September 2003 Frodo Baggins of *The Lord of the Rings* was third with $2.9 billion, Harry Potter was fourth at $2.8 billion, and Nemo of *Finding Nemo* was fifth at $2 billion. Pooh was first that year, with $5.9 billion, while Mickey trailed in at $4.7 billion. Winnie the Pooh product sales make up 20 percent of the *world's* character licensing business. (Disputes over the marketing rights to Milne's creation were at the center of the longest-running lawsuit in Los Angeles Superior Court, costing millions of dollars in lawyers' fees. Disney reported to the Securities and Exchange Commission that it could be liable for "as much as several hundred million dollars" if it lost the case. Other estimates put the number closer to $4 billion. Disney did not lose the case.)

Disney invariably sees merchandising spikes during its promotions for characters' anniversaries, and Pooh's eightieth anniversary in 2005 was no exception. A flood of new infant and toddler products rolled into retail channels. Retailers offered the Pooh activity ride-on with flashing lights and engine/horn sounds ($29.99); an interactive plush doll, Pooh Knows Your Name ($34.99); and more. In the infant electronics category, Toys "R" Us offered the Pooh CD Lullaby Projector, "with built-in nature sounds," which projected images and movements onto the ceiling ($49.99), and a two-channel, one-way family-radio baby monitor concealed in a Winnie the Pooh picture frame ($39.99).

Babies "R" Us offered a Pooh Microfiber Baby Diaper Tote ($24.99). Wal-Mart had a Pooh Plush Blanket ($13.84). A Classic Pooh Album ($29.99) was sold at craft and scrapbook stores; a Pooh sticker collage for decorating the album was sold separately ($4.99). At Target the Classic Pooh First Prints Kit ($12.99) included an ink pad and two frames to display hand and foot prints. There were Nexcare Tattoo bandages, Pooh Chapstick, Oral-B Stages 2 toothbrush, toothpaste, sunblock, and Nutri-Stix Vitamins. The Pooh & Friends Phonepocket ($19), sold "at specialty boutiques, Verizon Wireless stores and select department stores," was a cell phone carrier that attached to a diaper bag handle.

Leading the anniversary merchandising charge was the Disney Store. The chain, operated by the Children's Place, claimed in a press release that it would transform itself into "Pooh Headquarters." The announcement was hardly surprising. Since its relaunch in 2005, the Disney Store had gotten back into the newborn market, and that meant capitalizing on "Pooh as franchise," said company executives. The strategy has been enormously successful. The chain's merchandising department has found that customers think of Pooh as *the* newborn character, largely because he was a childhood icon for today's parents — and even grandparents. "As you have your own children or grandchildren, you want to introduce something from your history, something warm and secure," explained the general manager of merchandising.

PLAY AS WORK

The success of licensed characters in the newborn market represents a radical shift in the history of toys — indeed, in the history of early childhood. As important as licensing has always been in the toy industry, until recently it had never been terribly successful at penetrating two markets in particular: the educational toy market and the infant and toddler market. The bulk of licensed toys had always been associated with trendy fun or commercial schlock, depending on the demographic profile of the consumer. Historically, there has been a major cultural divide separating "educational" toys from what were considered novelties — essentially, any toys boasting whiz-bang features or inextricably connected to the popular culture of the day.

As Cross points out in *Kids' Stuff*, Buck Rogers and Shirley Temple toys sparked massive crazes in the 1930s, and the 1955 debut of *The Mickey Mouse Club* heralded the era of advertising toys directly to children. But the marketing of novelty toys such as these was always in stark contrast to the marketing of educational toys. Where the trendy toy shouted out its pop culture status, the educational toy was presented as a plain and sober creation built on solid learning principles — and built to last. The Shirley Temple doll was a dimple-cheeked, curly-headed cutie who spurred sales of other trademarked Shirley Temple items such as songbooks, purses, and coloring books; the faddish demand for her died as soon as the child star hit puberty. And children who did not grow up watching Shirley Temple movies may have liked the doll for her cherubic looks but would have no understanding of her special cultural appeal. In contrast, the educational doll was a sturdy soul whose mission was to teach little girls how to care for babies, sew clothes for them, and provide other necessities. According to early childhood educators of the day, the doll's very plainness was supposed to inspire in her owner a sophisticated level of creative play. In contrast, the celebrity doll's commercially constructed character was thought to hamper the freedom and quality of play. The educational doll was deliberately untrendy. She would be passed from older sibling to younger and even handed down through the generations.

The two toy camps conveyed the world views of the people selling them. From the start, there was a major divide between companies that saw their toys as educational and those that were out to make a buck off the latest licensed character. Louis Marx, dubbed the "toy king" by *Time* and *Fortune* and master hawker of novelty toys for the first half of the twentieth century, famously remarked that the only adults who gave children educational toys were "spinster aunts and spinster uncles and hermetically sealed parents who wash their children 1,000 times a day." In other words, they were a bunch of uptight bookworms, hell-bent on depriving kids of fun. The purveyors of educational toys, however, saw themselves as freeing the minds of youngsters from the vice of commercial exploitation, promoting deep imaginative play, and offering opportunities to accomplish work the children could be proud of and that would prepare them for a lifetime of productivity.

To a large extent, the division between novelty and educational toys reflected a cultural rift between the rising affluent classes and those they considered the hoi polloi, with the bourgeois opting for the educational, and everyone else going for trendy fun. When the celebrated early childhood educator Maria Montessori proclaimed that "play is the work of childhood," she was, on the one hand, trying to help stern adults understand that play was not frivolous and was necessary for intellectual development and character building. On the other hand, her insight can be understood as a philosophical extension of the middle-class preoccupation with self-improvement through work, rooted in Max Weber's Protestant ethic. If parents were spending even their free time bettering themselves, then so should children at play. As the century wore on, the two sides would intermarry on occasion. Fisher-Price built its business to some degree on brokering such unions, offering toddler pull-toys in the shape of Disney licensed characters such as Donald Duck and Mickey Mouse as early as the 1940s. But for the most part novelty and educational toys occupied separate spheres.

CORE AND "FRIENDS"

For infants and toddlers, noncultural toys had always outnumbered licensed novelties. Part of the reason was Piaget's belief that infants and toddlers themselves were noncultural, progressing through the universal developmental milestones of the first three years of life. They were not considered consumers of popular culture. Licensed characters had found their way into the toy boxes of very young children, however.

Disney licensed Mickey's likeness to Fisher-Price for use on infant and toddler toys such as bell chimes and sand pails in the 1930s; Disney's Winnie the Pooh became a staple of American nurseries in the 1960s, when Sears began selling Pooh merchandise. In 1982 Fisher-Price began promoting Adventure People, the first action figures for the zero- to three-year-old set and a precursor to the company's Rescue Heroes of today. By 1987 Playskool countered with First Transformers: chunkier, weaponless versions of the robot androids wildly popular with toddlers' older brothers. In 1990, plastic Big Wheel tricycles with licensed characters from blockbuster movies such as *Ghostbusters* and *Batman* were introduced. But since there were very few films or television programs designed specifically for very young children, licensing in the infant and toddler business was relatively modest.

By 2000, however, many toy companies had launched departments to manage the business of licensing TV characters. LeapFrog, for example, makes most of its licensing deals not with book publishers but with television studios, to use the likenesses of the characters young children recognize from *Dora the Explorer, Bob the Builder,* and *Thomas the Tank Engine.* According to the head of LeapFrog's licensing department, most licensing decisions are based on Nielsen reports of the two-to-five viewing audience. In the early 2000s the dominance of licensing compelled Fisher-Price to split into two divisions: one devoted to the toys and products designed in-house as original Fisher-Price products (known internally as "core" products) and the other to those derived from licensed characters, Fisher-Price Brands (internally called "friends").

PLAY PATTERN

Executives in the kids' entertainment business use the word "toyetic" to describe television characters that will translate well into toys — and Stan Clutton has spent the better part of his twenty years in the field chasing down that elusive quality. Clutton, the senior vice president of licensing and new business at Fisher-Price, still hasn't discovered the formula that transforms an ordinary TV character into a toyetic one. He was responsible for the development and promotion of the spectacularly popular Tickle Me Elmo, but even that toy didn't overly impress retail buyers when it was first shown at the International Toy Fair in February 1996. Caprice, says Clutton, sometimes weighs as heavily in the success of a toy as sophisticated marketing practices. But he has observed that several key factors contribute to a media property making a splash with children three and younger. First, repeat exposure is crucial. Very young children thrive on routine and familiarity, and encountering these characters over and over again breeds trust and attachment. The repetitive strategies of *Blue's Clues* were instrumental in this regard, changing the entire approach of programs aimed at very young children. But Clutton also notes that in the last fifteen years videos have played an important role in getting very young children to know television characters. Before VCRs, and now DVDs, became nearly ubiquitous, licensed characters could not have reached toyeticism in the infant and toddler business on the scale that they have. One of the most effective methods used by Fisher-Price's "friends" marketing team to determine the toyetic viability of a TV property is to send pilots of new educational preschool shows to mothers of very young children and ask them to keep a diary of their children's requests for repeat viewings. Do they ask for it often? Even an eighteen-month-old, says Clutton, can make himself clear.

The team also asks mothers to observe if the child integrates aspects of the television show into his play. Becoming integral to a young child's play pattern is vital. *Bob the Builder,* Clutton points out, is an excellent example of a show that feeds right into a play pattern. The combination of repeat viewing and play-pattern integration is such a powerful generator of sales that Fisher-Price has gotten into the video business. Since the "core" and "friends" split, the company has created videos starring the cartoon versions of its "Little People" and bundled them with Little People dolls and related toys, such as the parking garage and farm. It has followed the same strategy with its Rescue Heroes.

These videos are in the tradition of the PLCs of the 1980s. At the 2004 International Toy Fair, a Fisher-Price marketing representative summed up this strategy pithily. Holding up a Rescue Heroes action figure for toddlers in one hand, she cheered "Product!"; she then produced the accompanying video in the other hand, announcing, "Marketing!" Little People and Rescue Heroes are both marketed to babies as young as twelve months old.

The most important key to ferreting out a toyetic TV show, says Clutton, is the starring character, which must "pop" — that is, be visually arresting, easily recognizable, temperamentally exuberant. Of all the "poppy" characters for little kids, few are more toyetic than Dora the Explorer. By 2005 Dora had made more than $250 million in video sales alone. Her image is so ubiquitous that even two-year-olds whose parents don't own a TV know who she is. (One of the first twenty-five words my second child uttered was "Dora" — more like "Do-wah" — and she had never even seen the show.) Dora is an important component of Nickelodeon's merchandising empire. The success of Elmo as a licensed property alerted the commercial television and cable networks to the real money to be made in the infant and toddler market — as long as the product was "educational." For the past decade, virtually every media conglomerate has followed Sesame Workshop's example. In 1994, when Nickelodeon officially launched its preschool educational TV programming with *Blue's Clues,* the licensing business began to make serious inroads into the two markets that had eluded it: educational and infants and toddlers. Over the past decade, Nickelodeon's licensing muscle has bulked up substantially; in 2005 the company pulled in $424 million in licensing revenues from consumer products — an impressive 12 percent share of the cable network's $1 billion in operating profit for the year (in contrast to other networks' average of only 2 percent). Paramount and Nickelodeon make more than $1 billion in home video sales a year, with *Dora the Explorer* leading the list. Viacom's 2004 filing with the Securities and Exchange Commission noted that "other" revenues — meaning money from movie theaters, consumer products, and home entertainment from television and cable product sales — increased 20 percent, to $1.7 billion. One of the primary reasons for this striking jump, stated the report, was higher income from Nickelodeon consumer products and licensing. In a 2005 report, Viacom's cable networks' "other" revenues jumped 29 percent, from $695 million to $897.7 million.

It is little wonder that Nickelodeon has done so well. According to Viacom corporate materials, in 2005:

> Nickelodeon [reached] a total of 302 million households in 167 territories worldwide via 28 channels, 21 branded program blocks and two broadband services across Africa, Asia and the Pacific Rim, CIS/Baltic Republics, Europe, Latin America, and the United States. Programming is also aired on the third-party broadcasters in major territories around the world, increasing Nickelodeon's exposure to 669 million households.

It's the same story at Disney. In 2004, Consumer Products' operating income rose 39 percent — from $384 million to $534 million. Revenues increased 7 percent, thanks partly to a $73 million revenue increase in merchandise licensing, driven by strong performance of the Disney Princess brand, among other factors, and a $72 million revenue increase in publishing, which the report attributed to the success of *Finding Nemo* and other children's books.

THE ANIMARKETING TRIANGLE

There is big money in characters aimed at little people — so much money that marketers find it worthwhile to study infants and toddlers in depth. Every spring for the past several years, the Geppetto Group has led a scavenger hunt at Walt Disney World and the Epcot Center. The Geppetto Group is not in the business of organizing educational events for children, nor is this a kids' scavenger hunt. Geppetto is a New York–based marketing firm, and it charges marketers selling products or services to children more than five hundred dollars apiece for an expedition that the company calls "kid immersion." The brochure advertising the hunt describes it as an opportunity to "observe kids in action" and to "collect ideas, pictures, facts and props" at the theme parks. After the hunt, the brochure says, attendees will "regroup, compare notes, review insights and award our winners," as well as "derive intriguing insights you can use, important information you can share and valuable tips you can apply to your business."

At one particular scavenger hunt, the attendees first meet in a nearby Orlando hotel conference room to receive their assignments and to bone up on the Geppetto Group's key marketing tenets, which will serve as the framework for the day's hunt. One of these tenets is the "Kid/Mom Marketing Dynamic." The firm identifies nine "determining factors" that influence a brand's power in the marketplace: "purchase," "taste," "form," "packaging," "usage," "marketing potential," "competitive," "distribution," and "emotional connection." In each category, there is a balance of power between what a child wants and what his mother wants; in each case, either the kid has the greater influence, or the mom does. Observing and assessing the kid/mom dynamic at work at Disney World is one of the attendees' jobs. To aid in this assignment, fill-in-the-blank worksheets are distributed.

"HERE'S YOUR TASK: Scout out a situation where Mom is in a conversation, with persuasive intent, with her kid/s," instructs the Kid/Mom Marketing Dynamic worksheet. Attendees are to note specific instances in which the child wants — or the mom wants her child — to (a) "Go Somewhere"; (b) "Do Something"; (c) "Buy Something"; or (d) "Have Something." Attendees must answer the question "How does each get what they [sic] want?"; the four multiple-choice answers are "Manipulation"; "Persuasion"; "Negotiation"; and "Command/Demand." Finally, they must allocate ten points between mom and kid to calculate which person gained more in the exchange. The resulting ratio reflects who succeeded in the exchange — that is, where the balance of power lies in the Dynamic.

The highlight of every year's scavenger hunt is participants' observation of the form of marketing for which Disney is most famous: "Animarketing . . . we'll never look at Disney's characters or any brand spokescharacters in the same way again!" Animarketing is considered a specialty of the Geppetto Group; indeed, the firm's chief creative officer, Chris McKee, accepts credit for having coined the term. Animarketing refers to the practice of using "spokescharacters" (usually cartoon characters) to market products or services — or an overarching brand — to children. The Geppetto Group created such spokescharacters as Chester the Cheetah for Frito-Lay's Cheetos snacks, as well as Captain Velocity for Adidas. But Walt Disney World and the Epcot Center are perhaps *the* ideal locales in the world for observing animarketing in action.

The Geppetto Group's paradigm for successful animarketing is the "Animarketing Triangle." A slide in the presentation diagrams its components: "The Character" is at the top, "The Kid" to the left, and "The Brand" to the right. Each point on the triangle must have a strong connection to the two other points, the presenter explains, for the animarketing model to be effective. A worksheet provides this explanation: "A spokescharacter is effective for its brand when there is a relationship between: 1. The character and the child; 2. The character and the brand; 3. The brand and the child." Attendees are to consult this worksheet every time they observe a child interacting with a Disney character at Disney World. "What is the character relationship with the child?" the worksheet prompts. "What does the character represent for Walt Disney World? What does Walt Disney World represent to the child?" Underlined at the bottom of the page is what the Geppetto Group characterizes as "The Ultimate Question": "How does the character help strengthen the relationship between Walt Disney World and the child?"

Out in the field, a small group of seminar attendees stops at a gift shop on Disney World's Main Street, USA. One of the group's first encounters is with the mother of a toddler holding up two boxes, each containing a Disney Princess doll. "Which one do you want, honey? Let's make up our minds," sighs the mother. "'Rella," says the stroller-bound two-year-old girl, in definite tones. "Want *'Rella.*"

CRADLE TO GRAVE

Marketers are upfront about the power of an appropriately designed spokescharacter to attract toddlers. Speaking on the phone with a reporter more than a year after delivering the keynote speech at the Kid Power 2004 conference, Dave Siegel of WonderGroup is clear that character is everything to infants and toddlers. Certainly, animarketing undergirds any marketing campaign directed at children. "Good marketers realize that [young children] see characters and figures right away, and they want kids to recognize the product, and the best way to do that is through characters," he says. "For very young kids, every character you use has to be roundish, with big eyes, the theory being that young kids prefer round because round is safe, pointy is dangerous." And, more bluntly, "We know that kids point to characters, that's why we use them. That's why cereal companies use them. You do it for recognition. They [the children] don't know what the product is, but they recognize Tony the Tiger and Mickey Mouse."

"Cradle-to-grave marketing" emerged as a term and practice in the mid-1990s — the same period in which the White House brain conference drew national attention to the importance of the first three years of a child's life. As the term suggests, it refers to attracting a customer to a particular brand early on in life and keeping her loyal to that brand into adulthood and even old age. It has been estimated that corporations whose marketing campaigns appeal to a toddler can expect to collect as much as $100,000 from her over the course of her lifetime — starting with the money spent on her as a child and, later, the money she spends on her own children and grandchildren.

Whether marketers are *consciously* trying to develop long-lasting brand awareness in infants and toddlers is much disputed, even in the industry itself. Ask kids' marketers to discuss how they market to infants and toddlers, and they will almost invariably balk at the question. By far the majority maintain that they do not, that the marketing is directed only to the parents. They concede that an infant or toddler may recognize and point to a spokescharacter, with the result that the mother acquiesces and buys it. But, they say, since it has not been proven that infants and toddlers consciously associate a particular brand with the character, using spokescharacters to sell products to them cannot be considered "marketing," which is different from advertising or promoting. Marketing is a holistic strategy in which advertising is only one of many tools. It is a set of targeted processes for creating, communicating, and delivering to customers something of perceived value. In this light, using a spokescharacter to sell a product may represent an effort to catch a child's eye and make a quick sell to mom, say marketers. It does *not* represent an effort to develop overall brand awareness.

Many also argue that there is a crucial difference between spokescharacters (Tony the Tiger, say), whose only purpose is to sell a product, and a licensed character (Disney's Cinderella) that was created originally as a character in a movie or television show. The Geppetto Group's Chris McKee speaks passionately on this subject. Several months after his firm led the 2005 marketing scavenger hunt at Disney World, McKee emphasized vociferously that marketers do not market directly to children three and under. He argued that product spokescharacters resonate with older kids — five years old at the very youngest — and that they serve as ambassadors for the brand and that licensed characters, by contrast, are short-lived and typically not exclusively tied to a particular brand or product, so marketers use them to build a brand rather than to boost immediate sales. This means that licensed characters are less effective in the long term.

When asked how marketers do use characters specifically to attract toddlers to products, McKee answered this way: "Can marketers use characters to market brands to kids? That's a two-part question. They don't. They don't actively use their characters to market brands to kids because they're not marketing to them . . . Two- and three-year-olds certainly embrace characters. They [the characters] are the ideal in terms of what becomes meaningful for those kids, as much as a character represents the brand. What I love about characters is two- and three-year-olds develop such a strong affinity for them. You see the way they bond with these characters. They say, 'I love Blue!' from *Blue's Clues*, and then they ask for every single thing that has Blue on it. But I can't say marketers are using characters to sell their brand. Disney is out there selling Little Mermaid, but the Little Mermaid is not a spokescharacter for Disney like Ronald McDonald is for McDonald's. And even then, McDonald's doesn't target toddlers directly. They're simply not doing it. If a kid sees Ronald McDonald, I'm not so sure that that kid is making the connection between Ronald and the McDonald's brand. But if the kid loves Ronald and is in the store, he may then have an affinity for the place."

HIGH LEVEL OF RECOGNITION

Is it possible to verify scientifically that using spokescharacters and animarketing can be a direct route to building brand loyalty among young children? And if so, at what age would children begin to develop brand loyalty in this way? Sabrina M. Neeley and David W. Schumann decided to find out. Neeley is an assistant professor in the Department of Marketing at the Richard T. Farmer School of Business, Miami University, in Oxford, Ohio. Schumann is the associate dean for research and technology in the College of Business Administration at the University of Tennessee as well as a fellow of the American Psychological Association and a former president of the Society for Consumer Psychology.

Interested in the widespread — and controversial — use of spokescharacters in advertising to very young children, Neeley and Schumann set out to explore, in an experiment with tests and controls, whether spokescharacters could influence very young children's product preferences. The only other research on this topic — two academic studies —

had revealed that while a spokescharacter's behavior and voice could clearly have some bearing on a young child's attention to an ad and to the character and on recognition of, and even a positive attitude toward, a product, the relation between spokescharacters and a child's preference, intention, and choice of a product was not clear. "Although public opinion suggests that spokescharacters influence young children's product desires, academic research has generally failed to demonstrate this effect," noted Neeley and Schumann in the introduction to their 2004 paper, "Using Animated Spokescharacters in Advertising to Young Children: Does Increasing Attention to Advertising Necessarily Lead to Product Preference?" published in *The Journal of Advertising.*

Neeley and Schumann's study looked at the responses to animated spokescharacters of 150 two- to five-year-olds, evaluating the children's knowledge of, preference for, and choice of a particular product. As part of the experiment, Neeley created a mock ad with an animated mouse character that she designed herself to make sure the kids had never seen it before. She modified packages by removing labels and brand names of peanut butter cookies and Cheez-Its and assigning them generic names such as "cookies" and "cheese crackers." Going into the experiment, Neeley's hypothesis was that the spokescharacter's behavior in the ad would affect the children's attention most intently. She laid out three ad scenarios: the mouse shown eating the crackers; the mouse shown doing flips or jumping up and down but without touching the crackers; and the mouse shown standing next to the product and doing nothing. Neeley's theory was that if the character was shown eating the product, children would be more likely to recognize and also prefer the product after viewing the ads.

Surprisingly, that did not happen. It did not matter what the mouse did. The children's defining response to each scenario was simply *character recognition.* This finding was strikingly similar to that in Anderson's *Teletubbies* study. That is, the character's actions did not appear to influence very young children's comprehension of the larger narrative context. The chief piece of learning that very young children mastered from watching characters on television was the ability to recognize them.

Neeley switched gears. She decided to try to uncover a more detailed picture of how the two- to five-year-olds responded to the character and how the character affected their knowledge of the product. What would using the character mean in terms of recognition and recall, attitude toward and preferences for the food product being advertised? Neeley invited her subjects to watch fifteen minutes of TV programming — a puppet show with commercials "breaks," including the animated commercial she had made with the mouse. Afterward she used a set of flash cards she had designed especially to help the youngest, newly verbal (or preverbal) children indicate whether they recognized the mouse they had seen on TV on the flash cards' pictures. It used to be assumed that if a toddler had higher verbal ability, he or she had higher cognitive ability, too. But psychological research had shown — and Neeley's own work bore out — that this was not necessarily true. Neeley knew that using flash cards was often the best way of avoiding communication problems and getting information out of very little children easily and efficiently.

The children had what Neeley termed a "high level of recognition." That is, she would show them a picture of the mouse and ask, "Did you see this?" If the answer was "Yes," Neeley would then ask, "What was he doing?" Many of the verbal children would say, for example, "He was doing flips" or "He was eating cheese crackers" or "He was blue." The majority were able to correctly associate the mouse with the crackers. Neeley would show three different cartoon character animals (whom the children had not seen) along with the mouse, which they had seen. She would then show four other flash cards, each showing a different snack, and ask the children to point out which animal went with which food. Almost 71 percent of the young children correctly matched the mouse to the crackers. Even more striking was that some 88 percent said they liked the little mouse character.

Neeley wondered if the emotional connection would translate into a preference for the mouse character–related product. But when she asked them to choose a snack several minutes after they had seen the ad, only 15 percent said they wanted the cheese crackers. That surprised her. Neeley suspected that the children may have been confused about her question about preference, since so much of their session had focused on matching questions; she felt that the response reflected the little kids' trouble shifting gears cognitively rather than their feeling about trying the mouse character's cheese snacks. She decided to see what would happen after the character-snack association had had time to sink in. Neeley told the children that as a reward for being so helpful, they would be invited back for a party. When the children returned later, she allowed them to pick their own snacks and choose which ones they wanted to bring home with them. This time, about 19 percent chose the mouse character's crackers. In that short interim period, the character's stature had clearly grown in importance in the toddlers' and preschoolers' minds.

But what was most astonishing to Neeley was that the children in her study recognized the mouse character later — *even if they hadn't seemed to be watching the ad at the time.* Neeley had made a subjective measurement of how much attention they were paying to the TV ad when it was on, categorizing it as high-level attention (watching raptly); midlevel (some breaks to talk to peers); and little attention (walking around, playing, and so on). There was *no relation* between how much attention a child paid and his or her character recognition later. To Neeley this meant that just because a child is not watching the television does not mean he is not picking up on the message. Toddlers, especially, seemed able to formulate an impression, even though they couldn't verbalize it. At this age, Neeley observed, children don't understand what an ad is, and her subjects did not realize they were looking at an advertisement. They knew it was separate from the TV program, not part of it, but they did not understand the purpose behind the ad. They did not understand persuasion.

SPECIFIC TRAINING

In addition to working with television producers, Iris Sroka and her team at the Hypothesis Group work with marketers at companies ranging from Disney Consumer Products and Mattel to Philip Morris and Quaker Oats to help them develop and successfully market products to children. To get a meaningful sense of how children use — and feel about — branded products in real life, Sroka and the Hypothesis team often conduct at-home ethnographies, using many of the same techniques she uses to determine whether children are learning anything that can be described as "educational" from television. Broadly speaking, the term "ethnography" refers to the tools and methodologies anthropologists employ while embedded in a community whose way of life they wish to study thoroughly over time; ethnographic research was once the purview only of university anthropology departments. Today many advertising and marketing firms have ethnography divisions, often headed by an executive with a graduate degree in anthropology. Many companies that sell to kids conduct their own ethnographic research studies as a part of the earliest phases of product development. Fisher-Price, for example, conducts what it describes as "deep dives," or ethnographic research.

But many companies hire outside firms such as Hypothesis to conduct ethnographies, and whenever Sroka and her business partners are pitching their firm's services, they tout their expertise in this area. At a 2005 presentation to an audience of prospective clients — among them Tropicana, Warner Bros., the Cartoon Network, Pepperidge Farm's Goldfish division, Nick Jr., and Nickelodeon — Sroka and her Los Angeles counterpart, Jeff Seltzer, an experienced quantitative market researcher, stressed the value of ethnographic research. "It gives you a chance to look at the stuff around them [the children], their social and physical objects. How do they choose this specific thing from the chaotic pile in their room? You insinuate yourself into a home environment and see how kids *really* live. You can observe authentic, natural behavior in an authentic, natural environment." Seltzer nodded fervidly and added: "This is key for researching kids. Adults know when you're watching them; kids often don't have that level of sensitivity." Sroka rejoined: "But getting reliable information from ethnographic research relies on observational strategies. It takes specific training to be an astute observer."

Specific training is key to Hypothesis's ability to attract business. In pitching clients, Sroka highlights the psychological methods she and her team use to pull information out of children, as a way of differentiating her firm's expertise from that of its competitors. "You need to speak their language, and you need to listen very carefully for their language because kids often know more than their language allows them to communicate to us," she explained during her presentation with Seltzer. "That's why it is so important to work with people who, as we do, have backgrounds in educational and developmental psychology. When kids tell us something that seems confusing, because of our backgrounds, we'll know that it's because they can't, because of language or that they aren't ready cognitively for what you're presenting them with."

To get what she considers the most authentic market research from children whose homes she is investigating, she employs the same techniques that a child psychologist or other early childhood development professional would use during a developmental or psychological assessment. One of the most useful of these, she says, is scaffolding — the Vygotskian concept that young children need help from adults to build new knowledge, as well as to express what they know but may have trouble articulating. To the extent that an adult can calibrate his level and quality of help to the child's level of performance, scaffolding not only produces immediate results but also can help cement the skills required for independent problem solving in the future. For these reasons, scaffolding is viewed as important in early childhood development, particularly in group care or preschool settings. It is also, according to Sroka, what makes it so useful in conducting in-depth marketing interviews with children.

Upon entering a family's home for the first time, Sroka's team asks the child or children to give them a tour. What do they do in each room? How? When? The tour exercise, she said, is the first piece of scaffolding that her team erects. It not only gives the client rich and intimate details about the kids' lives, it gives kids the necessary scaffolding to ground themselves in a discussion with virtual strangers, to reflect on their routines and interests, and to begin to trust that the team is genuinely interested in their experiences and ideas.

But a tour can go only so far; children will open up to a certain extent before their "public" selves begin to erect barriers to protect their "private" selves from invasion. At that point the next piece of scaffolding is introduced: journaling. A solitary activity, journaling is generally thought of as a way for teenagers and adults to separate their inner, genuine thoughts from those that may be influenced by others. But journaling is used by experts in early childhood development, too. Preschool teachers often take young children's dictation in journal form, as a way of helping them anchor their personal ideas, feelings, and stories. Developmentally, this is considered important because from the time kids enter a group setting — whether preschool or a daycare — other than their families, even very young children start developing public personas that are distinct from their private selves. What a child says she likes when she is in a group may differ considerably from what she feels when she is alone.

"We find that kids are more likely to share their private selves with us through journals than by talking," Sroka explained to potential clients at her presentation. "The journals also help them organize themselves and their ideas and feelings, and they need this kind of scaffolding to get to what they're really thinking."

In a 2004 ethnographic study Hypothesis conducted for an electronics company, the client wanted to research the potential market for a new hand-held device. The client company knew that adults and teenagers were highly aware of brands in the electronics market and had strong brand allegiances. But the client wanted to know if younger children were aware of electronics brands. So that the kids could "express themselves more clearly, more authentically," Sroka and her colleagues designed a fill-in-the-blanks journal with the title "What is Your Dream Electronic?" The journal was divided into chapters, which the kids were invited to title themselves, except for the last chapter. The last chapter culminated in the "dream electronic": designing the perfect gadget. Sroka and her partners made it the last because "earlier chapters help ground them in the category." The gradual progression of the chapters provided the necessary scaffolding to produce the nuanced, intimate results the client was after.

When the journals were in, the Hypothesis team noted that the children's entries reflected a great deal of "brand sensitivity and understanding." Some children had drawn pictures of electronics, and many included hand-drawn brands and logos, such as the Motorola *M*. Brand awareness comes from a number of different sources, but an important one is parents, explained Sroka. Parents often hand down old electronic products to kids; rather than throw away an old cell phone when they trade up or change calling plans, parents will often offer their children the gadget to play with. Thus even very young children become "sensitized" to the brand logos on these devices, she said. But brand awareness also comes from companies marketing directly to kids, albeit to older kids. Even though iPods and MP3 players are marketed to teenagers, "kids are 'aspirational,'" said Sroka. "If a fifteen-year-old sibling has it, then the eight-year-old is sensitized to that brand now." That principle, she said, applies even with younger children. "As we always say to clients: 'If you want to get your product in the hands of a six-year-old, get it in the hands of a nine-year-old.'"

For children under five, however, building brand awareness requires a different tack. As Sroka explained in a separate phone interview, very little children do not connect with brands such as Kellogg's or Colgate; that level of abstraction is well out of their cognitive range. It is a fundamental Piagetian concept, she points out, that kids under three are completely concrete thinkers. Take the example of television programs. "*Sesame Street* is the uber-brand for the little kids and then behind it, sometimes, as they approach five years old, they begin to know that that's PBS Kids, or with SpongeBob, they start to understand that it's Nickelodeon." Adults, in contrast, tend to think of the uber-brand as Disney or Nick, with specific shows below those brands. "Kids do it in reverse, they build up from the concrete example." Their first attachment is not to brand but to character. Although infants and toddlers may be attracted to characters associated with cereals, like Tony the Tiger, the characters they become emotionally attached to are the ones they see on TV regularly. If children see those characters in a variety of forms and in different environments — in books, on backpacks and juice boxes — their attachment to them deepens. "Kids are living in a 360-degree world where brands are trying to create 360-degree experiences, where touch points for that brand are everywhere for the child: eating, wearing clothing, watching TV, playing with a toy," Sroka explained. "As [children] consume in a sort of 360-degree environment, as they consume a character or television property, it takes on the stature of brand."

"They know that character, and then the character *is* the brand," explained Sroka. "That's where the idea of brand starts."

6

##########

The Princess Lifestyle

I N 2OOO ANDY MOONEY had an epiphany at a Disney ice show in
Phoenix, Arizona. Mooney wasn't there for fun; he has no children.
He was there strictly to observe. Just months before, the Scottish-
born executive had been hired away from Nike by Disney's chief, Michael Eisner, to revamp Disney Consumer Products. Previously known
as the lackluster "ancillary products" division, it was essentially the
company's licensing arm, churning out Disney-branded products with
every new film release and theme-park opening. Disney Consumer
Products was, in a word, uninspired or, in another, incoherent. A twenty-
year veteran marketing executive at Nike, Mooney was aghast at this
state of affairs. In his mind, consumer products was about an airtight
brand image and the customer's deep emotional connection with that
image — not just slapping a character on a toothbrush or lunchbox.
The lifestyle branding for which Nike had become famous not only
made the company wildly prosperous in the 1990s, it also transformed
the marketing industry. Now consumers chose products on the basis of
emotional connection to a brand, not just to a specific item. Mooney
wanted to bring that same depth to the marketing of Disney characters,
to move them out of their knickknack ghetto and into lifestyle branding. As Mooney watched hundreds of little girls file into the skating

rink dressed as Cinderella, Jasmine, and Ariel, everything suddenly clicked. Each character represented a distinct personality and had its own following — a clique. But as a whole the group of characters represented a magical, glamorous lifestyle. Eureka!

Within a year of Mooney's revelation, all the Disney heroines were gathered under a single brand: Disney Princess. Snow White, Cinderella, Ariel (from *The Little Mermaid*), Belle (*Beauty and the Beast*), Sleeping Beauty, Jasmine (*Aladdin*), Pocahontas, and Mulan were now packaged as a group, to sell accessories ranging from underwear (a different Disney Princess for each day of the week) to dolls to dress-up clothes to books. The strategy paid off staggeringly well. In 2005 worldwide sales of products in the Princess line topped $3 billion, triple the $1 billion in 2002. Just four years after the launch of Disney Princess, a Disney marketing study revealed that 91 percent of moms with kids between the ages of two and five were familiar with the brand, and 26 percent called it one of their favorites. *Disney Princess* magazine had a circulation of 10 million in seventy-five countries (there are thirty editions); Disney Princess albums from Walt Disney Records reached platinum on *Billboard*'s Children's Chart; three titles are on the Top 25 chart. The Princess craze even altered the country's Halloween landscape. By 2005 the National Retail Federation reported that princesses outnumbered witches by more than two to one.

One reason for launching Disney Princess was, naturally, to extend the retail life of each character. No Princess would ever have to be retired when her big movie left theaters. Continually marketed as part of the exclusive clique, each Princess would stay in the public eye, retain and further cultivate a devoted fan base, and continue to pull in revenue via licensing and merchandising. But another insight driving Disney's move was that the KGOY phenomenon had infiltrated the Princess business. "Age compression" and Kids Getting Older Younger are terms used frequently in the kids' marketing business, referring to the phenomenon of today's grade-school children playing and acting in ways that adolescents did fifteen to twenty years ago, and so on down the age scale. The terms are relatively new in the marketing lexicon, but for nearly a century marketers have tried to capitalize on children's perennial yearning to be older than they are. The ubiquity, increasing volume, and variety of mass media have merely accelerated the trend, particularly in the United States. For example, in the 1980s, *Sesame Street*'s target audience was four-year-olds, whereas today's four-year-olds think the show is for "babies." In the 1990s, the Power Rangers brand targeted boys between six and eleven; by the 2000s, three-year-olds were a fan base. Disney had seen the KGOY trend move into uncharted territory. In the early 1990s, kids became consumers of Disney Classics (the company's catalogued movies) when they were about six years old. A little more than a decade later, children as young as eighteen months were customers.

Of all the Disney Princesses, Cinderella emerged as the brightest star. Cinderella's runaway success demonstrated another major influence of KGOY's penetration of the Princess business. Unlike older children, who became hooked to new characters and merchandising via new animated features, toddlers did not need blockbuster movies to win them over. Cinderella was a perfect case in point. Although her image was emblazoned on their hearts and minds, many of Cinderella's devoted little fans had never even seen the classic Disney film, partly as a result of a strategic decision Disney had made at the dawn of the VCR era. To maintain the premium status of its classic films, Disney has famously kept a very firm grip on their release, reissuing them in "special" editions only every seven to ten years. The latest re-release of Disney's *Cinderella*, this time in DVD format, was in October 2005, well after the Cinderella wildfire had spread among two- and three-year-old girls. But before the release, Disney unleashed more than 250 Cinderella-related products in virtually every major category, including toys, apparel, electronics, stationery, home furnishings, and accessories. Products featuring a "Magical Lights" theme were made available starting in September 2005, continuing to roll out over the holidays and into 2006. The company erected exclusive Cinderella boutiques in every Toys "R" Us in the

United States and set up center-aisle promotional displays in every Wal-Mart. "Disney has lined up Mattel, Kellogg's, Home Depot, and Jolly Time Popcorn as marketing partners in a campaign that will rival that of Disney's *The Lion King*," boasted a June 2005 Disney press release. As research psychologists had seen, once a toddler's environment was saturated with images of the Princess characters (from TV to supermarkets to libraries), she came to recognize them and then grew attached to them. She began to ask for them and wanted to look like them — or, at least, Disney wanted her to.

Looking like a princess was key to the success of the new toddler- and preschool-focused Princess business. According to industry analysts and Disney itself, a cornerstone of the Princess line was "transformation": dress-up clothes and accessories. The princess whom little girls most wanted to look like was Cinderella — but not the Cinderella of storybook fame or even of the Disney cartoon, who spent most of her life sweeping hearths in ragged peasant attire. The Cinderella that Disney was marketing in promotions and tie-ins everywhere was the gowned, bejeweled, glass slipper–clad belle of the ball. Snow White might have a cute frock, as did Belle, but in the rubric of many of her two- and three-year-old devotees, Cinderella was the "fanciest" Princess. And toddler girls didn't want to look just like *any* fancy Cinderella; they wanted to look like the *Disney* Cinderella. (My two-year-old emphasized this point one time while we were playing Cinderella. I tried to act out the part of the godmother from a Caribbean version of the story, *Cendrillon,* by Robert San Souci, but my daughter wasn't having any of *that.* She stamped her foot angrily and howled, "Not Cendrillon — I want Disney Cinderella!")

Cinderella's royal Disney-fied attire was easy to pick out from generic-brand princess wear. Every Disney Cinderella–branded dress-up costume and accessory — ranging from a gown of nylon satin and sparkly powder blue tulle ($65) to glittery clear plastic "glass slippers" ($16) to a plastic bejeweled wand ($12) and many other items — was adorned with her official logo: a plastic cameo of Disney's Cinderella. Cinderella products also now ranged from luxury goods to cheap novelties. At the "mass" end of the spectrum, one could buy any number of Cinderella trinkets costing little more than a dollar. At the "class" end, for several hundred dollars parents could treat their little girls to a "live" Princess party at Disney World, hosted by Cinderella "herself." As Mooney said, "the hottest ticket is the princess breakfast," either at Cinderella's Royal Table at the Magic Kingdom or at Epcot's Akershus Royal Banquet Hall. In the spring of 2005, Walt Disney World introduced the show "Cinderellabration." "Playing several times a day to an enraptured audience of little girls, it is the most lavish appearance yet by the Disney Princesses where little girls can meet their favorite Princess and dress up in regal attire including 'Cinderellabration'-inspired gowns and glittering tiaras," said a Disney press release. "In total, girls have access to 2 billion hours of immersion into the Disney Princess experience." Disney's Cinderella even carries an aura of prestige with grown women. The Cinderella theme wedding at Walt Disney World is the most popular; for $2,500, the bride is escorted in a glass coach, drawn by four ponies. Swarovski sells a line of Cinderella crystal jewelry that includes a $235 beaded choker and bracelet.

As some have pointed out, irony attended the marriage of KGOY and Cinderella. A 2005 *New York Times* piece declared that Disney's Cinderella was emerging as the polar opposite of the original Grimm's fairy tale character and even of the Disney movie Cinderella. Because toddlers were not connected to Cinderella through the story — and its moral — to them she was not a heroine whose modesty and kindness ultimately unmasked her stepmother's and stepsisters' crass materialism and cruelty. Their Cinderella was a vaguely beneficent celebrity, a wholesome supermodel. The article observed that "Cinderella lust causes some young devotees to behave more like her wicked stepsisters," reporting that two- and three-year-old girls competed on the basis of who had the prettier or greater number of accessories; fought over Cinderella costumes during play dates; and constantly demanded more additions to their cache of Disney Cinderella–adorned licensed products. Disney's Cinderella seemed to be the figurehead of an imaginary world, replete with beautiful "good things" — some more beautiful and costly than others — whose tightly branded aesthetic universe was in no way undergirded by a code of moral consequence. Cinderella was no longer the heroine of a story. In what might be the most radical extension of KGOY marketing to date, Mooney had transformed Cinderella into a lifestyle brand for toddlers and preschoolers that was every bit as vertically integrated as Nike.

Vertical and Horizontal

The classic business textbook *Marketing Management* defines a brand as an identifier for a particular company's group of products. To many people, a brand may simply connote a preferred type of toothpaste or tennis shoe. But many brands encompass a great deal more than a particular product. In the marketing business, developing a brand is a complex blend of art and science, with social and economic effects that are far deeper and wider than most of us consciously consider. Achieving such penetrating results is the goal of building "brand equity."

As a term and an idea, "brand equity" has received a great deal of attention over the past fifteen years, with Nike setting some of the most striking and successful examples. With the globalization of manufacturing and economics in general, a typical modern corporation can't stay competitive just by making a better or cheaper product. Rather, it must create a brand with which customers identify in some personal or emotional way. A person's attachment to a brand, regardless of the product's form, may be considered a measure of that brand's equity. In this way, brand equity is rather like karma; it can be good or bad, depending on how people behave in relation to it. Or as Kevin L. Keller, the E. B. Osborn Professor of Marketing at Dartmouth's Tuck School of Business, defined it in a 1993 paper in the *Journal of Marketing:* "A brand is said to have positive (negative) customer-based brand equity if consumers react more (less) favorably to the product, price, promotion, or distribution of the brand than they do to the same marketing mix element when it is attributed to a fictitiously named or unnamed version of the product or service."

There are essentially two ways to build brand equity: horizontally or vertically. Economists and marketing experts define horizontal brand differentiation means variations in the function or category of products, whereas vertical differentiation is variation in quality levels within a product category. In a 1998 article on brand equity in the journal *Marketing Science,* professors at the Wharton School of Business used Ivory soap to illustrate horizontal differentiation. The Ivory brand includes a sizable array of products, including bar soap, liquid hand soap, liquid dishwashing soap, and laundry detergent. But the differences among these products are in their formulation or form, not their quality. Because none of these products is marketed, or perceived by the customer, as "better" than the others in the line, Ivory's products are said to be horizontally differentiated. Vertically differentiated brands can be illustrated by Nikon's branding strategy. Nikon offers a range of cameras: point-and-shoot, digital, 35mm SLR, underwater, and so on. Within the 35mm SLR category, however, Nikon offers models that vary in quality from good to better to best. These models are considered to be vertically differentiated.

Brand equity has three components: brand associations, brand prestige, and brand image. If a customer associates Maytag with reliability, for example, then "Maytag" and "reliability" become synonymous in his mind. This positive association is obviously a boon to Maytag, and it contains a less obvious windfall. Since the interchangeability of "Maytag" and "reliability" helps a customer make his choice in the marketplace, that ostensible assistance underscores his belief in the brand's reliability. Prestige can also play a vital role in feeding the perception of brand value. The authors of the Wharton study pointed out that Mercedes is perceived as a prestigious brand in the United States primarily because of its high-end models, and this prestige rubs off on Mercedes' middle-market cars, too. Finally, the study argued that brand image can be seen as the umbrella for all other aspects of brand value; prestige, for example, can be viewed as a special instance of brand image. But customers have deeper emotional and symbolic connections to specific brands. Because Nike effectively associated its brand with exuberant self-expression ("Just Do It"), the brand would trump all others among customers who embraced that ethos.

Thanks to Mooney's expertise, Cinderella — and the Disney Princess brand as a whole — possesses all three building blocks of brand equity. Customers now associate "Disney" with the very word and concept of "princess." Thanks to its high-end offerings, Disney Princess products, especially Cinderella-branded items or events, have an aura of prestige. And there is a strong emotional connection. To capitalize on all three features of brand equity, Disney Princess should go vertical, the Wharton study concluded.

PERMISSIVES AND RESTRICTIVES

Taking into account Anderson's and Neeley's studies, as well as Sroka's field research, several key issues emerge regarding characters and the concept of brand. First, infants and toddlers clearly form attachments to characters designed to appeal to them as well as to those that conform, even if unintentionally, to a Piaget-inspired set of features. Second, the main thing that infants and toddlers learn from such characters, whether on television, juice boxes, or bed sheets, is the ability to recognize them — which should not be confused with actually learning anything "educational." Third, infants' and toddlers' attachment to characters deepens the more often they encounter them, no matter what the medium. Finally, the presence of such characters on a wide variety of merchandise seems to be toddlers' first experience of developing loyalty to an early concept of a brand. As Sroka said, the character *is* the brand. If, as the Wharton professors argued, the best way for marketers to develop brand equity is to take their brand vertical, in the kids' business this means taking the character vertical.

Disney's Cinderella is one of a growing pantheon of celebrity characters among babies and toddlers, including such superstars as Elmo, Dora, Blue, and Clifford, most of whom have entered young children's consciousness via television or videos. But because babies and toddlers do not spend money themselves, smart marketers must figure out how to grow a kids' product line vertically for parents.

For any company interested in selling products to or for young children, the Generation-X mother is a very tough gatekeeper to sneak past; companies need especially incisive marketing strategies to do business with her. There are many kids' marketing firms but WonderGroup's "Millennium Mom Segmentation Model" is notable for its precise partitioning of the subsets of Generation-X mothers. This model, which the firm developed in concert with Sabrina M. Neeley (the Miami University marketing professor who conducted the spokescharacter study), measures mothers' purchasing behaviors on a scale ranging from most permissive to most restrictive. Moms who are most likely to give in to their child's request for a product or most likely to be persuaded by an effective marketing campaign for a product are at the "Permissive" end of the continuum. Those least likely to acquiesce sit at the opposite, "Restrictive" end. The model divides the scale into six separate profile types, three permissives and three restrictives, and each type is further measured and labeled, with P1 representing the most permissive mother, P2 the next, and so on, ending with R1 as the most restrictive. The Millennium Mom Segmentation Model offers detailed profiles of each of these types, with ethnic and education breakdown.

Unfortunately for marketers, Permissives make up only 40 percent of Generation-X mothers as a whole. The model characterizes Permissives as follows: "indulgent"; "impulse shoppers"; "respond to brand"; "respond to kid requests" while shopping; "allow kids substantial freedom"; believe that "kids have rights, not responsibilities." P1 accounts for 7 percent of all Gen-X mothers. A P1 mother is "highly responsive to kid request, but does not have high income." She is "self-focused: not warm toward kids," and her attitude can be summed up as "keep out of my life." P1 moms are "lower income," "stretched to afford non-essentials," "conspicuous consumers and impulsive," "single moms." P2 moms, who account for 9 percent of the group, are, according to the model, "Heartland Moms, family-centric"; a "high percentage are Stay at Home Moms (SAHM)"; they are "middle- to low-income"; "62 percent non-white"; "second highest single Mom group"; "optimistic." P3 moms, who make up 24 percent of all Gen-X mothers, view purchases as a family "collaboration"; they "balance family/work" and represent the "highest percent full-time employed Moms." A P3 mom is "middle- to upper-income"; "allows brands and non-essentials"; "70 percent white"; "60 percent married"; "well-informed; politically active; health and nutrition conscious." P3 mothers are "the power group for marketers," notes Siegel, the president of WonderGroup. "If you don't own this group, you're out of luck."

However, marketers may be out of luck in general when it comes to appealing to Generation-X mothers. "Restrictives," the dark side of the Millennium Mom Segmentation Model, account for 60 percent of the moms. They are characterized as "purposeful shoppers"; "less responsive to kid request"; "don't like marketers — they think what we do is wrong"; "seek higher control over kids." R3s, 22 percent of all Generation-X moms, are the least restrictive. The R3 mother is the "evil twin sister of P3," says Siegel. "And dare I say . . . a 'bitch'?" She has a "low response to kid requests" while shopping but is emotionally "warm" toward her children. R3s represent the "most educated group" and have a "family focus." R2, 23 percent of Gen-X moms, "wants to give in to kids' requests but can't financially"; is "middle- to low-income"; "frustrated because she can't afford it, so she is annoyed with marketers"; "single-divorced Mom"; "less informed"; "a Wal-Mart shopper." R1, the most restrictive category, includes 15 percent of the group. "She *is* a bitch"; "very cold, very strict"; "self-focused."

With all these subtle gradations in purchasing behavior, WonderGroup says to prospective clients, it may appear that the only recourse is for marketers to pick a distinct niche and target it directly. But, the firm insists, that strategy is neither necessary nor advisable. Marketers must learn that they are potentially addressing all these groups at retail, and that Generation-X mothers generally are tough customers. But their armor, which these mothers built to protect themselves during their own childhoods, has a few chinks in it, and the chinks represent marketing opportunities. As with all armored creatures, the soft tissue underneath is extremely vulnerable.

THIS GENERATION'S CURRENCY

If you want to know what is unhealed from your own childhood, it's easy to find out: have your own kids. In *Generation X*, Douglas Coupland referred to such facile analysis — applying precepts from partially digested undergraduate psychology courses to one's own life — as "101-ism." Yet this pop-psych insight seems to be at the core of how purchase decisions are made in Gen-X-headed households. Even though this generation railed against the yuppie materialism of the Baby Boomers, the average Gen-X adult spends 18 percent more on luxury goods than the average Baby Boomer, according to a 2005 American Express Platinum Luxury Survey. According to marketers, the primary characteristic that most Generation Xers share is shopping. This generation, they say, identifies with peers less on the basis of political beliefs than on whether they drive a Volkswagen Passat station wagon, say, or happened to buy the same "Rhys"-style media console at Pottery Barn or prefer Marmot and REI outerwear to Lands' End or L.L. Bean. It is a generation that has integrated vertical lifestyle brands into their identities. "Consumption is this generation's currency," said Jane Rinzler Buckingham, president of the market research firm Youth Intelligence, in a 2005 interview with the *New York Times*. "They don't have government or causes to believe in, so the Gucci bucket hat is their currency instead."

Generation X spends an extravagant amount of money — to the extent of forgoing savings — on anything related to what they lacked as children: home. Upper-middle-class Gen-Xers are notorious for their lavish spending on what glossy magazines call "shelter," but they do it with a sense of thrift and virtue — relics from a childhood spent rebelling against the twin influences of empty homes and conspicuous consumption. "The emerging code of financial correctness allows bobos [bourgeois bohemians] to spend money without looking like one of the vulgar Yuppies they despise," David Brooks observed in his 2000 sociological study, *Bobos in Paradise.* "It's a set of rules to help them convert their wealth into spiritually and intellectually uplifting experiences."

Just as Generation Xers are determined to spend money they don't have on making the most comfortable, beautiful, high-quality "homey" homes to make up for a lack in childhood, marketing studies show that Gen-X parents are also determined to transform their relationship with their children through the shopping experiences that were a source of such conflict but also attention in their own childhoods. In fact, Gen-X parents often seem to take their philosophy of attachment parenting to the mall and supermarket. One study, conducted by Neeley in concert with WonderGroup, shows that Gen-X mothers are repelled by the "nag factor" that worked like such a charm with their mothers. Indeed, to a Gen-X mother, nagging embodies a dynamic from her childhood that she is striving to erase as a parent: division and manipulation born of neglect. These moms want to see themselves as consensus builders, which means treating their children as people whose voices deserve to be heard, people worthy of respect and dignity. They will include children as young as two — and even younger — in decisions ranging from buying breakfast cereal to acquiring a car or home.

Generation X's twin penchants for attachment parenting and shopping have also produced the rise in popularity of mini-me fashions in the past decade. To Generation-X mothers, the cutesy, froufrou baby clothes of the past were tacky and foolish-looking; dressing their babies in traditional infant clothes somehow translates to a deeper sense of objectification, a neglect of the babies' personhood. The Gen-X mother identifies with her baby and wants to dress her in the same kinds of outfits she herself wore. The rise of BabyGap, H&M, and Mini Boden reflected this trend at the mass-market level, as do DKNY Baby, Young Versace, Calypso Enfant, and Coach in the luxury market. But there is a deeper level to the symbiotic identification of Generation-X parents with their young children: the desire to return to their own childhood and fix it.

NEWSTALGIA

Take a walk through the women's clothing section of any Target store, and you cannot help but do a double-take. There, on racks next to the inexpensive designer knockoff jackets and twinsets are form-fitting tee shirts featuring the googly faces of Elmo, Cookie Monster, and Oscar the Grouch. A peek at Wal-Mart's selection reveals junior- and adult-size Care Bears and Strawberry Shortcake tees and matching thong underwear. Crack open an issue of *In Style* or *Star* from the past several years, and you'll spot photos of A-list Generation-X celebrities such as Jennifer Anniston and Sarah Jessica Parker wearing "vintage"-style Mickey Mouse tees. Edgy designers such Dolce & Gabbana, Hysteric Glamour, Religion, and others have come out with street takes on classic Disney characters such as Tinker Bell, Donald Duck, Alice (from Disney's animated *Alice in Wonderland*), and the evil queen from *Snow White*. Ultra-hip baby boutiques offer cotton rompers and onesies silk-screened with such 1970s Saturday morning cartoon classics as Wonder Woman, the "cuckoo for Cocoa Puffs" bird, and Underdog.

Marketers call it "newstalgia," defined by Urban Dictionary (www .urbandictionary.com) as "the love of old things from the past revived in what designers call 'the contemporary classic' from cars to TV shows." Although the term is not exclusive to marketers — it has long been used in the music industry and by car hobbyists to describe new songs or vehicles that capture the style of the 1950s and '60s — newstalgia (or, alternately, "newtro," as in "new retro") is often invoked in discussions of marketing to Generation X. Newstalgia has inspired film revivals of such 1970s and '80s lightweight classics as *Scooby Doo, Charlie's Angels, Starsky and Hutch, The Incredible Hulk,* and *The Dukes of Hazard.* It helped revitalize *Preppy Handbook*–era fashion houses such as Izod Lacoste and Lily Pulitzer and launch new prepster designers like Kate Spade and Le Tigre; it has sparked renewed interest in striped miniskirts, guitar-pick earrings, metallic disco bags, and ballet flats. Viacom's Nick at Nite, launched twenty years ago as a channel showing nostalgic Boomer reruns such as *The Dick Van Dyke Show* and *Mary Tyler Moore,* now runs the TV staples of Generation X's childhood: *Three's Company* and *The Facts of Life.* The VH1 music network has built its business around Generation-X newstalgia, with *Behind the Music,* which tracks the rise, fall, and current whereabouts of 1980s bands. Time Warner's Cartoon Network division launched Adult Swim, a late-night lineup of cartoons in the campy graphics style of those old Saturday morning cartoons, along with reconfigurations of the shows themselves. Robert Smigel's TV Fun House cartoon segments on *Saturday Night Live* featured "The Ambiguously Gay Duo," a bawdy take on '70s superhero teams. In the mid-1990s, after the enormously successful recasting of the marginal superhero Space Ghost in *Space Ghost Coast to Coast,* in which the chucklingly banal hooded specter hosts a celebrity interview show, a spate of similarly tongue-and-cheek retrofitted cartoons followed. One of the most popular, *Harvey Birdman, Attorney at Law,* resurrects the old Hanna-Barbera character (voice by Stephen Colbert). Once a superhero hack, Birdman now works at a white-glove law firm representing cartoon stars who have slipped out of the spotlight and into shady real-world entanglements. Harvey Birdman has represented Shaggy and Scooby, held on charges of drug possession; Fred Flintstone, when the feds look into his possible ties to the Mob; and Grape Ape, accused of steroid doping at the Laff-a-lympics.

Various cultural critics have argued that what separates Generation X's nostalgia from that of preceding generations is the absence of sincere emotional connection to actual events. That is, Generation X knows now, as it knew growing up, that the late 1970s and 1980s were a time of serious crap. Previous generations' nostalgia is rooted in achievement, triumph over hardship, social activism — some authentic, galvanizing experience. "Greatest Generation" nostalgia, for example, is centered on World War II, sacrifice at home, and the heyday of Big Band music; Baby Boomers gloat over memories of the civil rights, antiwar, and feminist movements. Not Generation X. Scared stiff and overwhelmed by the social problems surrounding them in the 1980s — "racial strife, homelessness, AIDS, fractured families and federal deficits" (as described by the 1990 *Time* cover story) — the latchkey kids of Generation X had just one galvanizing collective experience: TV. As adults, this generation seems to consume the newstalgia of today in much the same way it consumed 1980s popular culture as adolescents: with irony, ennui, and self-awareness.

But as parents, interestingly, Gen-Xers consume newstalgia in a completely unironic way. Like parents before them since time immemorial, these parents yearn to share with their children the playthings of their youth. It is just that Generation X's idea of play is inextricably tied to TV, licensing, and buying stuff "all sold separately." These parents' image of childhood is rooted not in activities or experiences but in buying the brands of their youth.

CONSUMER FRENZY WITH A NEW GENERATION

The Licensing Show, held annually at New York's Jacob K. Javits Convention Center, is the venue to hit up if you want to get a barometric reading of what is hot now or will be hot very soon in consumer culture. Unless you're in the entertainment or licensing business, the Licensing Show is like ground zero for feeling one's age. At the 2002 show, however, anyone born between 1965 and 1981 would have felt comfortably like a connoisseur. Mattel reintroduced its Hot Wheel cars; Hasbro was showcasing a monster-size Tonka truck. The Cartoon Network was promoting a $20 million resurrection of the '80s cartoon hit *He-Man and the Masters of the Universe*, complete with twenty-five He-Man licensed toys targeted to tie in with the show's comeback. Fox Broadcasting touted revivals of the Cabbage Patch Kids and Teenage Mutant Ninja Turtles. Strawberry Shortcake, the Care Bears, and My Little Pony were plastered on or dangled from every conceivable toy, garment, or accessory.

By 2005 many of these retooled properties had prospered. An American Greetings press release dated in November of that year announced: "In 2002, the instantly recognizable Care Bears made a grand exit from hibernation and grabbed national headlines by sparking consumer frenzy with a new generation of kids and teens, as well as parents who originally grew up with the cuddly characters." When the Care Bears were launched exactly twenty years before, American Greetings made $250 million in the first year from the furry team. The original *Care Bears Movie*, released in theaters in 1985, pulled in $23 million at the box office, making it the best-performing animated movie of its time. The Care Bears generated $1.5 billion in retail sales from 1982 to 1986 and was the dominant licensing property of the period. In 2001 American Greetings decided to test out the market for Care Bears newstalgia. The company repackaged old TV episodes and two feature films from the mid-eighties and released them on DVD, along with a line of its signature plush bears at Target, Toys "R" Us, and certain greeting card stores. Response was so spectacular that American Greetings started receiving calls from retailers. It was time to relaunch. The Care Bears entered the infant market in 2003 with bedding, sold at Wal-Mart. In April 2005 Care Bears diapers and pull-ups were added, exclusively at Target, followed by Care Bears infant plush toys, mealtime accessories, sippy cups and bottles, layettes, onesies, playwear, toddler bedding, toddler footwear, and accessories. From 2002 to 2006, the Care Bears brand generated over $2 billion in retail sales — not including home video and DVD sales. Care Bears maternity wear was introduced in 2006. Consumers were demanding it, explained the company's head licensing agent. Today's moms grew up with Care Bears in the '80s, she pointed out, and now Care Bears is a "comfort-food property."

Strawberry Shortcake followed a similar trajectory. American Greetings, the creator and owner of the brand, relaunched the 1980s character in 2003; by 2006, Strawberry Shortcake had generated over $1 billion in worldwide retail sales. As of April 2005 more than 5 million copies of eight *Strawberry Shortcake* DVDs had been sold. At Toy Fair 2006, American Greetings and DIC Entertainment, the worldwide licensing agent for the brand, announced a new line of branded merchandise, Strawberry Shortcake Baby. The companies' joint press release called it an "all-new extension of this evergreen girl's brand," which would include products for infants from birth to twelve months: apparel, layette, prewalker shoes, infant toys, crib mobiles, and other nursery decor. The release announced tie-ins with well-known diaper brands. "The success of Strawberry Shortcake these past few years has been extraordinary, and the program continues to grow and evolve. Strawberry Shortcake Baby gives us the opportunity to expand the brand to an entirely new consumer," said DIC's vice president of consumer products. Many other 1980s mass-market icons had revival stories, too, including My Little Pony, Cabbage Patch Kids, Smurfs, Teenage Mutant Ninja Turtles, Transformers, and Hot Wheels.

But the newstalgia campaign with the biggest impact promoted the defining saga of Generation X's childhood, *Star Wars*. With the spring 2005 release of *Star Wars: Episode III — Revenge of the Sith,* Toys "R" Us was stacking Star Wars merchandise from floor to ceiling, with special offerings from Playskool, Hasbro's toddler brand. There was the Star Wars Playskool Jedi Force Red Plush Lightsaber, a soft, clothlike sword; the Star Wars Playskool Jedi Force Figure set, including chunky Little People–like action figures based on favorites from the original movie, such as Chewbacca, Darth Vader (with Imperial Claw Droid), Luke Skywalker (with Jedi jet pack), C-3Po, and R2-D2; and a Darth Vader Mr. Potato Head called "Darth Tater" (followed by Artoo Potatoo in April 2006, labeled for children aged two and up). Burger King's Kids

Meals had rights to all the fast food tie-ins. The film, which had a PG-13 rating, featured scenes of grizzly violence in which light sabers chopped off limbs, children were killed, and the main character's face melted off in molten lava. In promotional appearances prior to its release, the filmmaker, George Lucas, underlined the violent themes of his final production. "It's much more dark," he said in a *60 Minutes* interview. "It's much more emotional. It's much more of a tragedy. I would take a ten-year-old to it or an eleven, but I don't think I would take a five- or six-year-old to this. It's way too strong." But in May, newspapers from the *San Jose Mercury News* to North Carolina's *News & Observer* reported that many parents were taking their preschoolers — even liberating them from daycare — to go see the movie. "Dark. Violent. Scary. They had heard the warnings. It didn't matter," read the lead paragraph in one such article. "They were going to this movie with their kids."

Why didn't the violence matter to parents? In the marketing terms delineated in the Wharton study, Generation X's emotional attachment to newstalgia seemed to qualify as the brand association that trumped all other purchase decisions. It did not have to do with prestige or reliability but with happy childhood memories. This brand association was so powerful that it overrode other, serious concerns: namely, that the movie was far too scary for little children. If the notoriously overprotective Generation-X parents could turn a blind eye to the violence of *Star Wars*, it was proof positive that newstalgia was powerful. *This* was brand equity.

A Growing Problem

Richard Dickson, a former Bloomingdale's executive, began to mull over brand equity when he became the senior vice president of global consumer marketing and entertainment for Mattel Brands in 2003. He was hired to manage Barbie, but when he looked at her, he saw a big, fat mess. There was nothing wrong with the fashion icon herself; she was unimpeachably fabulous. Barbie had been, after all, the best-selling fashion doll since the 1960s and still "owned" 91 percent of that market. Indeed, a Barbie was sold every three seconds somewhere in the world. But sales had begun to lag in recent years, and Dickson felt that the core of the problem was a vision thing.

Barbie was clearly a horizontal brand. Since her debut in 1959 she had appeared on backpacks, lunchboxes, CD-ROMs, digital cameras, videos, DVDs, nightgowns, and notebooks, to name just a few of the many Barbie products. But the licensing program, in Dickson's view, was in shambles. Barbie's overall look was not as tightly controlled as it should be. Although the international licensing program was successful, Barbie's appearance was completely inconsistent on different licensed products. A candy manufacturer in South America might license a particular image of Barbie, then modify or embellish the image to suit its purposes and stamp the picture on bags of sweets. Meanwhile, a Canadian company might license the same Barbie image but make changes to it before stamping it on a line of nightgowns. This sloppy management had the effect of muddying Barbie's brand identity. Barbie's look needed to be streamlined and absolutely consistent across all formats for her overall image to be clear and coherent. Licensees would still be able to choose from various images of Barbie. But if four different licensees wanted to use the image of Barbie Cali Girl — the Southern California beach hipster who broke off with Ken in 2004 — then each licensee would have to adhere to very strict guidelines governing virtually every aspect of Barbie Cali Girl's appearance. When she appeared in a print ad, for example, her likeness had to be framed by the exact decorative border designed by Dickson's creative team, according to the exact dimensions and color scheme specified by the company.

Dickson issued a phone book–length style guide detailing every conceivable scenario in which Barbie might appear in graphic form, along with specific requirements for her appearance in each case. Furthermore, every Barbie licensee was required to use the new Barbie logo: a classic-looking, cameo-style profile of the It girl herself. If the logo appeared on all Barbie licensed products, from backpacks and charm bracelets to umbrellas and board books, Dickson hoped it would become as recognizable as the Nike swoosh. His efforts paid off almost immediately. He was delighted when colleagues and competitors expressed amazement at how much of Mattel's money he was spending on advertising; Barbie's new pulled-together look and new logo were everywhere. But Dickson hadn't spent a dime. What seemed to be a massive and well-coordinated advertising campaign was simply a result of enforcing the style-guide regulations. With Dickson pulling the strings, Barbie was solving the $1 + 1 = 3$ equation. Now that the brand had a strong, integrated horizontal line, however, it was time to scale the other axis: it was time to take Barbie vertical.

Going vertical was necessary because over the years, Barbie's fans had gotten younger and younger. When she was "born," she had been positioned as a doll for girls between six and eight. Now, girls of that age were favoring Bratz, a line of dolls with massively exaggerated breasts, hips, and lips, wearing street gear and bling. There was even a line of baby Bratz dolls (called Bratz Babyz), which offered a $50 Cribz Playset, complete with tiki kitchen, disco room, sunroof, and aquarium. Although Mattel could not legally promote Barbie to children under the age of three because her tiny accessories are choking hazards, Dickson knew that the dolls were now popular with toddlers. A 2000 study by toy marketing specialists at the now defunct firm Griffin Bacal found that nearly two-thirds of the mothers interviewed reported that their children asked for specific brands before the age of three, while one-third said their kids were aware of brands at age two or earlier. Those that kids knew best included Cheerios, Disney, McDonald's, Pop-Tarts, Coke, and Barbie.

Barbie's popularity with toddlers could be attributed in part to KGOY. But KGOY flourishes most at the intersection of peer pressure and exposure to targeted marketing. That is what made Barbie's appeal to this group so perplexing. Where was the peer pressure among toddlers? Where was the targeted marketing? Where was the KGOY influence coming from? Certainly, older siblings' hand-me-downs could account for some of it. But as far as first-time Barbie customers were concerned, this form of KGOY could only be coming from aunts, godmothers, friends of their mothers — or their mothers.

ALL SOLD SEPARATELY

In one way, it was ironic. The women who were buying two-year-old girls Barbie dolls were mostly Generation Xers who had grown up in the 1970s and 1980s, back when Strawberry Shortcake and her cream-puff crew were marketed as innocent alternatives to Barbie. Even the word "Barbie" had been invoked in liberal circles as a euphemism for sexist values and general helium-headedness; among conservatives, "Barbie" connoted premature sexualization. Now, however, Barbie didn't seem so bad. Not only had she embarked on a few different career tracks in her life (doctor, businesswoman), but compared with Bratz, she seemed downright wholesome. But while some portion of the Gen-X mom customer base certainly figured that it was better to buy a Barbie than a Bratz, there were other reasons for the purchase. Girls who had either grown up with Barbies or been denied them were now eager to relive a piece of their own childhood by buying Barbie for their babies or by giving them a toy they themselves had coveted.

The Barbie brand seemed to have such a strong emotional pull for Gen-X women that they impulsively bought it without heeding the suggested age range. They didn't worry that Barbie might seem too mature or sexualized for little girls and didn't stop to consider that they had probably not played with Barbie until they were six or older. Nor were these mothers deterred, apparently, by the big warning label on each package cautioning that Barbie was not safe for children under three. Gen-X moms couldn't wait. In the rubric of the Wharton professors, the mothers' brand associations with Barbie were so positive and deep-seated it was as if "Barbie" and "happy girlhood" had become synonymous. This powerful connection trumped other important purchase considerations, such as safety, values, and age appropriateness. But just what was it about Barbie that forged this connection?

Dickson nailed it as aspiration. From the start, Barbie had been marketed as a grown-up ideal to which little girls aspired. By the time they entered first grade, children were socialized enough to know that Barbie embodied the teenage mystique: an idealized grown-up world in which girls bought their own clothes, drove their own cars, had their own *stuff*. Historians have pointed out that Barbie's chief mode of play — with her armada of dream houses, automobiles, outfits, and other accessories "all sold separately" — trained little girls in the mores of consumer culture, at a time when becoming grown-up was synonymous with materialism and affluence. Barbie's accoutrements always evolved to fit the style of the current culture, but her continuing allure was her aspirational lifestyle. In terms of vertical brand stature, aspiration was key to the Barbie brand's prestige.

Toddlers, of course, did not understand such nuances. As research had shown, babies and toddlers could recognize — and develop an attachment to — Barbie's face and logo if they were exposed to it regularly. They might even clamor for Barbie-branded items on the basis of that familiarity. But toddlers were not developmentally capable of understanding Barbie's deeper appeal as a representative of a glamorous teenage lifestyle. Indeed, part of the problem with Barbie's new toddler audience was that children that young didn't get the "sold separately" part of the marketing plan, meaning that sales would lag further. Like *Sesame Street*, Barbie was in danger of becoming "for babies." Dickson knew that four-year-old girls wouldn't want to play with toys associated with toddlers. If Barbie continued to appeal to younger children, her chief asset — the ability to inspire aspiration — would become moot. In a strange twist of fate, KGOY could end up relegating Barbie, the long-reigning queen of KGOY, to the Piagetian toy chest. She would become just another baby doll.

Perhaps the way to get Barbie's KGOY kingdom back might be via the customer base that had gotten Barbie into this predicament: Gen-X women. Toddlers might not understand Barbie's aspirational pull, but their mothers obviously did. That the Barbie brand associations remained so strong for Gen-X mothers suggested that even into their late twenties and thirties, they still yearned, in some deep way, to have a Barbie — which in a more primitive way meant they still probably wanted to *be* Barbie. And that gave Dickson an idea.

In October 2005 Mattel introduced Barbie Luxe, a line of couture jeans, shirts, handbags, and jewelry for women and teenage girls. Capitalizing on his clout as a former fashion executive, Dickson tapped labels such as Versace, Anna Sui, Anya Hindmarch, Citizens of Humanity, Judith Leiber, Nickel, Not Rational, Paper Denim & Cloth, Stila, and Tarina Tarantino to use Barbie as their "muse" in creating exclusive clothing and accessories — all with Barbie's new retro silhouette on a cameo pendant as the official logo. "Our target market is the fashionista," said Dickson, at a Barbie Luxe press conference. "From teens through adults in their twenties and thirties. It's not Mattel's usual target audience."

Dickson launched Barbie Luxe as he would any couture line: during New York's Fashion Week, amid underground campaigns and exclusive launch parties. "When a teen or twenty-something is carrying an Anya Hindmarch Barbie bag it'll reinforce Barbie as a relevant, cool brand for little girls," said Dickson. "Little girls are growing up faster than ever and looking to adults and teens for inspiration, and Barbie is their aspiration." To keep the brand truly aspirational, prices were deliberately set high: jeans were $176, and a three-quarter-sleeve hooded sweatshirt listed for $140. Dickson told reporters that Mattel was making a point of keeping Barbie Luxe as a specialty collection and the prices a bit out of reach. "Barbie has a special relationship with women," he said in an interview with Reuters that fall. "It takes them back to being a little girl and fantasizing about what they're going to be in the future."

But women were not fantasizing about their daughters being just Barbie-fabulous someday: they were fantasizing that they would be smart, successful, happy, *and* fabulous. To appeal to Gen-X parents, the treacly fun of Barbie — indeed, of any mass-market character — had to be balanced with the gravitas of an all-important accessory: a book. "We feel parents are more willing to buy something about reading, about learning," a Random House marketing executive explained. "So, if their daughter's into Barbie, they may buy a toy, but they'll also go for the book [because] it can help with their education, their future."

7

Anything to Get Them to Read

WANDER INTO THE KIDS' SECTION of a Barnes & Noble bookstore and you may find — among the oversize cardboard character cutouts and tables promoting seasonal or theme-based specials — a wooden train set. If you cannot find it, that may be because it's obscured by a thicket of intent little bodies gathered around a table that is just the right height. The train set features every accessory a little person might dream up: loopy tracks, trestles and drawbridges, perfect tiny trees and miniature buildings, and an array of train cars, including a steam engine, boxcars, a coach car, and a diesel engine. Venture closer to the table and listen to the kids. Most likely they will not be discussing what the different trains do but what "Thomas" or "Gordon" or "James" or "Wilbert" does. If one of these names happens to belong to one of the children at play, it is purely coincidental. The children are talking about the train characters belonging to the entertainment property Thomas & Friends, one of the most successful brands in the children's entertainment business.

As a toy, Thomas is targeted to boys from two to five years old, and even as young as eighteen months. As a brand, Thomas & Friends generates an estimated $500 million in annual retail sales. Thomas books have sold 25 million units in the United States, and worldwide book sales are approaching 80 million units. Thomas was not always such a high-revving engine. By the late 1990s, the property was close to stalling, until a marketing executive named David Jacobs took control and set Thomas on its present course, making comparisons to *The Little Engine That Could* at once hackneyed and appropriate.

Jacobs, an angular, bespectacled man in his fifties, has been in the children's entertainment industry for more than two decades. Starting as a U.S. representative at international entertainment trade shows in the early 1980s, he moved to Sesame Workshop in 1987. As the manager of consumer product licensing in Asia, he helped take *Sesame Street* to China. But reviving Thomas was not a trivial operation. When he started in 1998 as vice president and head of licensing at the New York office of the U.K.-based Britt Allcroft Group (then owner of Thomas & Friends, later renamed Gullane Entertainment), Jacobs was charged with unseating the Swedish toy company Brio as the top seller of toy trains for toddlers. Thomas had been popular as a children's television show in the United Kingdom in the 1980s and had had a good run on PBS in the early 1990s as a character on a show called *Shining Time Station*, but at this point the train had all but disappeared from American TV, and sales of Thomas toys were barely moving. Like every marketing executive in the toy business, Jacobs knew that the most efficient way to increase toy sales was to launch a television show starring the toy itself. But at the time, television producers were looking for fresh, new properties, so Jacobs would have to come up with another approach. He identified a core problem: Thomas was fuzzy on brand identity. What did Thomas really stand for? American boys had played with trains for more than a hundred years. But nowadays, even the little boys at whom Thomas was targeted were playing with action figures. Thomas not only had to differentiate itself from other toy trains but also had to make train play special again.

One way in which Thomas (and friends) stood out from the pack was that he had literary appeal, having begun life as a character in a 1940s British book series. If Jacobs could capitalize on this legacy, the parents most likely to purchase Thomas products at first would be college-educated and in the middle to upper middle class. Ultimately, to make money in volume sales, the products would have to appeal to a mass market. But if Thomas was restructured as a vertical brand, with the literary patina at the top trickling down to products lower in the chain, it could move from class to mass over time. Jacobs knew he would have to be careful not to oversaturate the market or alienate relationships with small independent toy stores; the "boutique," upscale appearance would be crucial to Thomas's brand image. Once that association was locked in, Thomas could be made more cheaply for the mass market. But the marketing strategy would have to convince parents not only that Thomas had educational value but also that it was at least equal to Brio in quality. Then Jacobs had what he considers a major *aha!* moment of his career: he would carry out this strategy through *books*.

In retrospect, the plan seems obvious. Books could be produced cheaply, but their educational status would greatly enhance the value of the Thomas brand. Entertainment properties inspired by book series invariably carry educational heft and "class" appeal. But to simultaneously boost sales of the train sets and accessories, Jacobs would have to promote the books and toys in the same retail environment. In terms of building educational brand equity, he reasoned, it would make more sense to get the toys into the bookstore rather than the books in the toy store. In 1999 Jacobs arranged to have Thomas train tables set up in the kids' sections of Barnes & Noble stores, which at that point were just beginning to expand their children's merchandising. Jacobs recognized, as did his colleagues at Barnes & Noble, that American babies, toddlers, and preschoolers were spending more time at the bookstore chain. The train tables offered a win-win: they generated interest in Thomas and kept children in the play area so that mom could shop.

Jacobs was right. Today, as he predicted, the Thomas brand does straddle the twin tracks of mass and class, with the high-end wooden train cars and engines selling for premium prices at Barnes & Noble and toy boutiques, and a low-end, die-cast plastic "Take Along" line selling at discount rates at Target. Thomas is now sold at Toys "R" Us, too, including the higher-end wooden railway pieces. And it finally made enough money for a television program based on story lines from the books. When television writers started coming up with new plot lines, the process reversed itself. A show once based on a series of books was now inspiring new books, which then sold to fans of the television show. In 2005, classic Thomas stories were reprinted, and by 2006 new stories from the new television show were published. As part of Thomas's sixtieth-anniversary marketing blitz, the parent company, HIT Entertainment, teamed up with the American Library Association to distribute anniversary-themed posters and bookmarks through libraries across the United States. As HIT North America's president, Pat Wyatt, said in an interview with a reporter in 2006: "Anything that gets kids to read, right?"

CHEWABLES

Jacobs's idea of using books to sell toys was an innovative strategy in 1999. But using toys or other spin-off merchandise to sell children's books is not new; the practice is almost as old as children's publishing itself. The pioneer children's publisher John Newbery (1713–1767) regularly bundled his books with gimmicky freebies — pincushions, balls, even headache tonics — to boost sales. But by the early 2000s, marketing synergies and spin-off merchandise (known as "merch") had become an extremely powerful force in publishing, and one of the fastest-growing areas within it was the infant and toddler category.

This trend took hold in a remarkably short time, considering that books for infants and toddlers had been in existence for barely twenty years. Under the aegis of the zero-to-three product industry, the baby book category was born in the 1980s, when academic research was demonstrating that children who were "bathed" in language from the start — spoken to, read to, engaged in conversations, encouraged to tell their own stories and share their thoughts — were far more likely to be able to read by school age than those who weren't. As a first step, parents were advised to read to their babies. It didn't matter that babies and toddlers never seem to sit still long enough to hear a story and can't understand much of it anyway; one of the precursors to literacy is regular exposure to reading. One problem, however, was that, aside from Mother Goose and sundry nursery rhymes, books written specifically for babies were scarce in the early 1980s. Furthermore, parents were concerned that expensive picture books would swiftly be mauled by children too young to realize that they were destroying property or to be disciplined for doing so. And babies and toddlers are just as apt to gnaw on books to soothe teething pains or simply express their immersion in the oral stage of development as they are to sit still for a lap reading. Parents worried that the push to develop preliteracy skills might translate into constant fishing trips into their babies' throats to extract wads of *Goodnight Moon*.

The publishing industry came up with a solution: "chewables." These short, sturdy, chunky cardboard books are made to withstand regular gumming, but for reasons of liability as choking hazards, this benefit could not be explicitly advertised. The books were never referred to as "chewables" outside of industry conversations; to consumers, they were marketed as board books. Although they had been around since the 1970s, board books didn't become big business in children's publishing — and staples in bookstores, libraries, daycare centers, homes, strollers, and car seats — until the 1980s. By the end of that decade, board books had become so important in children's publishing that many companies started reformatting older titles as chewables.

The 1990s saw a frenzy in board-book publishing. The White House brain conference and the focus on the importance of the first three years reignited the fervor for early reading. Publishers began mining every successful children's book they had ever published to see if it could be resurrected in board-book form. Longer storybooks were abridged and adapted to the format, but in many cases, they weren't successful. The original Winnie-the-Pooh stories by A. A. Milne, illustrated by Ernest H. Shepard did not work as board books because, many in the industry believe, the illustrations were too intricate and sophisticated to appeal to babies. Disney's Winnie the Pooh, however, worked perfectly because the Technicolor cartoon, with its googly eyes and simple lines, was more appealing to infants. But the popularity of the Disney version also resulted from the character's media tie-ins. And by 2000, media tie-ins had become a major part of children's publishing.

THEY'VE BEEN CORRUPTED

Natasha Cane, a thoughtful, open-faced woman in her twenties, is a juvenile specialist for the Brooklyn Heights branch of the Brooklyn Public Library. Part of her job is to arrange the books in their display cases, to direct young children and their caregivers to books they might enjoy, and to serve in a generally advisory role. Since 2003, when she took that position, Cane has made some changes to the young children's area. "I've tried to make this a more Barnes & Noble experience by pulling out all our Franklins, all the Arthurs, all the Maisys," she explains, spinning one of the racks holding books featuring TV characters. "It makes it more accessible, and it's what they're looking for. The kids can come in and say, 'Look Mommy, Clifford!' And go right to it and get instant gratification." She has found it difficult to get young children interested in titles that are not based on licensed characters. She laughs with resignation: "They've been corrupted!"

Like many of her colleagues, Cane has made an uneasy peace with licensed books, though she reckons that no librarian does so without some serious struggles. On the one hand, librarians are trained as cultural curators, helping point young readers to books that might open their minds to new forms of art and ideas, books that children might not find on their own. Cane worries that although licensed books usually have the kinds of images that very young children respond to —

primary colors, simple lines — the approach "makes kids more rigid," she says, and "mistrustful of stuff that's not packaged in a familiar way." She points to *Madlenka* by Peter Sis as a wonderful story with beautiful art: "A book like that can awaken a child's artistic sensibilities" in ways that a mass-market book can't. But Cane says that it is increasingly a challenge to interest a very young child in *Madlenka* because the character isn't a familiar brand. Cane recalls trying to share the children's classic *Blueberries for Sal* by Robert McCloskey with a group of preschoolers. The three-year-olds complained that something was wrong with the book. It looked "sick." When she asked them why, the children told her it was because the illustrations were in black and white.

Cane has noticed that the youngest children gravitate more and more toward books featuring licensed characters. Infants and toddlers watch a great deal of television, and when they come to the library they recognize and ask for these characters, if not in words, certainly in gestures and vocalizations that are unmistakable. "It's empowering to a two-year-old to recognize a character on a cover," Cane says. How can one discourage a toddler from picking up a book? She has adopted the stance of many other librarians with respect to the cross-pollination of movies, TV, and books: If it gets them to read, who is she to discourage them? "We're happy to see kids coming into the library," she explains. "If it has to do with a movie they've seen or the way a book is marketed, as mass-produced as it may be, if it gets a child to read then I'm a happy camper."

READING IS GOOD — RIGHT?

That was the opinion Daniel Hade had always held, too. An associate professor of children's literature at Pennsylvania State University and a former librarian, Hade — like many of his colleagues — had always believed that reading is good, whatever the form. Hade, an earnest, portly fellow in his fifties, was a freshly minted Ph.D. when the literacy studies of the 1980s were published, promoting the message that all reading was good reading. Born of the same research that inspired the board-book explosion, the recommendations from academia held that adults shouldn't restrict children to books. They should read aloud the ingredients on the breakfast cereal box, point out words on traffic signs, intone advertising tag lines on billboards. They should let infants and toddlers see that every part of their world is touched and defined by language. Certainly, no type of book should be discouraged. If children wanted to read only comic books or Golden Books based on television or movie characters, they should be encouraged to do so; at least they were reading. Purists might dismiss such books as merch, but they had to recognize that merch wasn't new. Wasn't this merch promoting reading, however obliquely? In fact, couldn't you make the case that a toy or a mobile or a printed crib bumper was, in a sense, a new interpretation of a story?

In 2002 Hade decided to conduct an exercise involving Curious George, whom Hade had adored as a kid. The chimp's inimitable combination of spontaneity, cheek, and guilelessness were so irresistible that as a boy Hade had religiously borrowed *Curious George* books from his local public library to keep up with George's adventures. Back then, reading books was the only way to do that. But by 2002, Hade realized, a young enthusiast could surround himself with Curious George. By doing a bit of window shopping, Hade discovered that a child could wake up in the morning to the ringing of his Curious George alarm clock, and if it was still dark outside, he could flick on his Curious George lamp. Clutching one of his many Curious George plush dolls, he could unwrap himself from his Curious George comforter and bed sheets. He could peek out from his window hung with curtains fashioned from Curious George cloth. Making his way to his Curious George dresser, he might stumble over some toys he'd neglected to return to his Curious George toy chest: his Curious George drum, spinning top, jack-in-the-box, train set, and a multitude of Curious George puzzles. He could slip on a Curious George tee shirt before looking in on his baby sister, sleeping in a crib lined with Curious George bumpers and fitted with a Curious George sheet. In the kitchen, he could reach for Curious George salt and pepper shakers to flavor his morning eggs on the Curious George plate placed on a Curious George placemat. He could check the time on a Curious George wall clock before grabbing his Curious George lunchbox and stuffing it into his Curious George backpack. At school he would find that his teacher had put up a Curious George wall-hanging alphabet and had set up the flannel board with Curious George felt characters. Next to the computer might be a Curious George mouse pad and a stack of Curious George CD-ROMs. At home after school, he could snag a cookie from the Curious George cookie jar, look at the Curious George calendar, and count the days to Halloween. Then he could put the *Curious George Flies a Kite* video in the VCR and dream about wearing his Curious George costume on Halloween, collecting candy in his Curious George pail. Hade found all these products, and more, listed on Amazon.com.

If Hade had conducted the same search in 2006, he would have encountered a new raft of Curious George products — and a whole new Curious George. Although Houghton Mifflin (also the publisher of this book) had published the original series, it did not hold exclusive licensing rights and was not the company behind George's celebrity makeover. The Curious George of Hade's youth, and the one whose likeness was emblazoned on so many licensed products, had been redesigned to coincide with Universal Studio's *Curious George* movie, which reached theaters in February 2006 (earning $58.3 million at the box office). In many ways comparable to Disney's makeover of Ernest H. Shepard's original Winnie-the-Pooh, the new George had bigger eyes, a more open, smiling face — a more cartoony look than the hand-sketched illustration of old. A TV series, narrated by William H. Macy, debuted on PBS Kids in the fall of 2006. Promotions abounded: a Tickle N Giggle doll, new books, a Bump N Go line of toddler push-along toys, storybooks with plush toy for two-year-olds and up, a new line of beanbag plush for three and up. There were five different toy-with-book items. "We've heard from parents, and they said they love the idea of a book with a toy," explained Joann McLaughlin, co–chief operating officer at Toy Biz (a licensee of Universal Studio's version of Curious George) at Toy Fair 2006. But, added a colleague, the merchandise launched around the movie "is just the beginning."

"Reading," wrote the journalist Tom Engelhardt in a 1991 article in *Harper's Magazine*, "may be harmful to your kids." Engelhardt argued that the publishing industry's new corporate stewards, such as Bertelsmann (Random House) and Rupert Murdoch's News Corporation (HarperCollins), were so dependent on revenues from the toys, clothing, and recordings spun off from children's books that reading had come to be an extension of "listening, viewing, playing, dressing, and buying." Reading children's books, he maintained, was just another way of shopping.

Like many readers, Hade — as he later described in a *Horn Book* article — did not take Engelhardt very seriously at the time. His admonishment had seemed extreme, and Hade, by his own admission, had never been particularly political. Even as a student in the 1960s, he preferred sitting in the corner of the library buried in a good book to striding with antiwar comrades or penning jeremiads against social injustice. But these developments in children's books bothered him. It was tempting to view all this merchandise as promoting reading, to see it as a good thing. But Hade was beginning to feel that the more powerful message to children was not "read" but "buy." Perhaps this trend signified something more than a change of scale in the business.

STRONG NAME RECOGNITION

The corporate mergers of the 1990s compressed children's book publishing into a small cadre of large houses: HarperCollins, Penguin Putnam, Random House, Simon & Schuster, and Scholastic. Except for Scholastic, the largest publisher and distributor of children's books, these houses were corporate divisions of large media conglomerates such as Viacom, the News Corporation, Pearson Corporation, and Bertelsmann. Other industry behemoths such as the Walt Disney Company and AOL Time Warner also owned children's book publishing houses. These corporations dominated book publishing in the United States, and they radically shifted the way business and marketing was conducted.

In the past publishers had expected to make profit margins of roughly 4 percent by relying on the intermittent bestseller, dependable backlists, and the sale of various rights. But the industry always felt it had a greater intellectual mission. Book editors and publishers alike considered it their job not just to turn out products that kept their business thriving but also to produce books that contributed something vital to cultural life. To conglomerates, this approach was quaint, naive, and unprofitable — or, rather, not as profitable as they wanted. The new corporate parents expected their publishing divisions to earn profits in the 12 to 15 percent range. In children's publishing, this expectation was met by mining backlists for well-known characters and stories, licensable properties with TV, movie, or toy tie-ins. Characters — whether they originated in children's books, television shows, or movies — were treated as licensed properties and appeared across a wide range of media. By the early 2000s, classic children's storybook characters such as Clifford the Big Red Dog, Arthur, Madeline, and Peter Rabbit had emerged as major licensed properties, with their own TV or video series and products ranging from backpacks and bed sheets to lunchboxes and alarm clocks. The annual reports from the big publishing houses openly began to acknowledge and promote their classic storybook characters as branded properties. Conversely, popular television and movie characters had become hot licenses, which conglomerates could either funnel into their own children's book divisions or sell at a premium to other companies.

In 1997, Scholastic decided to get into the entertainment business, so it formed Scholastic Entertainment Inc. (SEI). Today the division is responsible for TV, feature films, interactive products, DVDs, video, software, video games, and Web sites; it is also the licenser and marketer of

Scholastic properties worldwide. "The Company develops successful children's books and then builds these brands into multimedia assets," read a passage from Scholastic's 1999 annual report. "Scholastic has developed strong name recognition associated with quality and dedication to learning." Four years later the company had refined its strategy, highlighting the success of Clifford the Big Red Dog as a far-reaching vertical brand: "The *Clifford the Big Red Dog* series is part of a comprehensive brand marketing campaign, including home entertainment, consumer products, publishing extensions, such as television tie-in books, interactive media and consumer promotions, supporting Clifford's position as a leading pre-school brand." The report underscored Clifford's status in the marketing industry: "In connection with its branding campaigns, SEI (Scholastic Entertainment Inc.) has received numerous marketing and licensing awards, including a 2003 LIMA award for Clifford as 'Best Character License.'" Other publishers used similar language to describe their properties.

IT CAN CERTAINLY DRIVE SALES

From the corporations' point of view, the new zero-to-three book market opened up even more licensing and branding possibilities. Scholastic, which controls the children's book "club" market, acquired Baby's First Book Club in 2002. The infant and toddler market also gave publishers the opportunity to funnel their licensed properties into a dazzling variety of new book formats. "Chewables" may have been the mother format for babies and toddlers, but she rapidly produced litter after litter of new offspring: oversized board books, palm-size board books, board books equipped with stroller tethers, board books with padded covers, "touch-and-feel" board books using textured fabrics and other materials (think *Pat the Bunny*), board books with sparkly or foil papers, board books with embedded sound chips; board books with toys attached (wheels on a Tonka Truck board book, for example), puzzle board books, "activity" board books, lift-the-flap board books, soft cloth books; waterproof bath books, magnetic play books. All these formats could serve as vessels for licensed properties, and many have done so with great success.

In 2003 a list of the ten most popular board books for children three and under read more like a Nielsen TV ratings report than a roster of literature. Number one was based on *Winnie the Pooh,* then *Sesame Street,* with *Bob the Builder* in third, *Dora the Explorer* in fourth, and *Clifford the Big Red Dog* as number five; *Little Critters* ranked sixth, anything by Dr. Seuss was seventh, *Finding Nemo* was eighth, *Blue's Clues* ninth, and *Barney and Friends* closed the list at number ten.

By the early 2000s, preschool television and baby genius videos had acquired such a strong reputation as learning arts that they made even their tie-in books seem more educational than the average book. One of the fastest-growing sectors of children's publishing was board books tied to videos marketed as educational for infants and toddlers. By 2004 HarperCollins had purchased the license for Mommy & Me, Disney owned Baby Einstein books, and Bendon Publishing International began releasing *Brainy Baby* books based on the video series. Such titles could now wear two halos: one for the baby genius–type videos and the other for early literacy and books in general. "If you can affix your company or product line to an educational brand, it can certainly drive sales," acknowledged Ben Ferguson, Bendon's president, in a 2004 interview with *Publishers Weekly.*

Board books based on popular preschool shows, such as *Dora the Explorer,* sold themselves because they starred well-known characters. Books based on licensed characters or video series seemed to come with their own stamp of approval. For parents these books represented a safe impulse buy; toddlers clamored for them because they recognized the characters from television. Moreover, the flood of spin-off books into big chain stores helped strengthen the educational marketing claims of the TV shows, DVDs, and videos; the educational patina of books served to cement the shows' equity as education brands. (The strategy was also taken up by purveyors of snack and junk foods. General Mills, Mars, and Nabisco marketed their Cheerios, Goldfish, M&Ms, and Oreos board books as "counting" and "activity" board books for toddlers.)

SQUEEZED OUT

Corporate synergy in the media industry was not the only reason the licensing business was able to make such deep inroads into infant and toddler publishing. The demise of libraries also played a role. In this new landscape, public and school libraries, which had been major markets for children's books, could no longer generate enough revenue to sustain the conglomerates' requirement of a 12 to 15 percent profit margin. In the 1960s and 1970s, librarians trained in selecting age-appropriate books with a range of artistic styles, narrative forms, and graphic presentations made the purchasing decisions, and the federal, state, and local governments provided funding through a variety of initiatives. By the early 2000s, however, those funding sources had all but dried up; when money is tight, a school's media specialist is often one of the first to be let go. The new, more profitable markets for publishers were big bookstore chains and mass-market discounters, and the children's books they move most quickly are licensed books.

According to publishing sales executives, Barnes & Noble and Borders Books and Music — the country's largest booksellers — had not historically been heavy purchasers of licensed products. But by 2005 they had shifted course. One reason was that most of their customers were gravitating to the licensed stuff. As a sales executive for a midsize children's publishing house put it: "Most buyers grab what's familiar, what's easy. People either say, 'I had that book when I was a kid' or 'My kid is addicted to Power Rangers; he'd probably like a book about them.'" Because the chains have come to dominate the physical and economic landscape in the United States, children's book publishers now rely on sales to the chains. The more copies of a book that Barnes & Noble commits to buying, the better its chance of success. With the media tie-in books, those written by celebrities (Madonna, Jamie Lee Curtis,

John Lithgow, Katie Couric) and perennial classics such as *Pat the Bunny* and *Goodnight Moon* taking up so much shelf space, there seemed to be little room at the chains for children's authors and illustrators doing wholly original work. According to one publishing executive, "They're being squeezed out."

It is not, many in the industry hasten to emphasize, that no original books are being produced anymore. With roughly 10,000 children's titles coming out every year, there is still a lot of original material. But much of it isn't getting into the big chains in significant volume, which limits publishers' sales opportunities. For a book to avoid failure, it has to hit certain sales numbers. A trade book (one with an original story and illustrations) is not considered a failure if it sells 5,000 copies. But with mass-market books — the majority of licensed books — selling 5,000 would be considered a disaster. A mass-market book can sell 50,000, 100,000, or a million copies. Those numbers conform to the mold that Barnes & Noble, Borders, and other big chains appear to be creating: carrying fewer titles but selling more of them.

THEY FOLLOW INSTRUCTIONS

At the chains, licensed books and tie-in merch are often given prime toddler eye-level shelf space. Unlike independent bookstores, which often recommend books based on knowledge of the book (and, in many cases, of the customer), the children's section managers at mega-bookstore chains may not have any professional experience in children's literature or education, in libraries or bookstores, or even in selling books at all. Most such managers don't even decide how to organize their sections. Instead, they follow instructions from corporate headquarters. Boxes of new books arrive tagged with SKU identification numbers, which correspond to specific locations in the children's section. This system tells managers where, how, and for how long books are to be displayed. The section managers also do not make the purchasing decisions, which are in the hands of corporate buyers.

The buyer determines which books a chain such as Barnes & Noble will stock. Like the children's section managers, the corporate buyers of children's books may have no background in children's literature or education. In determining how many copies of a new title to order, they rely on the past sales performance of certain book series, authors, or illustrators; to be safe, buyers usually stick with the proven winners. Some conscientious buyers may scour the journals that review children's books for the starred recommendations and make at least some purchasing decisions based on that selection. But this strategy does not usually lead to chains stocking more books by small, independent publishers. In fact, it tends to further support the conglomerates. According to Hade's calculations, in 2000 more than 84 percent of the books reviewed in the *Horn Book Magazine* and more than 75 percent of those that received a starred review in *School Library Journal* were published by the big houses. As a point of comparison, just over a quarter of a century before, in 1967, the top eight children's book publishers accounted for just 34.4 percent of the reviews in the *Horn Book* and 38 percent of the starred reviews in *SLJ*. Since the success of a children's book largely rests on whether a chain stocks it, a great deal depends on this star system. One of the few points of leverage publishers have in convincing a bookstore chain to stock a title it might otherwise reject is to pay for expensive in-store promotions. But this costly practice is an option only for big corporate publishing houses.

In 2001 Borders, the country's second-largest bookstore chain, began a program of selecting various publishers to comanage each of its 250 book categories. Random House — publisher of *Dora the Explorer, Blue's Clues, Bob the Builder,* and *Thomas the Tank Engine* licensed books — was chosen as the first "captain" of books for children. An entire division of Random House was permitted to help decide which books, from all publishers, would be stocked, displayed, and marketed in Borders stores. "Category management," as this marketing practice is called, is now emerging as a major trend in the publishing industry. Publishers inform the chains of their bestsellers, sales figures, and analysis, and help them decide what to stock. A publisher pays Borders more than $100,000 for this privilege and the access to research — a price out of reach for most small to midsize publishing houses. Although Borders insisted it would have the final say over which titles were chosen, critics argued that when the supermarket industry adopted category management in the 1990s, "final say" amounted to little more than a rubber stamp response; the "captains" essentially chose to stock their own products.

THEY LIKE CHEAP

For publishers of children's books, mass-merchandising chains such as Wal-Mart and Target are increasingly important accounts. The baby genius trend of recent years seems to have motivated Wal-Mart in particular to devote more shelf space to books — and Wal-Mart has plenty of shelf space. Where Barnes & Noble might order a thousand copies of a board book, Wal-Mart can order a million. Because Wal-Mart wields such enormous buying power — and because, as it moves toward its goal of becoming a trillion-dollar company, one market segment it is looking to command is books — it may be edging into the uniquely advantageous position of single-handedly shaping the marketing and selling of children's books in the United States. According to publishing sales executives, Wal-Mart often asks, in exchange for a huge purchasing order, that the Wal-Mart logo be stamped on the cover of each book, a request many publishers find hard to turn down. Wal-Mart can also demand exclusive reprints of out-of-print titles or have books custom-published for its use only.

Of particular interest for the baby and toddler category is that the mass merchandiser sells a huge number of board books. It does not seek out specific authors or illustrators. As one sales executive for the publisher of a top-selling board-book series characterized Wal-Mart book buyers' sensibilities: "They like series, and they like cheap." Six or seven dollars is about the highest price for a board book sold by Wal-

Mart. This has further motivated publishers to funnel their backlists and every viable entertainment property into board-book format: if a publisher can produce a board book at a low price, it may be able to persuade Wal-Mart to carry a book it wouldn't otherwise have considered.

The board books that sell best at Wal-Mart are based on licensed products and media tie-ins. According to sales executives in children's publishing, Wal-Mart does more business with licensed products, even for the baby book market, than any other retail outlet. Wal-Mart "will do a lot less" with characters that have staying power, like *Sesame Street* characters, than with Spider-Man 2 because Spider-Man 2 is "right now." Wal-Mart stocks such books on low shelves so that even very young children will push parents to an impulse buy. "The only time a child drives a book purchase is when the book features a licensed character," one publishing sales executive explains. "Your kid riding in a shopping cart points at it, and wants it, so you buy it." Parents may be pleased, thinking that they are supporting their toddler's budding interest in reading. But make no mistake, the executive says, the child has not been attracted to a book; he has been drawn in by branding.

A Moral at the End

Amy Cohen (not her real name) is a freelance children's book author who describes herself as a "hired hand" or "the flack" for several publishing houses that produce books based on licensed characters and movie tie-ins. She has written more than fifty such books, many based on some of Disney's best-known characters, as well as books featuring popular stars from Nickelodeon and PBS television shows. "I think I get paid pretty well, considering it's low effort, and it doesn't take me a lot of time," she explains.

Cohen is commissioned by the publisher and is paid a flat rate for her work: no royalty deals, no copyrights. Books are sometimes "by" her or "adapted by" her, but just as often she gets no writing credit at all.

This does not concern her: she is less interested in making a name for herself as a children's book author than in making decent money for as little part-time work as possible. "I could take on projects that would pay the same but would be more time-consuming," she explains. "But why take on ninety-six pages for five thousand dollars when you can do two twenty-four-page storybooks for five thousand dollars?" Typically, she has three months to do a storybook and she tries not to spend more than fifteen hours total on each one. It's a manageable workload, she says, for a mother working from home with two kids. And even if she did make a concerted effort to achieve a level of eloquence or originality in her work, she does not imagine that many readers would notice or care. "These books are not sold on the writing," she says, with a smile that suggests the point is obvious. "These books are sold on concept and cover design. Buyers for a Wal-Mart or a Barnes & Noble don't say, 'Let me see how well-written the stories are.' The writing — and even the pictures — are, unfortunately, not that important."

Before she became a children's book author, Cohen worked as an editor of mass-market children's books at one of the large corporate publishing houses. She dealt with licensers shopping ideas to book publishers and toy makers at licensing shows. Much of the deal making took place at the Licensing Show, where entertainment studios enlist as many publishers and toy makers as possible to tie in with new TV shows or movies. The deals can be tantamount to gambling for a publisher that licenses a brand-new, unproven property; just like toy licensees, publishers try to predict whether the show will be a hit.

If Cohen's company deems a property potentially lucrative enough, it would approach a licenser with a contract offer. In a hypothetical but typical case, she explains, a publisher might propose paying a studio — Disney, for example — $100,000 and 5 percent of its net sales and maybe a five-year deal for a certain number of books in exchange for the rights to publish a book about, say, Ariel of *The Little Mermaid*. The deal might further stipulate that Disney would license only inexpensive formats (books that sell for under $12) to the publisher. Under that agreement, Disney Press would agree to publish only books sold above that price point. Naturally, the actual figures depend on how hot the property is. Publishers forecast how many copies they think they can sell and then figure out how much to pay for the license. After the license has been acquired, an editorial team at the publishing company and the licenser agree on the basic content, story line, or theme of the book; if it features a TV show character, the book will be based on a particular episode. The editor in charge then usually commissions a freelancer to write the book — at which point Cohen enters the picture.

Her job officially begins when the studio sends her a script of the show or movie on which the book is to be based. Cohen also receives a document entitled Defense of the Property, which explains the theory behind, say, *Blue's Clues* and why it's a good show for kids. She also receives a style guide or, as it is sometimes called, "About the Brand." Often more than one hundred pages long, the style guide describes in great detail how the property — Disney's Cinderella, for example — may and may not be represented in print. Cohen explains that the style guide gives an author the tools to "create a world with parameters that you have to obey." The story is supposed to follow the script of the movie or TV show episode the licenser has chosen, although she can sometimes add her own "moments" between scenes, minor elements that help move the story along — so long as she "follows the rules." One rule is that she must adhere to each character's brand identity, as specified in the guide. Each character has a complete biography and a set of restrictions that ensures that it is presented consistently in the many media in which it appears (Dumbo, for example, is never allowed to speak).

As little effort as Cohen expends on writing books with media tie-ins, she says that even less is spent on licensed board books for infants and toddlers. These are usually tossed off quickly by in-house editors, thus saving the publishing company the expense of hiring a professional writer. "You just pull out a few sentences or rewrite a few sentences — it's not worth commissioning someone to do it," Cohen explains. She doesn't usually meditate on what the books she writes offer their readers. "They are what they are," she shrugs. She does feel that they have introduced her, as a mother, to shows she would not otherwise have known about. And the books are harmless fun, she says. "Some days you just don't feel like reading a book that has a moral at the end, you know?"

8

Developing Character in Preschool

S HE CAN'T REMEMBER the specific date, but sometime in the
late 1990s Iris Sroka and her counterpart at Scholastic got together to brainstorm about what made *Clifford the Big Red Dog*
educational. They set their kids up in front of a video game and trun-
dled upstairs to her colleague's home office to talk about themes in the
book series by Norman Bridwell.

At the time Scholastic Entertainment Inc. (SEI) — the division responsible for the company's media, licensing, and advertising business
— was developing *Clifford the Big Red Dog* for PBS Kids as an educational program for preschoolers. The producers, Sroka recalls, wanted
to demonstrate that the TV show was based on an articulated curriculum that would guide the show's narrative as well as assure PBS's corporate underwriters and the parents of young viewers that the program
was based on sound educational principles. The producers needed to
have an expert in early childhood education look at the series, extract
the underlying philosophy, and distill this philosophy into a few cogent
tenets that TV executives and parents could absorb easily.

Sroka was an obvious candidate for the job. She helped determine that Clifford's purview was what academics call socioemotional learning: sharing, compassion, kindness, and cooperation. He helps children build character. Sroka and her colleague wrapped these concepts into a package entitled "Clifford's Ten Big Ideas": "Share"; "Be Responsible"; "Be Truthful"; "Be Kind"; "Believe in Yourself"; "Be a Good Friend"; "Have Respect"; "Help Others"; "Work Together"; "Play Fair."

A star was born — or, rather, born again. Clifford had been around in books for more than forty years, but starring on his own TV show shot him to superstardom. Since it debuted in 2000, *Clifford the Big Red Dog* has been a consistently top-rated show with children five years old and under. The series has been licensed for broadcast in more than eighty-five countries. Clifford became such a hit with the youngest of his young audience that in 2003 SEI launched a new show, or what it referred to as "a Clifford brand extension": *Clifford's Puppy Days*, which featured puppy versions of the regulars. Scholastic soon launched a whole range of baby Clifford products within its Sidekicks Baby line, featuring items ranging from Clifford's Puppy Days Attachable Jiggler (plush toy with bone and "vibrating mechanism") to Clifford the Small Red Puppy Stacking Ring Developmental Toy. Sidekicks offers Story-Book Collectibles, including Clifford Puppy Days plush toy with soft book. (In 2005 Scholastic launched Grow With Clifford, which the senior vice president of marketing and consumer products referred to as a "brand extension for infants and toddlers." Grow With Clifford products include baby wipes, diapers, bottles, bibs, pacifiers, melamine bowls and plates, baby formula, infant/newborn apparel, footwear, crib and room décor, and bath products.)

By 2003 there was no question that Clifford had risen to the pantheon of early childhood celebrities, able to take his place self-assuredly alongside Elmo, Big Bird, Blue, and Dora. He was proving to be a remarkably successful licensed character, too. Since his television debut just three years before, Clifford had become a multimedia powerhouse. According to the senior vice president, "Clifford became a full-fledged media brand with his own daily television series on PBS Kids and over sixty licensees in apparel and accessories, domestic and home furnishing, food & beverages, publishing, stationery and paper goods, toys, gifts, DVDs, and CDs. Managing the brand across all these platforms to ensure the integrity of what Clifford stands for has helped keep Clifford an evergreen property that continues to be a favorite with children, parents, and teachers." But the "Ten Big Ideas" would be able to pierce the heart of the preschool market: preschool itself.

FUN WITH CLIFFORD

Using the "Ten Big Ideas" as its centerpiece, Scholastic assembled a prekindergarten curriculum for sale to daycare centers, private preschools, and pre-K programs. Ellen Booth Church, a professor at the State University of New York, was a consultant. She had been an educational consultant to Scholastic since 1973 and had written children's books of her own. The curriculum components included the Clifford Hand Puppet; Clifford's Big Ideas Poster (ten in English, ten in Spanish); the Big Ideas Library (ten *Clifford* books in English; ten in Spanish); the Clifford video *A New Friend* ("based upon the award winning PBS series," according to the promotional copy); and the Bilingual Activity Book *Fun With Clifford*. The whole package was boxed and marketed as Clifford's Kit for Personal and Social Development: "Your resource for character developing lessons and activities," according to the marketing materials.

The Clifford kit was sold as part of a larger curriculum package with a price tag of about $2,600 apiece, putting it out of reach for most independent daycare centers but making it an attractive option for some of the larger chains. The Children's World chain of daycare centers (which merged with the Michael Milken–owned Knowledge Learning Company at the end of 2004, making it the nation's largest daycare chain) purchased the Clifford curriculum and began promoting it vigorously. "When it comes to preparing your child for school success, you expect the best and Children's World understands," stated the company's Web site at the time. "That's why we're pleased to bring you our new Pathways pre-Kindergarten Program, filled with fun and educational activities carefully designed to help bring out your child's natural curiosity and encourage a lifelong joy of learning. Developed by Scholastic, the curriculum uses themed learning units that incorporate reading, writing, math, science, social studies and more." The Clifford component of the program, the Web site went on to promise, offered "materials on building character like learning respect," as well as cooperation and responsibility.

The Clifford curriculum was designed for children of pre-K age — that is, four- and five-year-olds. But Clifford was obviously a runaway hit with toddlers. Scholastic began to receive requests from daycare centers: Could the curriculum be scaled down to teach two-year-olds? Toddlers recognized Clifford from TV, and whenever they glimpsed the posters on the walls of their center, they would point and vocalize with delight. Moreover, as teachers sheepishly admitted, Clifford was a gentle-handed disciplinarian who could produce instant results, often sparing teachers from wading into a confrontation between children who didn't really understand why they shouldn't grab, hit, or bite. Teachers reported that often all they had to do was invoke Clifford as an example or point to his likeness on a poster, and children would fall into line. Here was a character who could model character-building behavior for children and command instant respect and cooperation: why *not* start two-year-olds on a Clifford regimen?

It might work, mused Ellen Booth Church, talking on the phone one hot summer afternoon in 2005 from her home office in Ithaca. But there was one problem. Clifford's entire message is centered on building character: sharing, compassion, responsibility. Toddlers are not developmentally capable of learning empathy — that is, imagining how another might feel — until they are at least two and a half. The problem would be, said Church, that toddlers could not really learn what the Clifford curriculum was designed to teach. They would, however, certainly develop a strong bond to Clifford as a character.

RECEIVE OR FAIL TO RECEIVE

More than half of American children under the age of three spend most of their waking hours in the care of people other than their parents and in places other than their own homes. "Second only to the immediate family, child care is the context in which early development unfolds, starting in infancy and continuing through school entry, for the vast majority of young children in the United States," reported the authors of *From Neurons to Neighborhoods: The Science of Early Childhood Development,* a landmark 2000 study produced by the National Research Council and Institute of Medicine, which amassed the data. In daycare programs, "most children first learn to interact with other children on a regular basis, establish bonds with adults other than their parents, receive or fail to receive important inputs for early learning and language development, and experience their initial encounter with a school-like environment."

In public policy, daycare programs are not considered educational settings. Teachers and caregivers at such programs are not legally required to have any formal educational training in the care of young children or in early childhood development. Professionals working with children in grade school, middle school, and high school must complete extensive coursework in educational theory, practice, and technique, must have not only a bachelor's degree but also special academic certification, before they are permitted to enter a classroom in a professional capacity. Not all caregivers and teachers at daycare centers or preschools, however, are required to have those credentials. This means that caregivers may not understand what types of activities contribute to the development of preliteracy skills or have any formal knowledge of how young children develop physically, emotionally, or cognitively.

They are not all legally required to know that most infants are able to sit up by the age of six months or that most children do not speak their first words (other than "mama" or "dada") until they are eighteen months old. They are not required to know that toddlers are not developmentally capable of learning empathy until they are at least two and a half.

The only regulation of the vast majority of daycare programs is state licensing, which provides guidelines covering basic health and safety issues. As one leading authority on regulatory issues in child care explains, "Licensing is not a definition of quality, it is a threshold defined by the state to reduce the risk of harm." In 1992 the American Public Health Association and the American Academy of Pediatrics, with the support of the Maternal and Child Health Bureau of the United States Department of Health and Human Services, published the National Health and Safety Performance Standards, detailing recommendations, guidelines, and regulations for the care of young children in centers and family daycare — but these standards were never federally mandated. The only daycare centers that have implemented both basic protections and standards are Head Start and the Department of Defense daycare system, which is the largest employer-sponsored system in the world.

Some states use the National Health and Safety Performance Standards as a model for their own licensing regulations. In all states anyone caring for children in a licensed group setting must submit to a criminal background check, but other licensing requirements vary from state to state. Essentially, anyone who can comply with the regulations in his or her state can hang out a daycare or preschool shingle. Many outfits, however, do not bother with licensing. According to the National Research Council and Institute of Medicine, "Virtually every systematic effort to characterize the quality of child care in the United States has [found that ab]out 10 to 20 percent of arrangements fall below thresholds [of adequat]e care."

A MARKET FAILURE

Shedding light on these issues was a central goal of the Clintons' 1997 White House Conference on Early Childhood Development and Learning — the brain conference. If most of the country's infants and toddlers were spending a large part of their lives in daycare programs, the conference organizers maintained, there had to be some minimum standard of quality care. There was no question that high-quality care was critical to healthy development. According to a report published by the U.S. Department of Health and Human Services (DHHS), two things were clear. First, high-quality child care had scientifically measurable, positive outcomes:

> Both correlational and quasi-experimental research has found relations between structural quality and child performance. For example, children in classrooms with lower child:adult ratios were better able to understand, initiate, and participate in conversations, had better general knowledge, were more cooperative, and in their interactions with each other showed much less hostility and conflict than in settings where there were more children to each adult. On average, preschoolers perform better on standardized cognitive tests when their caregivers are better educated and trained — for example, if they have at least an associate arts degree in a child-related field. The children also have better language skills, are more persistent in completing tasks, and in general are more ready for school.

Another report, the National Institute of Child Health and Human Development's (NICHD) *Study of Early Child Care and Youth Development,* reported that high-quality child care during the first three years was related to children's language skills at age three. Even *after* filtering out particular characteristics, such as the family's economic status or the child's temperament, the study demonstrated that children enrolled in higher-quality programs as preschoolers demonstrated better math skills through second grade; that effect was even greater for the children of less-educated mothers. In terms of socioemotional development, the NICHD report demonstrated, there was no question that children whose caregivers were more involved with and invested in them during the preschool years had fewer behavior problems in kindergarten.

The problem, according to the director of the federal Child Care Bureau and others in the field, was that market forces alone had not supplied enough high-quality daycare options to satisfy demand. Since the 1970s, when the loss of manufacturing jobs required many women to work to sustain family incomes, demand had been accelerating. The dearth of adequate child care meant that many mothers opted to go on welfare rather than place their infants and toddlers in subpar daycare centers. With the 1996 welfare-reform bill came the double requirement that mothers work rather than stay home with their young children and pay for child care out of their own pockets. It was presumed that market forces would meet this need at an affordable price, if mothers had enough information to make informed decisions. But for many working families — especially low-income families — finding affordable, high-quality child care was virtually impossible. According to the Urban Institute's 1997 data from the National Survey of American Families, 60 percent of working families with children under three had to pay for child care, in many cases even if it was provided by relatives, friends, or neighbors; families often had to rely on a patchwork of local caregivers, which by definition is not stable, high-quality care.

The DHHS report pronounced the daycare industry a "market failure": "a situation in which a market left on its own fails to allocate resources efficiently," as defined by economists. In the daycare sector, the report stated, the market had failed for two primary reasons. The first was parents' lack of information. Because daycare providers are mainly small businesses, it is time-consuming and complicated for parents to pull together information about their comparative quality, cost, and availability; once they do, they are uncertain how to assess it. "Considerations of convenience, time, and access mean that parents may limit their search to small geographic areas," stated the report. "These problems may be particularly acute for low-income families and for those who need care for odd-hours employment."

A second cause of market failure was what economists call "externalities," meaning effects that go beyond the primary consumers. High-quality care is important not just for the parent and child but for society in general. The benefits "include lower costs for later schooling, as children enter school better prepared to achieve; future reductions in crime as juvenile delinquency diminishes; increased productivity and lower need for social services as working parents face fewer child-related absences or terminations and remain more securely attached to the labor market," the report explained. "The family and social costs of poor-quality, unsafe, and unhealthy child care are equally apparent." To these traditional causes for market failure, the authors of the DDHS study added a third: "imperfect capital market." In other words, parents of young children, who tend to have low incomes relative to their permanent incomes, may face borrowing constraints that reduce their ability to pay for high-quality care. The answer, the report asserted, was federally funded programs for early daycare. But even after the brain conference, and all the publicity it received, virtually nothing changed.

EMERGING PRACTICES

Today, as in the 1990s, the National Association for the Education of Young Children (NAEYC) — the largest professional organization for teachers and caregivers of children under the age of five — offers the gold standard for nationally recognized accreditation program for day-care centers and preschools. NAEYC-accredited centers follow what are called "best practices" in early childhood care. This means that the people staffing these programs are there not just to keep children safe but to support their physical, cognitive, and socioemotional development. Caregivers at an NAEYC-accredited center are supposed to know, for example, that an infant should spend a few minutes a day on her tummy to develop her neck, back, and arm muscles. They are supposed to know that very young children need time to "phase in" to a new group environment, to feel safe and comfortable with the unfamiliar adults who will be caring for them. They are supposed to know that because toddlers aren't capable of truly empathizing with their peers, they can't be expected to understand the importance of sharing and should not be punished for not understanding that.

The NAEYC accreditation process, which is exhaustive, is entirely voluntary, however. Before applying for accreditation, a center must engage in a yearlong self-study process to find out how its offerings compare with the NAEYC's standards. The center must then open its doors to an extremely thorough assessment by NAEYC to determine whether the best practices in early childhood care are being met. NAEYC accreditation is costly for daycare programs and preschools, which are the most cash-strapped of all schools. Not surprisingly, most such programs do not undergo the accreditation process; less than 5 percent of all programs in the United States are NAEYC accredited. Furthermore, that accreditation may not be proof of excellence. Several variables that NAEYC cannot control or keep reasonable tabs on can influence the quality of child care. Some beneficial practices, such as talking with young children casually when they're eating, are so rarely practiced in group care that NAEYC does not believe it is fair to withhold accreditation from a program that does not observe them.

High staff turnover is also a major problem in the field, and that can hurt the quality of any daycare facility. To feel safe, very young children must develop steady relationships with trustworthy caregivers; these adults, who are essentially their surrogate parents, are critically important to infants and toddlers. But caregivers who are not adequately compensated and not encouraged to develop in their professional efforts generally do not stay long on the job. Even at NAEYC-accredited centers, very young children are often routinely left in the care of people who are virtual strangers.

CHARACTER EDUCATION

In the current educational climate, the word "character" often takes on a double meaning. It can mean moral fiber; it can mean a cartoon character. When Children's World advertised its purchase of Scholastic's Clifford curriculum using phrases like "building character" and "character developing lessons," the company did not intend the pun. Indeed, "character building" was invoked deliberately. As part of the guidelines for his landmark No Child Left Behind legislation, President George W. Bush had explicitly supported what he called "Character Education." In his foreword to the proposal, President Bush wrote that "these reforms express my deep belief in our public schools and their mission to build the mind and character of every child, from every background, in every part of America." The No Child Left Behind law stipulated: "Additional funds will be provided for Character Education grants to states and districts to train teachers in methods of incorporating character-building lessons and activities into the classroom."

No Child Left Behind — and its character education component — was not designed to address curriculum or standards for daycare programs; it was directed at pre-K, elementary, and secondary public schools. The law, which compelled all public schools to comply with specified academic standards, divided many in the educational community. Each state's department of education publishes a book-length list of guidelines, which teachers and heads of schools must comb through and cross-reference with their teaching plans to make certain that they are in compliance. Advocates argue that there must be some measurable threshold of achievement and competency for both students and teachers. Opponents believe the law leads to a "drill and kill" model of teaching, with students encouraged to study simply to pass the state-administered tests rather than stretch themselves intellectually, think creatively, and enjoy learning for its own sake. The gulf between the two camps widened further in 2003, when some states' pre-K programs, serving four- and five-year-olds, were obliged to conform to such standards.

The application of standards-based curricula to pre-K children was controversial in the field of early childhood development. If a pre-K program was judged on the basis of its children's performance on standardized tests, teachers might rely too heavily on a scripted curriculum based on narrow lessons, drills, and worksheets. Most research on knowledge acquisition suggests that it is primarily through play that young children learn problem solving and creative thinking — all the kinds of open-ended experimentation they will need to learn math, writing, science, and reading. Another objection was that standardized testing of four- and five-year-olds is known to produce invalid results. Small children are easily sidetracked, and singling them out and removing them from the classroom to administer an exam can make them apprehensive or frightened. Finally, most standardized tests miss the important nonacademic lessons that young children learn in pre-K programs, such as social and emotional skills, the very abilities that the programs were developed to help children master.

But government funding of pre-K programs was estimated to grow from $2.54 billion in 2002–2003 to more than $3 billion in the 2005–2006 academic year, and with that growth came increasing demands for accountability and results. As a result, many preschool programs were forced to spend more classroom time on skill building and testing. In 2005 the $6.84 billion Head Start program for low-income preschoolers began administering basic skills tests to children entering kindergarten, to demonstrate how programs receiving federal monies help children progress. Many cash-strapped preschool programs also began looking for ways to earn additional resources by appealing to No Child Left Behind's promise of extra funding for character education. A school that engaged in character education often promoted it as a core part of the curriculum.

By 2005 the standards-based trend had begun to trickle down even further. The daycare industry began to feel pressure to assure parents that their infants and toddlers would be prepared for pre-K. But there were no clearly articulated, appropriate curricula for the nation's daycare programs. As Joan Lombardi, the former director of the federal Child Care Bureau, has written, state licensing — with its emphasis on basic health and safety — seldom acknowledges the importance of an underlying curriculum. According to most early childhood educators, a high-quality "curriculum" for toddlers generally means a program that supports and encourages them as they progress through their developmental stages. Such a curriculum is generally constructed around Piagetian principles, with the Vygotskian understanding that each child is unique and may need different kinds of support. But, as Lombardi acknowledged, "even federally supported child care, which serves more than one million low-income preschoolers a year, has no requirements or support for curriculum or supervision." That and the lack of teacher training "must change if child-care programs are to become educational environments."

It seemed as if the Clinton and Bush administrations' different messages about early childhood education had been conflated by mid-decade. From the Clintonians came the belief that children were better equipped to learn between the ages of zero and three than at any other time in their lives. The Bush administration put forth the conviction that children could develop character at that age. The result was confusion and controversy about what constituted a well-balanced curriculum for infants and toddlers. Many daycare providers have little or no background in early childhood development or education, so the interpretation of an appropriate curriculum was left to market forces.

HONEST ABE

The lobby of Young Minds Inspired, Inc., in midtown Manhattan is relatively nondescript. The walls are whitish; the furniture is unremarkable. The very plainness of the backdrop, however, forces visitors to turn their attention to the waiting area's only decoration. Lining the wall facing the entrance are twelve little white shelves, and atop each one is a small bowl containing a single Chinese fighting fish. Each creature lies motionless in its vessel, looking like a purplish rubber feather. Their stillness is so strange that I wonder aloud if they are real, or alive. The receptionist chuckles at the question. "Oh, they're alive, all right — we just have to keep them separated," he says with a wink. "They don't play well with others, if you know what I mean."

The president of Young Minds Inspired — or YMI, as it's known — is a fiftyish man named Joel Ehrlich. As I interview him in his office, Ehrlich keeps his hands loosely folded in his lap, his expression cool. He clearly pays attention to everything, however. His eyes are closely trained on my movements and stay fixed for a beat after I stop talking, seemingly to catch any subtext that might be read through body language. Satisfied, he leans forward in his chair, smiles, and opens his arms magnanimously. "Let me start at the beginning, tell you my story, how I got here — okay?" he says, with the breezy self-confidence of a performer who knows that this is not a question. It all started, Ehrlich says, with the best job he ever had. Back in the 1970s, just out of college, he wanted to be an actor. But like most young actors, he had a tough time finding paying work. He drifted here and there, not knowing what to do with himself — fast on his way, he says, to becoming a full-time waiter. On a whim, he decided to sign up as a substitute teacher with the New York City public school system. He thought it would be fun! Well. He was assigned to teach U.S. history at a school in the South Bronx. He went prepared with a lesson plan, expecting the kids to sit at their desks and listen. Forget it! They couldn't have cared less. They were talking, chewing gum, passing notes. Ehrlich found it depressing and disillusioning. The kids were supposed to be studying the Civil War — one of the most important events in United States history! How could he get them interested? How could he even get their attention?

The next day Ehrlich came to class dressed as Abraham Lincoln: "Honest Abe." He put on the suit, the beard — the whole thing. He refused to answer to "Mr. Ehrlich"; he was Abraham Lincoln or Mister

President. All day — and for the rest of the unit on the Civil War — he played the part of Lincoln, encouraging students to ask questions and answering as he believed Lincoln would have done. The kids loved it, he says. They got excited about the subject, they participated in class, they wrote papers, they did their homework. Ehrlich ended up winning a Teacher of the Year Award. Ultimately, he decided there wasn't enough money in teaching, but what he learned, he says, is that kids learn best when they are being entertained. That, in a nutshell, he says, is the basis for YMI.

OUR TARGETED DISTRIBUTION SYSTEM

YMI is a marketing company that works with corporations such as Kraft Foods, the Walt Disney Company, 20th Century Fox, Barnes & Noble, the pharmaceutical company Pfizer, and many others to promote products to children in school. YMI's target audiences range from toddlers in daycare programs to college students. YMI was founded in the late 1970s by Roberta Nusim, now Ehrlich's business partner. Before joining the company, Ehrlich spent more than twenty years in marketing and publishing. A recipient of *Brandweek*'s Youth Marketer of the Year Award, he served as a marketing and publishing executive at Cahners Publishing in the American Baby/Healthy Kids division, as well as at Warner Bros., DC Comics, and Marvel Entertainment Group. For most of its nearly thirty years in business, YMI stood for Youth Marketing International. Recently, however, the company changed its name to Young Minds Inspired. But YMI still walks in both worlds.

The YMI Web site aimed at teachers (www.youthmedia.com) characterizes the company as having "long been an award-winning educational presence in today's classroom." This site goes on to encourage educators and caregivers to download the "free materials created by YMI's educational experts," which are "designed for specific curriculum areas and target grade levels from preschool through college in the United States and around the world." Instructors are exhorted to "integrate them into your lesson planning and you can use our site as a valuable source for a variety of other information and resources to make your curricular planning easier." Another YMI Web site, www .youthmarketingint.com, which is aimed at corporate clients, characterizes the company's business in a different way. It describes YMI's expert service as a "targeted, effective, and cost-efficient marketing vehicle." The site goes on to tell prospective clients that "based on your marketing needs, YMI will develop an in-school, curriculum-based program" that will "integrate your brand into lessons and activities that students will spend *hours* interacting with in a positive and meaningful way"; "give your message special credibility and importance to young people as well as their parents, by having teachers they admire and respect present these materials in the classroom"; "extend your message beyond the classroom via take-home activities"; and "deliver the message that your company values learning and cares about families." The site promises that "our targeted distribution system can deliver your program to every school in the U.S. and beyond or to selected schools based on geography, market size, proximity to retail locations, ethnicity, and/or income level."

YMI promotes its clients' marketing objectives to children and their families through a range of commercially based and sponsored products that it pitches to schools as a free "curriculum": teacher's guides, activity worksheets, posters, interactive games, videos, book covers, competitions, and "other grade-appropriate materials." The materials are tied to the client's product to boost brand awareness, sales, or, in the case of filmed or video entertainment, viewer ratings. While YMI targets students up to college age, Ehrlich says that its biggest business is with daycare centers and preschools. This is not because the numbers are so impressive; the target audience among older children is far larger. YMI estimates that its marketing materials can reach 28 million elementary school students; 23 million secondary school students; and 15 million college students. Compared with these numbers, the daycare and preschool business is much smaller. According to YMI, there are about 117,500 preschools and daycare centers in the United States, with 823,000 instructors. The company estimates that more than 8.3 million American children attend some kind of daycare or preschool program. But the daycare market is successful, says Ehrlich, because the younger the target audience, the more open it is to accepting an advertising message as truth.

Ehrlich elaborated on this point at a 2004 kids' marketing conference. An executive from Reebok pointed out during his presentation that she doubted YMI's approach would work for her company because high school students would consider materials coming from their teachers as uncool — and for the athletic footwear and sportswear business, whose most critical market is teenagers, being seen as uncool would poison Reebok's brand equity. Ehrlich acquiesced. "Kids are much more influenced the younger they are," he said. "The preschool teacher controls their environment, and when she brings them our product, the kids accept it, and they get excited about it." In sum, said Ehrlich, "The younger the kid, the more positive the response."

One of YMI's most successful in-school marketing programs was centered on American Greetings' relaunch of the Care Bears. In 2003 the company hired YMI as part of its marketing strategy to reintroduce the brand to the very young children of Generation-X parents. The result was YMI's "You're Never Too Young to Care!" curriculum. "The Care Bears are perfect ambassadors of caring and sharing, serving as an appropriate resource in aiding young children's social and emotional development," stated YMI's letter to preschool teachers. The packet, which included a poster, coloring-book sheets, and other activities, suggested that teachers "engage children in expressing their emotions as they identify with various Care Bears personalities." YMI suggested that caregivers teach preschoolers new lyrics to the tune of "Frère Jacques": "Fall or winter / Spring or summer / Anytime of year / Whether home or here / Is just right for caring / For loving and for sharing / Caring time is here / Let's give a Care Bears cheer!" Teachers were encouraged to celebrate what YMI called "National Care Week," during which children were to do something altruistic and parents were encouraged to take their children to toy-store chains for particular toy promotions. On every one of the activity sheets "designed to be taken home to the parent or guardian," the highlighted reminder appeared: "Help your child remember all year to care and share. Take your child to meet a Care Bear at your nearest Toys "R" Us or Geoffrey's Toys "R" Us."

Under the Target Audience heading in the Care Bears curriculum kit, the text read: "This kit is designed for preschool students. Simplify the material as you see fit for younger children." One of its newer programs promotes the television show *Boobah*, created by the *Teletubbies* mastermind, Anne Wood. "Dear Preschool Teacher," reads YMI's Boobah curriculum. "Welcome to a unique educational program that meets national standards in physical movement, creative expression, and language arts."

SAFE STEPS

Ehrlich cut his teeth on marketing to the daycare industry as an executive at Marvel Entertainment, Inc. The company had purchased a small in-school marketing firm called Cover Concepts, which offered cash-strapped public elementary, middle, and high schools free book covers with advertising on them. But by the mid-1990s, Cover Concepts saw the potential of marketing to preschools and daycare centers. Some estimates said that U.S. households with preschool children spend more than $100 billion a year. No one had tried to get a piece of that business by going to the daycare centers themselves, however. To Cover Concepts' founders, Michael Yanoff and Steve Shulman, targeting daycare programs looked like a terrific business opportunity. Parents of infants and toddlers were hungry for information about their children; daycare centers, notoriously the most impoverished of all school settings, would likely accept freebies. Thanks to the White House Conference, the nation's eyes were turned to the all-important first three years of life. Anything a company could market as developmentally appropriate or educational would probably be well received.

The only problem was that infants and toddlers did not read textbooks. Cover Concepts came up with a solution: a quarterly magazine called *SafeSteps* that preschools could distribute for free. The magazine featured safety tips for parents and coloring pages for preschoolers, alongside ads for products like Mott's applesauce, Golden Books, and Plymouth Grand Voyagers. It also delivered to advertisers a very desirable demographic readership: 87 percent of its 1 million readers were female, 80 percent were between twenty-five and forty-nine years old, 65 percent had a household income of more than $30,000, and 5 percent were college graduates.

To build its distribution channel, Cover Concepts put together a network of more than 22,000 daycare centers that were willing to receive — and pass along to toddlers and their parents — product samples, coupons, and other promotions. Rather than viewing themselves as helping the marketing company disseminate its promotions, many daycare centers considered such freebies a service that Cover Concepts was extending to *them*, as well as to the children's families. That perception was a coup for Yanoff and Shulman. When Cover Concepts sent daycare centers free samples of its clients' food products — such as Kellogg's Nutri-Grain bars — the children often developed a taste for them, and many centers began buying the product as a regular snack treat. When Cover Concepts requested that program directors put a copy of *SafeSteps* into each child's cubby to take home at the end of the day, many administrators did not mind at all. The magazine seemed useful to new parents, they reported, and it was free. When Cover Concepts asked program directors for demographic data on the students to pass along to the advertisers in *SafeSteps*, many handed it over without question. Most student profiles contain information on the children's gender, age, family-income levels, and Zip Codes anyway, and Cover Concept's request seemed so innocuous that directors didn't consider it necessary to tell the children's parents that they had disclosed the information. The only piece of data most daycare centers could not furnish was the child's ethnic background. Unlike public schools, preschools don't usually track that information. Cover Concepts did not consider this to be a major stumbling block; they could track it down themselves so long as they had the names.

The preschool program significantly enhanced the value of Cover Concepts' database, its most powerful selling point with advertisers. For one thing, advertisers could now reach more children and their families; Cover Concepts' network reached 2 million preschoolers. But even more valuable, the specific demographic information allowed them to sculpt their messages more precisely to the audience they wanted to target. Gatorade, for example, used Cover Concepts' information on a school's ethnic makeup to distribute book covers showing Hispanic, African American, and what the company referred to as "mainstream" themes. Nike used the data to advertise in urban schools. McDonald's used it to distribute ads within a tight radius of its restaurants.

By 2006 the daycare and preschool marketing program at Cover Concepts was flourishing. Daycare centers wanting to sign up were warned on the company's Web site that requests outstripped supplies: "Because of the increasing demand for our products, only daycares with a minimum of 50 kids will be eligible." And Cover Concepts, along with marketing clients' products in the form of free samples and advertising, was now producing teacher's guides with "lesson plans" and curricula based on such products as Bubbilicious bubble gum.

Extra Credibility

Disney had a problem. The company was in the early phases of launching its preschool television division — Playhouse Disney — and it needed educational brand equity. Nick Jr.'s landmark programs *Blue's Clues* and *Dora the Explorer* had convinced parents and the public at large that it was possible to create educational television for three-and-a-half-, four-, and five-year-olds. Sales from licensed merchandise had convinced Disney executives that educational preschool television was a major business category. Although Disney had done extremely well with Baby Einstein, the company had taken pains to downplay the fact of its ownership of the baby video line and ancillary products. With the launch of Playhouse Disney, however, the corporate ties were transparent, and marketers were concerned that the Disney name might corrupt the educational reputation that Playhouse Disney was working to cultivate. The idea of tying each TV show to a preschool curriculum and hiring Scholastic to package it seemed to be the perfect way around potentially negative public relations.

In addition to developing its own curricula, Scholastic hires itself out to corporate marketers who wish to target children in daycare or preschool programs and their parents. Providing such services is the purview of the division called Scholastic 6 & Under Custom Marketing. The following is an excerpt from its promotional materials:

> Scholastic 6 & Under Custom Marketing reaches parents where their kids are: childcare centers, preschools and kindergartens. The time between 0–6 is when parents are most involved with their children's daily activities. So your message is delivered by the single most persuasive and irresistible person in their life — their little one. And when that message is educational and creative, your brand resonates even more profoundly. And because you're working with Scholastic, the single most trusted brand with parents, your message achieves extra credibility.

The division's success stories include the Ronald McDonald Reading Corner. The client's objective, according to the promotional materials, was "to utilize Ronald McDonald to promote early literacy in school and at home." To achieve the objective, "Scholastic created a pre-packed 'lending library' that delivered popular classic children's books to 22,000 preschools and Kindergartens around the country." The results: "Ronald's Reading Corner reached over 1 million children and their families with this program. Survey results indicated that 95% of teachers said that the program 'helped their students get excited about reading.'"

Scholastic also creates and packages preschool curricula for media conglomerates wishing to promote their television shows to very young children and their families. When Disney signed on with Scholastic, company executives appointed Lauren Rees to manage the project. Rees has the warm and cheery manner of a preschool teacher herself, but she is the senior marketing manager for the Disney Channel, of which Playhouse Disney is a division. Since Disney considers the distribution and management of the preschool curriculum a marketing initiative, Rees is charged with coordinating such efforts. According to her, Disney chose Scholastic because, according to market research, it wears an untainted educational halo. For Disney, that kind of brand-equity association was crucial. "We didn't want to seem as if we were just shilling for Disney," she explains.

For Disney, hiring Scholastic to create preschool curricula based on its entertainment properties is in many ways similar to hiring a freelance children's book author like Amy Cohen to write licensed books. Disney sends Scholastic's team a video of the show on which the curriculum will be based, along with extensive style guidelines, and Scholastic creates a set of materials. The preschool curriculum Scholastic developed for Playhouse Disney's *Jojo's Circus*, for example, included a set of "Activity Cards," oversize flash cards "for kids to recognize and imitate the movements of Jojo and her friends"; a poster featuring Jojo, which promotional materials referred to as a "Jumping Chart and Star Stickers for kids to keep track of how high they can jump"; and a video. The letter to teachers opened: "Dear Educator/Child Care Provider: At Playhouse Disney, we believe that imagination and learning go hand in hand. We're dedicated to building the developmental competencies that preschoolers need to enter school settings with more skills and confidence."

Anything That's Free!

Rees and the marketing team started out in 2003 by shipping educational kits based on the Playhouse Disney show *Stanley* to 75,000 preschools and daycare centers culled from Scholastic's mailing list. Launching a television show in such settings taught them several important pieces of strategy. First, preschools and daycare centers made excellent — free — test sites. Second, it sent a very powerful message to young children and their parents: if the teachers are using this TV program as part of their lesson plan, it is educational. Parents would be more likely to let their children watch Playhouse Disney at home and also more likely to buy the licensed products associated with the shows. Finally, by launching these shows in preschools, the Disney brand itself became gilded with that educational patina. Parents who had thought of Disney as harmless commercial schlock now perhaps had newfound respect for its educational initiatives; parents who loved Disney's fun and magic were delighted to discover that the company was secretly adding educational materials to its products.

The plan worked. It worked so well, in fact, that having Scholastic develop and package in-school materials became integral to Playhouse Disney's overall marketing strategy. According to Rees, every new television program that Playhouse Disney creates is launched first in preschools during its first year or season. Not until year two or the second season, she says, does Disney begin marketing and advertising directly to consumers.

Rees herself has been a bit surprised by the success of the program. When Playhouse Disney first started marketing its television shows in preschools and daycare centers, Rees was concerned that teachers and caregivers would object to the commercial nature of a curriculum based on TV. But there has been very little protest. The key, Rees says, is that while Disney pays Scholastic a respectable amount of money to produce and package the Playhouse Disney educational kits, the preschools and daycare centers don't have to pay for anything. "Teachers love it because it's free, and these preschools and daycare centers don't have a lot of money," she explains. "They say, 'We'll use anything that's free!'"

Focus groups conducted by Scholastic showed that the majority of teachers and caregivers who received the curriculum were overwhelmed by its depth and breadth. Most teachers did not really want to delve into all the activities and suggestions for further exploration. What they really wanted, Rees says, was to be told more explicitly what to do. In the focus groups, teachers and caregivers said they wanted to be told which activities were for younger kids and which were for older. They wanted to be told which activities were "standards-compliant," and they wanted those items to be highlighted.

Still, of the 250,000 kits based on *Stanley* and *Jojo's Circus* that Disney sent out to daycare centers and preschools in 2003 and 2004, as well as those based on Disney's 2005 preschool show *Little Einsteins* (a brand extension inspired by the Baby Einstein series), Rees estimates that just about all were used in some way, though far less than the Scholastic-Disney team might have imagined. What she has learned, again through focus groups and response cards, is that most teachers just kept the video of the TV show to pop in the VCR for "a rainy day activity" or "whenever." But even more important, Rees says, most teachers and caregivers put up the poster featuring the TV-show characters in a place where the children can clearly see it every day. "That's a win for me. As long as they put up the poster, we have exposed them to our product," she explains. "They're getting exposure to the character and the idea that it's educational. That's really the goal, as far as marketing goes."

Not all daycare centers and preschools want Disney's television promotions in their classrooms. Rees says that the centers and schools that are opposed to Disney's presence tend to be those that are less concerned with academic structure and achievement and more interested in building a curriculum around the children's interests. "The schools that are more, kind of, haphazard don't use it [the Disney materials] as much. The kind of teacher that's going to say 'Hey, Johnny found a bird's nest on the way to school — let's look at that' doesn't usually go for our stuff."

Full Acceptance

Another client of Scholastic's is Alice Cahn, the former PBS Kids executive who introduced *Teletubbies* to babies and toddlers in the United States. She is now vice president of programming and development for the Cartoon Network. In August 2005 Cahn launched a new block of daily preschool television programming, called *Tickle U*. A year before the launch, Cahn had preempted potential condemnation of her role in championing another controversial type of television for young children: with *Tickle U*, the criticism would likely be that it was baldly devoid of educational content. In a presentation titled "The Kids Are All Right," delivered at the Youth Marketing Mega-Event in the spring of 2004, Cahn defended the decision to plunge into this new territory. "We ended the last century with an acceptance of the fact that TV had to be educational for preschoolers; that while kids watching it was a given, parents still had doubts about TV's worthiness as a 'playmate' and would only be happy as long as the content was informational/educational. The next wave is a full acceptance of TV as an accepted part of preschoolers' lives and with that, a freedom to expand into a broader definition of programming content."

But as Cahn knew from her experience with *Teletubbies*, it was important to have the backing of academics when venturing into potentially taboo territory. And it was one thing to speak to a conference full of kids' marketers about the acceptability of noneducational television programming for toddlers. But parents apparently still needed assurances that the program had some educational value.

Cahn lined up a child development advisory board for *Tickle U* that included Ellen Wartella, the former dean of communications at the

University of Texas, who had helped defend *Teletubbies* during its launch in 1998. But Cahn wanted to walk the educational line carefully, for she knew that Gen-X parents were also walking it carefully. Anything that smacked of overt academic instruction was on its way out; wholesome socioemotional development, however, was on its way in. Moreover, Cahn recognized an opportunity to carve out a good niche from the growing schism between the early childhood education experts who believed that play was the most important developmental stimulation and the Bush administration's plan to measure preschoolers against national standards.

In enlisting her board, Cahn's pitch to child development experts was that very young children did not need academic instruction, that the insanity in the wake of the baby genius phenomenon, and now the trickling down of No Child Left Behind rules, would have a deleterious effect. Very young children did not need a "standards-compliant curriculum"; they needed to play. This plea appealed to Jeffrey Goldstein, a professor at the University of Utrecht, an expert on the importance of play to children's health and development. It also appealed to Kathy Hirsh-Pasek of Temple University, the coauthor of *Einstein Never Used Flashcards,* in which she and her colleague Roberta Michnick Golinkoff offered a research-based argument against the baby genius phenomenon and in support of safe, open-ended play. Cahn also assembled research papers on the importance of humor in cognitive and socioemotional development and uploaded them to *Tickle U*'s Web site. Then she hired Scholastic.

In conjunction with *Tickle U*'s August 2005 launch, the Cartoon Network's parent company, AOL Time Warner, paid Scholastic to produce a preschool curriculum based on *Tickle U* shows. The curriculum materials, sent to more than 20,000 preschools mined from Scholastic's database, featured the same elements as Playhouse Disney's kits, including the key element: the poster promoting the shows' characters. The goal of the curriculum, according to promotional materials, was to help very young children develop a sense of humor.

Conclusion:
A Defense of "Nothing"

THE CITY OF OBERLIN has the lowest per capita income of any city in Lorain County, Ohio. Although it is home to the prestigious liberal arts college of the same name, many of the professors live in the outlying, affluent suburbs of nearby Cleveland, where the public schools rank higher than Oberlin in national test scores. About 20 percent of Oberlin's population lives below the national poverty line. Some 24 percent are families with children under eighteen living at home; half of those families are headed by single women. Oberlin is ethnically diverse, as it has been since the nineteenth century, when it was one of the stations along the Underground Railroad. Oberlin's population is 19 percent African American, compared with the national average of 12 percent; many families are biracial.

If you live in Oberlin, have young children, and work outside the home, chances are your children attend the Oberlin Early Childhood Center (OECC). Founded in 1968 as an experimental summer program for low-income preschoolers, OECC grew quickly and has for many years served as the city's only early childhood education center with full-day services. The center cares for babies as young as three months and offers after-school programs to children of school age. OECC is open from 6:30 in the morning until 6:00 at night and is closed only on national holidays. In many ways, the real heart of the Oberlin community is not Oberlin College, it is OECC.

Although Oberlin is officially a city, it looks and feels like a small Midwestern town. People know one another and are involved (for better and for worse) in one another's lives. That concern for others is why OECC's executive director, Nancy M. Sabath, became worried in 1998, when many mothers started pulling their young children out of OECC because they couldn't afford the tuition. Sabath, a steel-haired woman in her sixties, has a sharp, sober manner and gives an impression of having boundless, determined energy — the kind of person who responds to an intolerable situation by immediately drafting a plan of action. This situation struck Sabath as intolerable. She noted that for three-quarters of the families whose children attended the center, the welfare-reform bill had either reduced or cut off funding for child care; these families simply could not earn enough from their jobs to make up the difference. They were stuck with the horrendous dilemma familiar to low-income parents everywhere. With their present jobs, they couldn't afford high-quality child care, but if they found work that paid even slightly better, their welfare assistance would be cut off. And welfare reform had also made it more difficult to find better-paying work; increased work requirements, along with the cancellation of support for full-time college study and child care support, made getting a college degree nearly impossible.

Sabath knew these people well. Of the twenty-three families she was most concerned about, eighteen were headed by single mothers. All but four had been victims of a husband's or boyfriend's physical or substance abuse, with the result that several of the men were in prison. But except for brief periods — during pregnancies, after the birth of a child, or when laid off — fifteen of the eighteen mothers had always worked full-time, before and after welfare reform. The other three were in full-time college programs. Some of the families had never received any public assistance except for child-care support and health-care benefits. If there was a way to help these families cover the difference between what they could afford and what public assistance offered, Sabath was confident that most of these mothers would be able to pull themselves out of dire straits. The children themselves needed consistent care from the center's teachers and staff, who knew and loved them. Of poverty's many harrowing effects, the instability of child-care arrangements is one of the worst. And as studies have shown, it has serious consequences for young children's development.

So Sabath and her colleagues wrote a grant proposal to the Nord Family Foundation, and it was accepted. OECC proposed not only to subsidize tuition for low-income families but also to conduct a three-year study of the effectiveness of tuition assistance and follow each family's progress toward self-sufficiency. The results of the study, published in 2003, were very positive. As a direct result of the tuition assistance, nine of the twenty-three families were able to make ends meet, while seven were still struggling but were considerably better off financially and emotionally than before; seven families had left the program because of unemployment or other (often violent and harrowing) family circumstances. For more than two-thirds of the families, the study reported that "stability and security in child care arrangements have resulted in more stability and security in employment and reduced stress level for parents, as demonstrated by interviews and observations, and improvements in the children's physical, social, intellectual and emotional development as documented by interviews and evaluations of teachers and therapists." Sabath is now undertaking to introduce the program to Ohio legislators in hopes that it may serve as a state — or even national — model.

WHAT IS MISSING FROM THIS PICTURE?

At the same time, Sabath was concerned about the center's educational approach. She felt that the thinking might have become stale, too prescriptive. The classrooms were decorated mostly with posters sent by educational companies or with the usual cast of cartoon characters. Teachers directed the activities, rarely with any input from the children, and usually revolved around such predictable themes as traced-hand "turkeys" for Thanksgiving. Sabath wondered if OECC could better help the children and their families by listening more carefully *to them*.

Through a colleague in the state education system, Sabath had been learning about an approach called Reggio Emilia, for the northern Italian city where it had originated after World War II. Emerging from the rubble of the war, the mothers of the city had joined together in the collective belief that to prevent the violence and intolerance of a system such as fascism, all children, even the very youngest, should be treated with dignity and deep respect. The city's teachers, parents, and the community at large made it a civic priority to listen to children, to honor their many ways of communicating ideas, and to support their impulses to deepen their knowledge together. For more than twenty-five years, Reggio Emilia has devoted 12 percent of the city budget to its child-care center for children six and under. What particularly appealed to Sabath about the Reggio Emilia approach was that a school did not have to buy any preapproved materials or train teachers in a specialized method. Rather, it had to be willing to cast aside preconceived notions of early childhood and to rigorously observe what the children are *actually* doing rather than what adults think they *should* be doing. This approach also welcomed input from and participation by the children's families and the community.

The Reggio Emilia approach seemed like a perfect fit for the community-based, culturally diverse, and cash-strapped OECC. And because many of its families and students had suffered violence and discrimination, they certainly deserved a forum in which their ideas, feelings, and backgrounds could be dignified. But when Sabath approached her staff with these ideas, a wall went up immediately. Many of the teachers were put off by what sounded to them like a high-flown, "European" philosophy. Some of the staff had bachelor's degrees, some did not; all felt intimidated. This wasn't some fancy private Manhattan preschool, they argued; this was poor, rural Ohio! Sabath persisted. Did that mean, she asked, that they were not entitled to think as deeply or question their own assumptions with as much intelligence and nuance as Italians? OECC had to decide whether it wanted to be simply a daycare center or whether it wanted to become an early childhood education center, and staff members had to decide whether they were just caregivers or teachers as well. If they wanted to be teachers, they had to commit to thinking carefully about their mission and philosophy, and how to integrate these into the curriculum. Sabath said she would support their decision.

Staff members thought about it, discussed it with one another, and in a few weeks reported back to Sabath that they did want to be teachers. For the next six years, the staff met while the children were napping to discuss their mission and philosophy. They started by asking what seemed like basic questions, which they had never really addressed head-on before. For example, "What is my image of the child?" "What is my role as a teacher in children's learning?" "What is a project?" "How do we facilitate children's learning to deepen the experience?" and "When I leave at the end of the day and look over my shoulder I ask, 'Did the child make an imprint on the classroom today?'"

The hard work really started when OECC received a grant to hire Sonya Shoptaugh, a Reggio educational consultant, to work intensively with the teachers. Shoptaugh brought her digital camera and took pictures of the children and teachers for a day, then gave a presentation. One of the first photographs she showed was of the infant room. It showed a crammed tableau of brightly colored plastic toys, posters, mobiles featuring Disney characters, and stuffed animals. "What is missing from this picture?" asked Shoptaugh. No one had an answer; nothing seemed amiss. Shoptaugh prompted again, then gently ventured: "Where is the baby?" It took the group several minutes to locate the infant, who was ultimately spotted near a slide. He had been virtually invisible against the backdrop of all that *stuff.* What did this say, wondered Shoptaugh, about how we see children? Are we really seeing *them*, or are we seeing the *stuff*?

The day the cartoon posters, mobiles, character-based books, and toys were removed, the head teacher of the infant room cried. She felt as if, in dismantling the room, they were ripping apart her whole idea of what babies liked, how babies saw the world, what stimulated their interest. She hated the experience, and she hated the stripped-down room. But soon something interesting happened: she and her fellow teachers began really *noticing* what the babies were doing. They saw that the babies were interested in different textures, so the teachers offered them various materials to experiment with. The head teacher documented the babies' explorations with digital photographs and brief annotations, so parents could see what they were interested in. Parents were fascinated, and they, too, began noticing their children's interests in new, fresh ways.

In the two-to-three-year-old room, one teacher realized there was very little evidence of the children's work, and nothing in the classroom was organized so that the children could access materials on their own. Overnight she removed everything from the walls. When the children came in the next day, they gazed at the walls in quiet wonderment. "I've never seen two-year-olds so quiet before!" the teacher chuckled. As she and the children began rearranging the classroom together, she noticed that tantrums and conflicts seemed to wane. Another teacher in that room noticed that the children had been talking about roller coasters, which they had seen advertised on television as attractions at a local amusement park, where some older brothers and sisters were allowed to ride. The class began a long-term project of building their own model of a roller coaster. The teacher documented the children's planning process, their "blueprints," and the assembly process. "It's not finished," she emphasized. "It is a work in progress."

Reflecting on the Reggio-inspired journey at that point, the teachers were honest. The approach was hard and frustrating, they said, and they often wondered whether it was worth it — and even whether they agreed with it. But the Reggio approach always challenged them to think in completely new ways, and it was always interesting. What is more, it had definitely helped them grow as teachers, and they could see the difference in the children.

NONE OF US ARE BAD PEOPLE

As I was working on this book, I was very moved by Sabath's example. Not only has she put enormous effort into supporting the teachers and families in her community, but she has also been willing to dismantle her preconceptions about what children need so she can do a better job of helping them. As a reporter and a parent, I feel that I underwent a comparable process over the three years it took me to complete this book. In the midst of reporting and writing, I was often asked about my personal opinions regarding the issues I was covering. It's a fair question, but my usual answer was, first, I'm just a reporter — definitely not an expert — and my only goal is to follow the trajectory of the zeitgeist; and, second, I could not have an informed personal opinion until my research was completed. This two-part response may sound like a dodge, but it did represent my cast of mind. It was very important to me that this book be shaped by asking questions, not by confirming preconceived answers. I am glad I clung to that ethos, because what I learned turned out to be very different from what I had initially imagined.

I think I expected to find some villains, especially in the marketing industry. I did not find any — no one, at least, who was fully conscious of the damaging effects of his or her work. Even in obnoxiously named business presentations such as "Marketing to the 'id' in 'Kid': Appealing to Kids' Emerging Personalities" (presented by the marketing firm boing and its client Burger King), during which marketers discussed exploiting elementary school children's struggles to find their emerging public selves so that the company could convert them from "McBabies" to Burger King "big kids," with the speakers showing an utter lack of irony or self-consciousness. The only truly cynical, self-aware remark I heard was one attributed to Rachel Geller, chief strategic officer of the Geppetto Group. At the firm's 2005 scavenger hunt (described in chapter 5), a young woman stopped in the middle of her presentation and said to us, the paying audience, that she used to worry that her work for the Geppetto Group would undermine parent-child relationships. But Geller had told her that she was, in fact, doing kids a favor: "Rachel said, 'It's good for kids to learn how to manipulate — that's how you get ahead in this world.'" The young woman told us that she had accepted Geller's assessment, and then continued with her presentation of the Kid/Mom Dynamic.

Most of the people I interviewed volunteered that they felt twinges of guilt or uncertainty every so often, but not so often or intensely that they felt compelled to stop and take inventory of their motives or actions. Some kids' marketers prefaced their remarks to me by cataloging their charitable work for children with disabilities. One even said he suspected that the increased incidence of childhood autism would ultimately be linked to our "sped-up" culture, citing the omnipresence of TV, the Web, video games, and even KGOY itself. Sounding concerned, he said that young children with unusual sensitivity to sensory integration (the medical term for turning sensory input into useful information) must be in a constant state of short-circuiting as a result of all the audiovisual "noise." Other marketers simply clocked in from nine to five (or, more typically in that business, from ten to six) and hadn't really thought about how their work might be changing the culture. "You know, none of us are *bad* people," said one marketer over lunch at a French bistro in Manhattan. "We're all just doing our jobs, and we don't really get a chance to think about how all the pieces add up until we have a conversation like this."

In this respect, I guess they are like many of us — or certainly like me. Until I did the research for this book, I did not really think about how all these commercial, psychological, and cultural influences added up to create this sprawling subdivision of the landscape of early childhood in

America. As Julie Aigner-Clark had said to me, I had no idea it would end up becoming such a huge phenomenon. My former editor at *U.S. News & World Report*, the wonderfully curmudgeonly Avery Comarow, advised me early on to "ask all the questions that any other reasonably intelligent, skeptical person would ask if they had the access to the same information as you do." That's what I tried to do. Now that the data are in, the question is what can and should be done about the commercialization of early childhood.

WHAT TO DO

First, the effect of screened media (particularly television and videos) on very young children is clearly an important health issue, and it should be treated as such by the government and health care professionals. Screened media influence the environment of most American babies and toddlers almost as much as air quality and nutrition do. Legitimate peer-reviewed academic research is beginning to show that foreground television does not have a positive educational impact on babies and toddlers. Thus it is unconscionable for hospitals to send new mothers home with complimentary videos from Baby Einstein. But the practice continues, almost unchallenged. Educating new mothers about the effects of videos and TV on babies and toddlers should be part of well-baby checkups. Medical schools, hospitals, and pediatricians should be trained about these health concerns. (In the summer of 2006 I was visiting a friend and her six-month-old baby boy at New York–Presbyterian, the university hospital of Columbia and Cornell, which ranked sixth in *U.S. News*'s 2006 list of Best Hospitals. The baby, in the critical care unit, was surrounded by infants who had been born with birth defects, drug addictions, and so on. On every hospital crib was a brand-new Baby Einstein toy and video.)

Second, given the widespread and extraordinarily powerful influence of professionally produced programs for babies and toddlers, it is imperative that more federally funded studies explore their effects. One

Columbia University health professional (who requested anonymity) told me she feared that the reason babies seemed so riveted by *Baby Einstein* videos was that they were actually slipping into what could be described as a low-level seizure state. That is only a hunch, but it is the hunch of a professional whose career has been spent working with children who have sensory-integration problems. Her idea should be studied. In 2006, Cornell economists found a high correlation between cases of reported autism and television watching by very young children. This finding ought to be pursued to see if there is a *causal* relationship. The lack of scientifically valid, well-publicized research has allowed self-interested companies to market unsubstantiated suggestions and outright claims as truth with very little challenge, except from a few commercial watchdog groups that are generally dismissed as alarmist. Indeed, a representative from a toy industry association I met at a conference organized by the Campaign for Commercial-Free Childhood (CCFC) told me that the public and the industry would never take such groups seriously until research was done that backed up their contentions. But legislation to provide funding for such studies has been stalled in Congress for years. The Children and Media Research Advancement (CAMRA) Act — introduced by senators Joe Lieberman, Sam Brownback, Hillary Rodham Clinton, and Rick Santorum and reintroduced in March 2005 — would give the National Institute of Child Health and Human Development $10 million in the first year and $90 million over the next five years to examine the role of all forms of electronic media on children's cognitive, social, physical, and psychological development. Passing this legislation ought to be made a priority.

Government may need to intervene in other ways, too. Citing the lack of evidence that screened media are beneficial for babies, CCFC filed a complaint with the Federal Trade Commission against Baby Einstein and Brainy Baby in May 2006. The watchdog group's complaint charged that two of the leading producers of videos for infants and toddlers were violating Section 5 of the Federal Trade Commission Act by marketing their videos as educational for babies. But broader measures should be taken, too. All the major networks and preschool channels are on the record as being fully aware that babies and toddlers watch their programs, even though they are meant for three-and-a-half-, four-, and five-year-olds. Given what research has revealed about how children under two process television, these networks and channels should be obliged to issue warnings before every program, advising parents that the content is not suitable for babies and toddlers.

A complex, and hugely important, issue that might motivate the industry to take such precautions is the role of foreground television and videos in advertising and marketing. The Children's Advertising Review Unit (CARU), the marketing and advertising industry's self-regulating body, is supposed to keep tabs on all advertising directed at children and to issue warnings to offenders. But critics charge that because CARU has no enforcement power, it is usually ineffectual, and has been since it was founded in the mid-1970s. Senator Tom Harkin of Iowa has noted, "CARU, frankly, has become a poster child for how not to conduct self-regulation." CARU should be obliged to consider the research conducted by Anderson, Barr, and Neeley, among others. Without question, more research is needed to explore this issue, but if other studies confirm that what infants and toddlers learn primarily from foreground television is how to recognize TV characters, then much of what is shown on television constitutes advertising to infants and toddlers.

Because of the ubiquity and impact of character licensing, such shows may prove to be what many educators and academics believe they are — the PLCs of the infant and toddler set. If so, they would be in violation of the Federal Communications Commission (FCC) rules limiting the amount of commercial material on cable channels during programs designed for children twelve years of age and younger. On January 1, 2006, the FCC issued rules that would classify a channel's promotions of its own programs as commercial material unless the programs are educational and informational as defined under FCC rules. The current FCC rules, however, do not define what is considered educational and informational for babies and toddlers and clearly do not take into consideration the extant research.

Third, licensing itself has become a form of advertising to children under eight and especially to babies and toddlers. The most obviously damaging form is the marketing of junk food. In February 2006 CCFC, the Center for Science in the Public Interest (CSPI), and parents from Massachusetts announced their intent to file suit against Viacom and Kellogg to stop them from marketing junk food to young children. As part of their case, the plaintiffs pointed out that Viacom's and Kellogg's brands have infiltrated nearly every aspect of children's lives. Findings from CSPI showed that twenty-one out of twenty-one — 100 percent — of Kellogg's Web sites for children promote foods that have little nutritional value. Another study found that 98 percent of Kellogg's Saturday morning television ads were for foods with poor nutritional content. In twenty-eight hours of Nickelodeon programming, of 168 food commercials, 148 (88 percent) were for junk foods. Nickelodeon has partnered with both McDonald's and Burger King, and its characters can be found on many packages of fat-heavy fast food. Junk food is advertised constantly on Nick.com and Nickjr.com, which are among the most popular Web sites for kids. "Television commercials and Internet advertising combine with brand licensing, in-school marketing, promotions, contests, and advergames to sabotage parents' best efforts to raise healthy children, turning kids into miniature lobbyists for products such as SpongeBob SquarePants, Wild Bubble-Berry Pop Tarts, and Dora the Explorer Fruit Snacks," the study stated.

THE PRINCESS GAME

But there are many effects of marketing influence that government cannot control. In a 2005 study at Brigham Young University, researchers found that girls as young as four years old show signs of engaging in the type of catty, manipulative "queen bee" behavior that was once the domain of adolescent girls. According to the study's authors, some pre-school girls will spread rumors about their peers, select certain class-mates for the silent treatment, and essentially do whatever works to exert and preserve their influence. While the study did not tackle the question of how queen bees are born, one of its authors hypothesized that many of these young girls have controlling parents who show them by example that manipulation pays.

The study did not address the influence of commercialization on queen-bee dynamics, but one need only summon up news reports of, or personal experiences with, the Disney Princess phenomenon to rumi-nate on its role in exacerbating, or even generating, these harsh social relations. Several of the little girls at my children's nursery school in-vented the Princess Game. Every day during free-play time, the girls would assume various roles in one of the Disney princess stories. A queen bee emerged in the group and became the one who decided which princess the group would enact each day. She then made a rule that only girls wearing dresses could play the Princess Game. Then the rule changed, and only girls wearing dresses the color of that day's Dis-ney princess could play. If the Princess Game was devoted to Cinderella, only girls wearing *powder blue* dresses — the color scheme of Disney's Cinderella — were allowed to join in. Naturally, girls who had never been exposed to Disney's princesses began to demand the products; even parents who did not want to give in felt they had to so that their daughters would not be excluded from the social group. The dynamics of exclusivity and manipulation grew to the point that several parents and teachers had to work together to change the situation. The girls were three years old.

I'll Show You the Man

Part of the problem is us. Much to my humiliation and amusement, I identify with the marketers' profiles of Generation-X mothers described in this book. I often found myself either laughing out loud or on the brink of welling up as I sat in on marketing presentations or read marketing reports and business books detailing the paradoxical, quixotic, and often poignant attributes of the Gen-X mom. True to the national average, my parents were divorced at the dawn of the Reagan era. I did not become a latchkey kid until I was eleven or so (until then we had live-in babysitters, usually graduate students), but my brother and I ate our fair share of TV dinners unsupervised in front of crummy '70s and '80s TV. My brother was a *He-Man* and *Teenage Mutant Ninja Turtles* aficionado, and we were both huge *Star Wars* fans, collecting every conceivable action figure, model vehicle, and weapon. We lobbied for an R2-D2 ceramic cookie jar, which, when filled, contained such convenience-store favorites as Oreos or Chips Ahoy! I remember with ebullient clarity the day my mom caved and bought me a Barbie "head" whose stiff, flaxen locks you could roll up with a little pink plastic curling wand and whose eyelids you could lacquer in Cheryl Tiegs–esque aqua eye shadow.

As adolescent malcontents, my brother and I gravitated to *Repo Man* and *Suburbia,* while our clean-cut counterparts quoted *The Breakfast Club* and *Pretty in Pink.* But the characters were, essentially, the same: '80s kids with nowhere to assuage their fears and no culture to replace their anomie. When I graduated from college in 1991, Joan Ganz Cooney was the commencement speaker. Most of the people in our class were born in 1969, the year *Sesame Street* went on the air. In a moment of uncharacteristic Generation-X corniness, we all spontaneously sang "Can You Tell Me How to Get to Sesame Street?" as Ganz Cooney took the podium. It would have been unbearably saccharine had not so many students been weeping.

So the marketers' assessments of Gen-X women as mothers made sense to me. The commercialization and neglect of young people results not only in fears of abandonment and bank-breaking shopping habits in adulthood to fill the void but also in a deep, neurotic sense of attachment to, and protection of, one's own children and home. Noted. My next response was: How could we, of all people, have been such suckers? Weren't we supposed to be suspicious of marketing, advertising, and corporate interests? We were said to loathe the yuppies' self-aggrandizement and consumption and to be defiantly independent in all our decisions. But we had become, apparently, the most involved, compassionate parents America had ever seen, even pushing our workplaces to give us more time with our families. How could *we* have opened the door to our children's rooms to marketers?

Psychology has at least a partial answer. However much distance Generation X has put between itself and its childhood, it is still almost impossible to be objective about one's early life. In some ineffable way, early childhood is the most primitive gauge of one's emotional barometer. As the old saw goes, "Give me the boy until he's seven, and I'll show you the man." Of course, the influences are far more complex than that, but all those formative years of latchkeys, PLCs, the nag factor, and the relentless compulsion to acquire products sold separately did have some long-term effects. At first it looked as if Generation X would lead a cultural backlash against yuppie materialism. As the journalist Nina Munk pointed out in a *New York Times* business piece in the summer of 2005, marketers had struggled to understand the inscrutable, disillusioned Gen-Xers in their twenties and had finally characterized them as cynical and anticommercial. "I don't buy things if they're advertised," a twenty-four-year-old sneered to the *Los Angeles Times* in 1993. Munk wrote that in the 1990s it was a "useful fiction, the idea of Generation Xers — a way to create a homogeneous group out of 48 million people who, in hindsight, may have had very little in common except their youth." At the same time, the idea gave Generation X something to rally around: "We stood for something. We were defiant! And independent! Marketers were struggling to understand the real us! We were worth something," Munk wrote. But as Generation X has grown older and started having children, that old Psych-101 maxim about experiencing one's own childhood wounds via one's children seems to have pushed its way to the fore. We didn't get stable homes, we didn't get our parents' attention, but we did get them to buy us *stuff.* According to marketers, that's what we are still doing: buying stuff. Munk wrote, "We finally do have something that unites us: shopping."

What kind of effect does this have on our minds, on our sense of self? If a person is surrounded by marketing messages early enough, does she internalize them without realizing she has done so? John Seabrook, author of *Nobrow: The Culture of Marketing, the Marketing of Culture,* described his take on this phenomenon in an interview for a documentary on PBS's *Frontline:*

> The "marketer within" [is] a core concept [in understanding youth culture]. You have a group of people who grew up mainly through television, absorbing a marketing voice, absorbing that pitchman's voice almost before they knew language. Studies have shown that two-year-olds can recognize the difference in volume and tone of the commercial voice on television and know it intimately in a way that they don't respond to the editorial voice. And you internalize that voice, so that marketing no longer seems like an alien external manipulative force; rather, it's just part of your world. It's part of something that goes on inside you and outside you.

Seabrook describes a phenomenon that began in Generation X's childhood: the feeling of being soothed, of having one's anxieties assuaged by the comforting "voice" of marketing. It is another bit of 101-ism that if Generation X suffers from obsessive, albeit unconscious, pangs of fear, abandonment, and insecurity, then their reflexive attempt to relieve such neuroses is through buying stuff — especially stuff for the home or children.

Marketing culture has even farther-reaching, deeper consequences. For one, it doesn't encourage critical thinking. The marketing industry's goals are to mirror back to people not who they actually are but who they would like to be, to confirm that their ideas are the right ideas, and to instill a sense that every problem has a simple solution. As American culture has become increasingly dominated by marketing, its Gen-X citizens have also become the least informed in history. In his 2004 book, *Tuned Out: Why Americans Under 40 Don't Follow the News,* David T. Z. Mindich, a former CNN assignment editor turned journalism professor, writes that less than 20 percent of Americans under the age of forty read a newspaper every day, compared with more than 70 percent of older Americans. The upshot, Mindich writes, is that "America is facing the greatest exodus of informed citizenship in its history."

I believe that this trend is related to Generation X's general *sensibility,* carried over from a chaotic childhood in the 1980s: the world is scary; TV shows are safe. The shows Generation X grew up with, PLCs, are marketing messages, and having internalized them so early on, Generation X naturally gravitates to them, whether they realize it or not. Indeed, that may be one of the chief reasons for the rapid spread of the baby genius media virus. Viewed in this light, the Fox News personality "news man" Bill O'Reilly and Baby Einstein's founder, Julie Aigner-Clark, have something in common. The many viewers who identify O'Reilly as one of their own, perceiving him as the edgy barroom contrarian they themselves might like to be, tend to believe what he says and do not question the legitimacy of his positions. Similarly, Gen-X mothers who like, or aspire to be like, Julie Aigner-Clark believe what she says, even though there is little reason to do so. In the marketing culture to which Generation X seems especially susceptible, the division between image-doctoring and news, sales pitch and fact, is fuzzy. Furthermore, this culture breeds a strange kind of conformity, in which ignorance is accepted and the questioning of any secular orthodoxy is viewed with suspicion or distaste. It is as if anyone or anything that presents an idealized picture of who we would like to be, confirms our ideas, and instills a belief in simple solutions deserves our loyalty. That rigidly conformist, question-averse sensibility may be one of the most insidious legacies of the "marketer within."

COMMERCIAL-LENGTH ATTENTION SPAN

But there are other troubling legacies. When *Sesame Street* debuted, much was made of its short, commercial-length segments. They were designed that way because producers believed that preschool children couldn't attend to TV for a longer period. Thanks to the research of Anderson and others, this belief has been disproved. But the format it spawned, which lives on in other venues frequented by young children, contributes to the sense that little kids must be kept busy and entertained at every juncture. Indeed, there is a profitable cottage industry dedicated to keeping children's eyes glued to screens, and it is installing itself anywhere toddlers are found. Sales of minivans skyrocketed in 1999 when General Motors started offering flip-down LCD players in the back seats of its Oldsmobile Silhouette line. Now LCD players are dealer-installed options on most minivans and sport-utility vehicles. Parents who fly on JetBlue can quiet their babies and toddlers with free TV in every seat. If you're traveling by train, automobile, or a different airline, you can take along a portable DVD player or a toy like Hasbro's handheld gizmo, VideoNow, which plays thirty-minute cartoons. You can even stay in Nickelodeon-themed hotels.

Supermarket chains have also joined the never-a-dull-moment business. At Stew Leonard's, a chain in Connecticut and New York, children are entertained by costumed characters called Daphne the Duck or Wow the Cow wandering the aisles. If they look up, they can watch animatronic bananas and celery sticks singing and dancing on a suspended stage. When the grocery bill hits $100, the cash register moos. Stew Leonard's makes another *cha-ching* sound at corporate headquarters: the chain made it into the 1992 Guinness Book of World Records for having "the greatest sales per unit area of any single food store" in the United States. No wonder it has spawned so many imitators. At supermarkets across the country — from Giant to Safeway, Superfresh to Kroger — a toddler can now "drive" a plastic race car attached to the front of a standard-size shopping cart, push her own pint-size cart, or gawk at Chuck E. Cheese–style robots.

DOING NOTHING

If the contrarian playwright A. A. Milne were alive to see the state of the house at Pooh Corner — festooned with matching curtains, bedding, educational software for toddlers, TV series, and more — he would probably want to board it up forever. Milne did seem to have a prophetic inkling of the Pooh mania that would follow his death in 1957, for in the second Pooh book, *The House at Pooh Corner,* published in 1928, he tried to kill Pooh off. In the closing scene, Christopher Robin explains to an uncomprehending Pooh that he's growing up and will soon have to bid farewell to his playmate from his nursery days.

> "Pooh?"
> "Yes, Christopher Robin?"
> "I'm not going to do Nothing any more."
> "Never again?"
> "Well, not so much. They don't let you."

Today it is harder for even the youngest children to enjoy doing Nothing, which used to be one of the staples of early childhood. Take your pick of Gen-X neuroses: perfectionism, fear of abandonment (and fear of perpetrating it), attachment to the marketer within, commercial-length attention span. Whatever the cause, Generation-X parents seem clearly worried that their children might feel uncomfortable doing Nothing and thus must be occupied. If a mother needs to take a shower, she pops in a baby video because she finds it deeply (and perhaps unconsciously) unacceptable that her infant might have to occupy himself for ten minutes and might cry. When a family with a two-year-old takes a car trip, parents worry that the toddler may throw a temper tantrum or become melancholy and isolated; she must be "stimulated" by watching her favorite programs on a portable TV screen. A fussing baby is distracted with an electronic mobile playing Bach and Mozart rather than being picked up and cuddled or having to figure out how to soothe herself by sucking on her toes.

Constant busyness has consequences. As they get older, these children begin to feel the stress of nonstop motion. According to a 2005 report, titled *Xtreme Parenting*, from the public relations firm Porter Novelli, the children of the oldest Generation-Xers (and youngest Baby Boomers), now eight and older, are known as Generation Y. Even though they are growing up very loved, they are full of anxiety. As the report's author, Wendy Watson, states:

> Since infancy, they have been scheduled and enrolled. Two-year day care waiting lists, infant music classes, and routine "play dates" were the norm in their developmental years. "Now that these children are in school, their time outside of the classroom is spent in extracurricular activities such as karate, soccer, ballet, and French class. At the same time, overscheduled Gen Y kids feel more frazzled than generations before them. This drives them to seek out less structured activities that allow down time, individualism, and personal expression.

Transient boredom, sadness, and isolation have never before been viewed as such high-stakes issues as they are by Gen-X parents. Such feelings are part of life, and even very young children need opportunities to discover who they are and what they are capable of doing on their own. But Generation X, raised on a heavy diet of loneliness, has developed severe allergies to normal doses as adults. Marketers say Generation X shops compulsively to stem their childhood fears of abandonment. To reverse that legacy, Gen-Xers overstimulate, overschedule, overshop for, and overobsess about their own children. Eager to relive the happy parts of their childhood, these parents unwittingly invite KGOY and commercialism into their babies' and toddlers' lives. It is both understandable and poignant. But it does not have to be this way.

One of Generation X's most remarkable, and inspiring, characteristics is that in spite of all its ironic snickering, the group seems to be true believers — and incredibly committed parents. If Gen-Xers could emerge from the crap and anomie of their childhoods with such heart, it may be proof that people are capable not just of enduring but of prevailing. And if that Faulkner reference feels too gooey, more proof comes — again — from the marketing industry. By all accounts, the old adults-are-clueless-and-mean-and-kids-are-smart-and-fun advertising does not work with today's 'tween children. The reason, according to marketers, is that Generation X's kids love their parents; they *like* spending time with them. As Porter Novelli's Wendy Watson wrote, "X-treme parenting has forged a strong bond between Gen X parents and Gen Y kids. Parents wield heavy influence, and their kids respect and honor their opinions. In fact, when asked who their top role models are, these kids almost always cite mom or dad."

To vaccinate against the baby genius virus — and all its insidious successors — may require participating in something many of us are uncomfortable with: doing Nothing. In Pooh's and Christopher Robin's world view, doing Nothing is different from doing nothing. Doing Nothing means that adults and their young children have periods of unstructured time when they can see what just unfolds. Doing Nothing isn't mediated by television, classes, computers, or educational ("learning") toys. For a parent, doing Nothing involves watching and listening to see what the young child gravitates to on her own and following her lead, with no agenda or goal in mind. Doing Nothing lets parents and children play and connect with each other in their own way — and lets each one discover what that means or does not mean. Doing Nothing is going to the market to buy food for dinner. It's relaxing in the park or backyard — doing nothing or doing something. Whatever else, doing Nothing isn't overthinking; it's just hanging out.

To adults, this may not seem like much, but to babies and toddlers, it is the foundation of life. Doing Nothing is critical for human development, for it provides the environment in which focused attention — the form of concentration that is so important to very young children's cognitive and emotional growth — is born and thrives. Research psychologists and early childhood educators insist that a diet of structure and stimulation actually starves children's imagination, curiosity, and ability to relax. Furthermore, as Anderson showed in his studies, the high signal-to-noise ratio generated by the backdrop of TV obstructs "private speech": the monologues toddlers act out to describe what they're working on and what they see, the antecedent to the inner voice we unconsciously use as adults to process our thoughts, feelings, and behavior. Take away a child's ability to create her own private speech, and the marketer within may move in to fill the void.

All the early childhood experts I spoke with said that spending time hanging out together is the best possible thing parents can do for their young children's development — and it's the one thing the American government will not let them do. Nearly 75 percent of mothers work outside the home. Just to keep their income level the same, parents now have to work more than five hundred more hours per year than they did in 1979. Yet the United States is the only industrialized country that refuses to provide for paid child leave. In *The Motherhood Manifesto*, Joan Blades and Kristin Rowe-Finkbeiner point out that 163 countries give mothers paid leave on the birth of their children; 45 countries offer paid leave to fathers, too. Australia guarantees a year of leave to all new mothers. In Canada, mothers get fifteen weeks of partially paid parental leave to recover from childbirth; an additional thirty-five weeks of partially paid leave can be taken by the mother, the father, or both during the first year of the child's life. In Sweden, family life is even more protected: mothers get almost a year of paid leave.

In the absence of state support, American parents have to pay for child care, which leads to massive wage reductions, especially for mothers. Indeed, it is not news that women with children earn less than anyone else in the United States. "Even after controlling for differences in characteristics such as education and work experience," writes the Columbia professor Jane Waldfogel in the *Journal of Economic Perspectives*, "researchers typically find a family penalty of 10–15 percent for women with children as compared to women without children." The situation doesn't seem to be improving. According to the U.S. Census, women lost a cent an hour between 2002 and 2003, earning 76 cents to a man's dollar — with mothers bearing most of the wage penalties. This disadvantage has serious consequences. Studies reveal that one-quarter of "poverty spells" — periods when American families' income cannot cover basic living expenses — begin with the birth of a baby.

All working parents, regardless of socioeconomic background, can relate to the agonizing problems brought about by these circumstances. If you work outside the home, you worry about whether your young children are being cared for kindly and competently by the people you pay so that you can go to work. If you stay at home to raise your children, you forgo Social Security earnings, paid vacation time, and company contributions to health insurance — and decrease the likelihood of finding employment at your previous level. Either way, the vast majority of parents are stressed and strapped for cash. Nothing *isn't* free.

But it should be. Earning it will involve lobbying for paid family leave; flexible work hours; universal, standards-based child care; health insurance for all children; and fair wages for all working families, especially single mothers. But for Gen-X parents — who in their twenties had "nowhere to direct their anger, no one to assuage their fears and no culture to replace their anomie" — fighting for the right to do Nothing with their children may be the perfect cause célèbre.

I think of the experience of Teresa Acevedo, a director of Tucson-area Head Start programs, who discussed her center's adoption of the Reggio approach at the 2004 NAEYC conference in Anaheim. By far the majority of young children in the Tucson program are Mexican American, and Acevedo's slide presentation documented excited families who had been invited to share their traditions at the center. At one point, Acevedo shook her head, looked up from the podium, and remarked in a bewildered tone, "I don't know when or why we accepted the idea that educational experiences have to come from a catalog!" She clicked to a slide depicting the center's stunning desert surroundings. "We weren't even taking advantage of, or even paying attention to, the natural beauty around us," she said. Then there appeared a picture of children playing as the afternoon sun sliced through thick, cottony clouds. "But then," she said, "we went outside."

NOTES

BIBLIOGRAPHY

ACKNOWLEDGMENTS

INDEX

Notes

I collected a great deal of the material for this book in first-person interviews and observation (attending conferences, marketing presentations, and so on), but I also did a lot of background reading. Sources for specific passages and facts cited in the text are given here. Other reading, however, fell into the category of background, which is documented in the bibliography.

Introduction

1 *power-lunch landmark, Oceana:* During the course of my research, I conducted lunchtime interviews with a number of executives, researchers, and other marketing professionals, some on the record, some on background, but always on my tab. Oceana is one of the restaurants where I conducted such interviews. This one took place in 2004.

3 *majority of American households:* See Victoria J. Rideout, Elizabeth A. Vandewater, and Ellen A. Wartella, *Zero to Six: Electronic Media in the Lives of Infants, Toddlers, and Preschoolers* (Menlo Park, Calif.: Henry J. Kaiser Family Foundation and Children's Digital Media Centers, 2003), p. 3: "In a typical day, 68% of all children under two use screen media (59% watch TV, 42% watch a video or DVD, 5% use a computer and 3% play video games) [for] 1 hour.

"It's Like Preschool": See www.noggin.com.

The channel was started: "CTW Finds Its Cable Outlet: A Venture with Nickelodeon," *Current,* May 4, 1998.

The term "preschooler": My interviews with mothers and marketers, 2003–2006; see also www.nielsenmedia.com.

Few eyebrows are raised: My interview with Francie Alexander, Scholastic's chief academic officer, 2004; see also "Preschools the Newest Forum for Advertising," *Washington Post*, Oct. 18, 2003, and "Targeting the Toddler Market," *New York Times*, July 11, 2003.

3–4 *in collaboration with Scholastic:* Scholastic corporate materials and my interview with Francie Alexander.

Very young children: My interviews with marketing executives. See also a prescient article on marketing to toddlers through television: "Get 'Em for Life," *Multichannel News*, Feb. 8, 1999, which provided great leads and marked the start of the industry's momentum.

"zero-to-three" . . . "cradle-to-grave": These terms and the phenomenon are widely accepted, according to my interviews with marketing executives, as well as reports in newspapers and trade publications. See, for example, Susan Tompor, "More Parents Just Say No to Pitches Targeting Kids," *Harrisburg Patriot*, Mar. 17, 2003.

$20 billion a year: I arrived at this figure by combining several sales estimates. The first set was supplied by Tim Dowd, senior analyst for Packaged Facts, a division of MarketResearch.com. Dowd estimates that for the zero-to-three group, toy sales in 2005 were $2.3 billion (other research firms estimate $3.2 billion); home furnishings and accessories (everything from cribs to strollers to lamps) were $4 billion; and apparel $7 billion. Dowd noted that because purchases for toddlers can skew older, sales figures for zero to five should also be considered. According to him, the total infant/toddler/preschool market (zero to five) in 2005 was toys, $5 billion; home furnishings, $8 billion; and clothing, $16.8 billion. Second, the industry publication *Licensing Letter* estimates the entertainment and character licensing market at around $14 billion annually, a figure that has remained steady in the last three to four years; although there are no age breakdowns, it seems safe to assume, conservatively, that the zero-to-three market accounts for at least $1 billion. Third, according to a usatoday.com article in April 2005, sales of nontheatrical children's DVDs, driven by established TV (Nickelodeon, PBS Kids) and toy brands (Mattel's Barbie), will surge from 11 million units in 2003 to 51 million units in 2007; the article noted that in 2004, consumers spent $2.7 billion on children's and family videos, about 17 percent of the $15.9 billion total spent on videos, mostly DVDs.

5 *study conducted in 2000:* The study was conducted by the now-defunct New York marketing firm Griffin Bacal.

KGOY: This term, and the phenomenon it describes, is widely accepted, according to my interviews with marketing executives, as well as newspaper and trade publication reports. See Paul Kurnit's collected presentations on kids' marketing at www.kidshopbiz.com.

"It's dribbled down": Quoted in "First Impressions," *AdWeek*, Mar. 24, 2003.

White House Conference: Many of the early childhood experts with whom I spoke — including Alison Gopnik, at the University of California at Berkeley, Daniel Anderson, at the University of Massachusetts, and Joan Lombardi, former director of the federal Child Care Bureau — were attendees, presenters, or organizers at the conference. All of them said that the baby genius phenomenon was a major unintended consequence of the event. My reporting for *U.S. News* and *Time Digital,* on smart toys and lapware, also bears out this conclusion. Conference materials are on the Web at http://clinton3.nara.gov/WH/New/ECDC. For a contrarian take on the conference, see John T. Bruer, *The Myth of the First Three Years* (New York: Free Press, 1999).

6 *Baby Einstein Company was founded:* My interview with Julie Aigner-Clark, June 25, 2005; "Bringing Up Baby Entrepreneur: Julie Aigner-Clark Hits the Tot-TV Jackpot with Baby Einstein," *People,* May 22, 2000; "Mom's Baby Vids Sharpen New Minds," *Billboard,* Oct. 3, 1998.

passionate curiosity: Baby Einstein product catalog, 2004.

7 *estimated $25 million:* This figure was widely reported in newspapers and news and business magazines.

steamroller executive: Interview with Aigner-Clark, June 25, 2005.

"Can Lightning Strike Twice": Brochure of the 2004 Youth Marketing Mega-Event, an annual kids' marketing conference hosted by the Institute for International Research.

8 *"It's one of life's":* "Bringing Up Baby Entrepreneur."

30 percent: Rideout, Vandewater, and Wartella, *Zero to Six,* p. 7.

Disney market research: Baby Einstein product catalog, 2004, pp. 11, 19.

more than half: Rideout, Vandewater, and Wartella, *Zero to Six,* p. 8.

9 *television in their room:* Ibid., p. 7.

61 percent: Victoria Rideout and Elizabeth Hamel, *The Media Family* (Menlo Park, Calif.: Henry Kaiser Family Foundation, 2006), p. 7.

88 percent do: Ibid.

The median time: Rideout, Vandewater, and Wartella, *Zero to Six,* p. 6.

fastest-growing segment: "Equity Marketing Named Master Toy Licensee, North America," *PR Newswire,* Feb. 17, 2004.

drastically shifted: According to my interviews with toy industry executives and observers, conflicts over what makes a toy "educational" — and what buyers think will sell — have pervaded the infant and toddler toy industry for the past decade or so. See Julie Rawe, "The Quest for a Super Kid: Geniuses Are Made, Not Born — or So Parents Are Told. But Can We Really Train Baby Brains, and Should We Try?" *Time,* Apr. 30, 2001; "A Smart Toy Guide (Parents Not Included)," *Time,* Apr. 30, 2001; "The Race to Raise a Brainier Baby; Parents Clamor for Educational Toys — to the Tune Of $1 Billion," *USA Today,* June 25, 2002; "A Brief History of Smart Toys," *USA Today,* June 25, 2002; "Parents Turn Toys That Teach into Hot Sellers," *Wall Street Journal,* Nov. 27,

2002; "Fisher Price Looks to Educational Toys," Reuters News, Mar. 23, 2004; "Smarter Toys, Smarter Tots? Parents Spend $2.8 Billion Per Year on Educational Toys for Infants and Preschoolers," *Christian Science Monitor*, Aug. 20, 2003; "Fisher Price Takes Edu Toy Fight to the Crib," Reuters News, June 21, 2004.

10 *Nick Jr.'s top executive:* Johnson quoted in "Get 'Em for Life."

date back at least to the 1920s: This statement was informed in part by interviews with the fantastically interesting Penn State historian Gary Cross, as well as by Ann Hulbert, *Raising America: Experts, Parents and a Century of Advice About Children* (New York: Knopf, 2003), chap. 4, "The Era (and Errors) of the Parent."

11 *The developmental gap:* Daniel Anderson of the University of Massachusetts verified this statement.

Piaget first showed: My crash course in Piaget's work was provided by college-level psychology textbooks; academic research papers; interviews with university research psychologists; and the excellent summaries in Alison Gopnik, Andrew N. Meltzoff, and Patricia K. Kuhl, *The Scientist in the Crib* (New York: HarperCollins Perennial, 1999).

12 *"problem-solving deficit disorder":* Levin used the phrase in my conversations with her in 2004–2005; see also www.pbs.org/opb/thenewheroes/parents/parents_2.html.

Marie Anzalone . . . reports: Interview with Marie Anzalone, June 24, 2004.

University of Massachusetts study: Daniel R. Anderson and Tiffany A. Pempek, "Television and Very Young Children," *American Behavioral Scientist* 48 (2005): 505–22.

13 *American Psychological Association:* Brian L. Wilcox et al., *Report of the American Psychological Association Task Force on Advertising and Children* (American Psychological Association: Washington, D.C., 2004); on the Web at www.apa .org/pi/cyf/advertisingandchildren.pdf.

They may recognize: Ibid., p. 5.

extensive study: Juliet B. Schor, *Born to Buy: The Commercialized Child and the New Consumer Culture* (New York: Scribner, 2004), questionnaire, p. 144.

Defining "consumer involvement": Ibid., p. 149.

14 *socioeconomic, educational, or cultural:* Ibid., pp. 147, 167.

clear causal and reflexive: Ibid, p. 167.

"Higher levels": Ibid, p. 170.

16 *just as a biological virus:* Douglas Rushkoff, *Media Virus! Hidden Agendas in Popular Culture* (New York: Ballantine Books, 1994), pp. 9–10.

Rushkoff's book: Rushkoff spoke at several business/New Economy conferences I attended, and as a senior editor at *U.S. News* at the time, I often heard business and marketing executives cite Rushkoff's theories enthusiastically. In his follow-up book, *Coercion: Why We Listen to What "They" Say* (New York:

Penguin Putnam, 1999), Rushkoff claimed to be shocked at how his theories had been bastardized by "them" — essentially, those in the business of institutional persuasion and coercion.

1. Learn Something New Every Day

23 *It is March 2004:* LeapFrog's public relations team invited me to spend several days at the company's headquarters in Emeryville to get an inside look at how the LeapFrog Baby line is researched and designed. I met with the division's top managers, learning how academic research shapes toy design and how prototypes are vetted by fellow producers and tested in the LeapFrog Lab. Also I was able to observe — and talk to staffers about — the culture of the company.

24 *Winnicott argued:* Donald W. Winnicott, "Transitional Objects and Transitional Phenomena," *International Journal of Psychoanalysis* 34 (1953): 89–97.

25 *Parents often view:* "Meet You at the Sandbox — After Class," *Washington Post,* Apr. 30, 2006.
140 videos or DVDs: "Want a Brainier Baby?" *Time,* Jan. 16, 2006.
According to the NPD Group: David Allmark, senior vice president and general manager of Fisher-Price Friends, at Toy Fair 2006.

26 *LeapFrog's advertising tag line:* www.leapfrog.com.

27 *According to LeapFrog's:* My interviews with LeapFrog executives and producers in March 2004 and interview with Pam Abrams, then vice president and editor in chief of Scholastic Parent and Family Publishing, in 2004.
Just seven years: LeapFrog press release, Feb. 13, 2003; Lynda M. Applegate and Christopher Dede, "Learning from LeapFrog: Creating Educational and Business Value," Harvard Business School case study, Nov. 13, 2003; "Big Battle for Young Minds: Fisher-Price Poses Challenge to Leapfrog," *Los Angeles Times,* Dec. 23, 2003.
high-level toy designer: I was granted an interview with this designer on condition of anonymity.

28 *The company pays a number:* Per my March 2004 visit.

30 *one of the most expensive:* Ibid.; see also "LeapFrog's Great Leap Forward," *Fast Company,* June 2003; LeapFrog Toy Fair 2006 press kit; Applegate and Dede, "Learning from LeapFrog."
According to the company: Liz Einbinder, LeapFrog PR representative, 2006.

31 *the infant or toddler affects:* My observations and those of Maryanne Buechner, whose research and reporting I am deeply grateful for, at International Toy Fairs in New York City, 2004–2006.
A brand manager explained: Buechner's interview with LeapFrog's Lara Dorjath at Toy Fair, February 2006.

key piece of market research: My interview with Adam Biehl at Toy Fair, February 2004.

32 *"researchers say that neurobiologists":* Carnegie Task Force on Meeting the Needs of Young Children, *Starting Points: Meeting the Needs of Our Youngest Children* (New York: Carnegie Corporation, 1994).

33 *there were no data:* John T. Bruer, *The Myth of the First Three Years: A New Understanding of Early Brain Development and Lifelong Learning.* (New York: Free Press, 1999); esp. pp. 77–78.

34 *"Whether or not":* Reiner quoted in Bruer, *Myth*, pp. 10, 20.

"Children aren't just valuable": Gopnik, Meltzoff, and Kuhl, *Scientist in the Crib*, p. 208.

36 *"some minimum threshold":* See conference materials at http://clinton3.nara.gov/WH/New/ECDC; Bruer, *Myth*, p. 51; Hulbert, *Raising America*, p. 310.

Kuhl's 2003 experiment: "Brief Exposure to Mandarin Can Help American Infants Learn Chinese," University of Washington press release, Feb. 17, 2003.

inspired by Kuhl's research: "Mom's Baby Vids Sharpen New Minds."

37 *"shown that music education":* Mary Schmich, "Magic of Mozart Is All in the Mind," *Chicago Tribune*, Oct. 15, 1993; "Certain Music Can Enhance Brain Functions," *Boston Globe*, Aug. 14, 1994; "Studies Show the Brain Is More Alive with the Sounds of Music," *Seattle Post-Intelligencer*, Mar. 28, 1996.

study seemed odd: "Mozart and the SATs," *New York Times*, Mar. 4, 1999; "Mozart Fails on Reasoning Tests," *Times* (London), Aug. 4, 1999; "The Loose Screw Awards: Psychology's Top 10 Misguided Ideas," *Psychology Today*, Jan. 1, 2005.

Don Campbell capitalized: "Holiday Title Wave Breaks with Kingly Lions, Barney, and Mozart," *Billboard*, Aug. 22, 1998.

38 *governor Zell Miller asked:* "Newborns to Arrive with Music," *Augusta Chronicle*, June 24, 1998.

Soon Florida, Colorado: "Warm Welcome Program Delivers the Sound Benefits of the Mozart Effect to Colorado Newborns," *Business Wire*, Sept. 17, 1998; "Babies Off to Smart Musical Start," Knight-Tribune News Service, June 28, 1999.

39 *experts at the conference:* Hulbert, *Raising America*, p. 42.

"What Is to Become": Quoted ibid., p. 88.

40 *Arnold Gesell:* Ibid., p. 158.

toys would enhance: Gary Cross, *Kids' Stuff* (Cambridge, Mass.: Harvard University Press, 1997); 1946 Playskool ad.

41 *Nobody took this advice:* "Study Probes Generation Gap," *Children's Business*, May 1, 2004.

golden age: Gopnik, Meltzoff, and Kuhl, *Scientist in the Crib*, pp. 20–21; Hulbert, *Raising America*, p. 300.

Researchers in the 1980s: See, in particular, "Making Baby a Shade Smarter,"

Seattle Times, Dec. 3, 1984; "Games and Giggles Toward a Better Baby," *Washington Post*, Sept. 10, 1985; "Those Amazing Newborns Are Complex," *Houston Chronicle*, Feb. 14, 1986; "Whatever Happened to the Silence of the Womb?" *Chicago Sun-Times*, Feb. 20, 1986; "Parents Are Rarin' to Start Infants on the Fast Track," *Chicago Sun-Times*, Apr. 17, 1986; "Value of Touching: Contact Can Feed Human Psyches," *Chicago Sun-Times*, Aug. 17, 1986; "The Final Word — We Hope — on Parenting in the 80s," *Washington Post*, Oct. 19, 1986; "Infants and Brain Growth: A New Study Contends There Is Neurological Growth After Birth," *Newsday*, Sept. 2, 1986; "IQ Booster Is Teacher's Smartest Idea Yet," *Orlando Sentinel*, Nov. 27, 1987; "Children Read Their Scribbles," *Washington Post*, Sept. 17, 1987.

42 *buzzword was "competent":* Hulbert, *Raising America*, pp. 304–5.

power-suited mothers: Ibid., pp. 295–96.

43 *established assumption:* My interviews with Daniel Hade, associate professor of children's literature at Penn State University, January and June 2004; Kathy Hirsh-Pasek, professor of psychology at Temple University and director of the Infant Language Laboratory, June 2004; and Anne E. Cunningham, associate professor of cognition and development at UC Berkeley, March 2004. See also Kathy Hirsh-Pasek and Roberta Michnick Golinkoff, *Einstein Never Used Flash Cards* (Emmaus, Pa.: Rodale Press, 2003), pp. 100–102.

Prenatal University: "Doctor Teaches Parents to Talk to Unborn Babies," *Chicago Sun-Times*, Jan. 5, 1986; "School for Babies in the Womb: Hayward 'College' Seeks to Give Kids a Jump on Learning," *San Francisco Chronicle*, Aug. 26, 1987.

44 *auditory stimulation in utero:* "Some Coos Babble in the Making of a Superbaby," *Los Angeles Times*, July 1, 1986.

time-squeezed superwomen: "Bringing Up Baby," *Globe and Mail*, June 4, 1983.

45 *Pregaphone was launched:* "Some Coos Babble."

Playskool and Fisher-Price: Cross, *Kids' Stuff*, pp. 141–42; www.fisher-price .com/fp.aspx?st=161&e=playlab&site=us.

Fisher-Price's PlayLab: I am very grateful to Fisher-Price for inviting me to spend two days, in April 2004, at its headquarters in East Aurora, New York, a small upstate town near Buffalo. There I spoke with Kathleen Alfano and spent a morning observing children at PlayLab. I also spoke with several toy designers in the infant and toddler division, as well as with Shelly Glick Gryfe, director of marketing research. I learned a great deal about the effect of the social sensibilities of the parents' generation on toy design and marketing messages as well as about the history of Fisher-Price.

headed by Jim Gray: I interviewed Gray during my March 2004 visit to Leap-Frog, as well as at the 2005 Kid Power Xchange conference.

46 *state-of-the-art facilities:* As I observed during my visits to both facilities in spring 2004.

"*That's our way*": Conversations with Fisher-Price public relations representatives, spring 2004; PlayLab's orientation video tape.

database of thousands: Jim Gray, Kid Power 2005 keynote speech.

Even the most enthusiastic: Interviews at LeapFrog headquarters, March 2004.

47 *term borrowed from academia:* The Nebraska Department of Education offers a particularly cogent definition of Scope and Sequence: www.nde.state.ne.us/READ/FRAMEWORK/index.html.

"*secret weapon*": I am grateful to the LeapFrog Baby executives — in particular, Adam Biehl, senior brand manager for infant/toddler/juvenile products, and Craig Hendrickson, senior brand manager for preschool products — who shared the Scope & Sequence with me — decoding it and explaining plans for its larger role in potentially guiding state-wide curricula — during my March 2004 visit to LeapFrog headquarters.

49 *2004 annual conference:* I attended this conference and spent time in many different seminars, as well as walking around the exhibition hall, interviewing vendors — including Disney and Scholastic — and conference attendees about their field.

LeapFrog already sells: LeapFrog visit, March 2004.

Its parent company: Corporate press release announcing merger, Jan. 2005: www.kindercare.com/pdf/Final-Merger01-05.pdf.

50 *Today the company operates:* www.knowledgelearning.com/aboutus/index.html.

fast-tracking: LeapFrog visit, March 2004. See also www.leapfrog.com/content/parent_guides/pg_ttdiscoverybk.pdf.

2. "*There's a New Mom in Town*"

52 *As Dave Siegel:* I attended the Kid Power conferences in 2004 and 2005 and took detailed notes during keynote speeches as well as the dozens of marketing seminars and presentations. Siegel's presentation was among the most nuanced and research-based.

53 *Generation X comprises:* Paul Kurnit of KidShop, presentation at Kid Power Xchange conference, 2004.

oldest born in 1965: Date spans provided by KidShop, WonderGroup, and other marketing firms.

"*They have trouble*": David M. Gross and Sophronia Scott, "Proceeding with Caution," *Time*, July 16, 1990.

Douglas Coupland's 1991 novel: Douglas Coupland, *Generation X: Tales for an Accelerated Culture* (New York: St. Martin's Press, 1991).

54 *Today two-thirds:* Siegel, keynote address, 2004.

Forty percent were latchkey: Census Bureau report cited in Marie Winn, *Chil-*

dren Without Childhood (New York: Pantheon, 1983), p. 121; Diane Ravitch, "In the Family's Way," *New Republic,* June 28, 1980, p. 24.

Some observers estimate: Maria T. Bailey and Bonnie W. Ulman, *Trillion-Dollar Moms: Marketing to a New Generation of Mothers* (Chicago: Dearborn Trade Publishing, 2005), p. 57.

"Generation X went through": "Study Probes Generation Gap," *Children's Business,* May 1, 2004.

According to a report: Kenneth Keniston and the Carnegie Council on Children, *All Our Children: The American Family Under Pressure* (New York: Harcourt Brace Jovanovich, 1977), p. 7.

55 *Indeed, the 1980s marked:* Interviews with marketers; licensing seminar, Toy Fair 2004.

While the sponsors: I am in debt to — and a great admirer of — the historian Gary Cross, who highlighted this turning point in the history of childhood and marketing in America. See, in particular, Cross, *Kids' Stuff,* chap. 7.

Concern that advertisers: Federal Trade Commission, *FTC Staff Report on Television Advertising to Children* (Washington, 1978).

By 1987 about 60 percent: Cross, *Kids' Stuff,* pp. 199–200.

release in 1977 of Star Wars: Ibid., pp. 202–3; licensing seminars at Toy Fair and KidPower; interviews with marketers.

Disney had always timed: Buechner's interview with a Disney public relations representative, June 2006; see also Cross, *Kids' Stuff,* pp. 106–7.

56 *products had grossed:* Cross, *Kids' Stuff,* p. 202.

the story of American toys: Gary Cross was kind enough to meet with me in person at Pennsylvania State University in State College during the summer of 2004, to discuss these ideas further.

58 *70 percent are married:* Siegel's keynote address, 2004.

getting married is not: Bailey and Ulman, *Trillion-Dollar Moms,* p. 61.

59 *national support group:* Single Mothers by Choice Web site: http://mattes.home.pipeline.com/faq.html.

The 2005 National Study: Press release, Oct. 13, 2005: www.familiesandwork.org.

"Of the 92% of employers": Ibid.

60 *32 percent:* Siegel's keynote address, 2004.

Gen-X mother deciding: Baby food example from Bailey and Ulman, *Trillion-Dollar Moms,* pp. 59–60.

Friends are extremely: Ibid., pp. 65–66.

61 *Gen-X mothers . . . watch:* Phone interview with Playhouse Disney executive Nancy Kanter, Dec. 13, 2004. Testimonials are from the Baby Einstein Web site.

63 *she had sold 40,000:* "Mom's Baby Vids Sharpen New Minds."

more than $1 million: "Baby Videos Spell Big Money: Mom Turns 'Einstein' into Million-Dollar Enterprise," *Denver Post,* Mar. 12, 1999.

by 1999: "Baby Einstein Company Ships Its 1 Millionth Unit," *Video Business,* Nov. 15, 1999.

rung up $4.5 million: "Bringing Up Baby: Entrepreneur Julie Aigner-Clark Hits the Tot-TV Jackpot with Baby Einstein," *People,* May 22, 2000.

But Disney has tried: My interview with Kanter.

Aigner-Clark appears: Interview with Julie Aigner-Clark, June 25, 2004; "Bringing Up Baby Entrepreneur"; "Mom's Baby Vids Sharpen New Minds."

64 *As the marketers:* Bailey and Ulman, *Trillion-Dollar Moms,* p. 61.

65 *Gen-X mom says:* The market research on Gen-X mothers rebelling against the baby genius phenomenon while still susceptible to it is culled from my interviews at LeapFrog, Fisher-Price, Kid Power, and Toy Fair. See "Gen X Moms Put Emphasis on Fun Toys," *Washington Post,* Feb. 29, 2004.

more than 85 percent said: Bailey and Ulman, *Trillion-Dollar Moms,* p. 67.

66 *Fisher-Price learned:* Fisher-Price marketing researcher Shelley Glick Gryfe supplied this fascinating example of marketing and advertising the Slumber Time Soother during my visit to East Aurora in April 2004 and supplied confirming details during a phone conversation in August of that year.

70 *Look at the photograph:* Interview with Gryfe, April 2004.

3. "It's Like Preschool on TV"

71 *In 1968 an icon:* The history of *Sesame Street*'s beginnings are primarily from Edward L. Palmer and Shalom M. Fisch's chapter "The Beginnings of *Sesame Street* Research," in Shalom M. Fisch and Rosemarie Truglio, eds., *"G" Is for Growing: Thirty Years of Research on Children and Sesame Street* (Mahwah, N.J.: Lawrence Erlbaum Associates, 2001), pp. 3–22. Over the two years that I was conducting research and writing this book, many people at Sesame Workshop — especially Rosemarie Truglio, Lewis Bernstein, and Ann Kearns — answered my questions about Sesame's beginnings, research processes, outreach projects, and licensing model. I am grateful to them for their help.

72 *By the 1960s Piaget's:* My survey of Piaget's and Vygotsky's work was provided by college-level psychology textbooks such as Carol Garhart Mooney, *Theories of Childhood: An Introduction to Dewey, Montessori, Erikson, Piaget, and Vygotsky* (St. Paul, Minn.: Redleaf Press, 2000); academic research papers; interviews with university research psychologists; and the excellent summaries in Gopnik, Meltzoff, and Kuhl, *Scientist in the Crib.* See also the Web site of the Jean Piaget Society, www.piaget.org.

75 *By 1968 research by Nielsen:* Fisch and Truglio, *"G" Is for Growing,* pp. 3–22.

77 *Daniel R. Anderson had recently:* In February 2004 Dan Anderson spent an entire day with me at his offices and lab, discussing his earlier key experiments and demonstrating the setups for current ones. He also spent many

hours on the phone and answering my e-mails over the next two years to update me on his research results and explain matters that were unclear to me. He also pointed me in the direction of the handful of colleagues at other universities working on similar research, which was extremely helpful.

78 *Brain scans of adults:* D. R. Anderson et al., "Cortical Activation While Watching Video Montage: An fMRI Study," *Media Psychology* 8 (2006): 7–24.

82 *PR material for* Dora: Nickelodeon press material, as quoted in Sally Beatty, "Couch Tater Tots: In Battle for Toddlers, TV Networks Tout Educational Benefits," *Wall Street Journal,* Apr. 1, 2002.

But marketing television: "*Blue's Clues* Trickles Down to Babies," *Children's Business,* Feb. 1, 2001; "Guilt Free TV," *Newsweek,* Nov. 2002.

Similarly Disney: Playhouse Disney Web site; interview with Playhouse Disney consultant Renee Chernow O'Leary, lead educational consultant to Playhouse Disney, December 2004.

83 *To verify such educational:* Interviews with Iris Sroka, April 2005, and fact-checking confirmation, July 2006.

85 *Even* Sesame Street: My interviews with Truglio in 2004.

By their own admission: I interviewed all these executives, and all reported that they knew babies and toddlers were watching their preschool programs but did not test that age group.

86 *Even the producers:* Interview with Rashmi Turner of Baby Einstein at Toy Fair 2004.

Teletubbies *had a lot:* For the history of *Teletubbies,* I relied on interviews with university research psychologists who study media and very young children, as well as on several good articles in *Current:* "*Teletubbies* in Britain: Craze, Controversy and Consumer Frenzy," Dec. 15, 1997; "Eh-Oh!: Bridging Real World and Toddler Fantasy, *Teletubbies* Reaches Youngest Audience," Feb. 16, 1998; "Alice in Blunderland," Mar. 16, 1998; "Tubbies Bring New Charges of Commercialism to PBS," May 4, 1998; "Is Tinky a Gay Role Model for Boys or a Purple Toddler in Full Play?" Feb. 22, 1999.

87 *"The AAP strongly opposes":* Quoted in "Tubbies Bring New Charges."

88 *Even a provocative 2004:* Dimitri A. Christakis et al., "Early Television Exposure and Subsequent Attentional Problems in Children," *Pediatrics* 113, no. 4 (Apr. 2004).

89 *Anderson figured that:* Interviews with Anderson.

90 *"they only watch videos":* On the baby video business in the late 1990s and early 2000s, see "Non-Talking Video Big Hit with Babies and Toddlers," *Denver Post,* June 26, 1999; "Bringing Up (Bilingual) Baby — Marketers Rush to Meet Demand for Toys, Tapes, and Classes," *Wall Street Journal,* Oct. 6, 1999; "Baby Videos Aim to Stimulate Young Brains," *Video Store,* Dec. 5, 1999; "Smart Baby Products Reeling In Parents," *Washington Post,* Mar. 3, 2000; "With Baby Video, Family Business Born," *St. Petersburg Times,* Oct. 8, 2000;

"Babies Are Bundles of Love, Joy — And Money; Give New Parents a Helping Hand by Stocking These Videos for Babies, Toddlers," *Video Store*, Oct. 12, 2003.

91 *One of the few:* Judy S. DeLoache, "Becoming Symbol Minded," *Trends in Cognitive Sciences* 8, no. 2. (Feb. 2004); www.faculty.virginia.edu/deloache.

93 *In 1999 Anderson read:* Interviews with Anderson; excerpts of the AAP's press release are in "AAP Discourages Television for Very Young Children," *Pediatrics*, Aug. 2, 1999.

4. A Vast and Uncontrolled Experiment

94 *In 2003 Anderson:* My interviews and visit with Anderson, February 2004, February 2005, and May 2006. See also Daniel R. Anderson and Tiffany A. Pempek, "Television and Very Young Children," *American Behavioral Scientist* 48 (2005): 505–22.

98 *In 2003 a team:* "Yes, Babies Do Watch TV," *New York Times*, Jan. 24, 2003.

In 2004 Deborah L. Linebarger: Deborah L. Linebarger, "Young Children, Language, and Television," *Literacy Today*, Sept. 2004. The full academic study is Linebarger and Dale Walker, "Infants' and Toddlers' Television Viewing and Language Outcomes," *American Behavioral Scientist* 46 (2004).

100 *Another study:* Bernard G. Grela, Marina Krcmar, and Yi-Jiun Lin, "Can Television Help Toddlers Acquire New Words?" paper presented at the annual meeting of the American Speech–Language–Hearing Association, Chicago, 2003.

In late 2003 the Henry J. Kaiser: See Rideout, Vandewater, and Wartella, *Zero to Six.*

101 *In a paper titled:* See Anderson and Pempek, "Television and Very Young Children."

Rachel Barr, an assistant professor: Barr spent an entire day with me in the spring of 2004 at her offices and lab, detailing her key experiments and demonstrating the more current ones. She verified my reporting of her findings on the phone and explained matters that were unclear to me. She also recommended that I speak to colleagues at other universities, most significantly, Judy DeLoache. I also referred to the summaries of Barr's research findings at her official Georgetown University Web site: www.elp.georgetown.edu.

5. Elmo's World

110 *It was Elmo:* The information on Sesame Workshop and the Elmo phenomenon comes from my interviews with Kearns and Truglio. Kearns spoke with me over lunch in September 2004; Truglio and I met in person, spoke on the phone, and communicated by e-mail from June 2004 to fall 2006.

112 *Elmo's stardom reached:* Interviews with Kearns and Truglio and my interview

with Fisher-Price's Stan Clutton, August 2005. See also "The Untold Toy Success Story: Elmo's Evolution Is a Surprise to Those Involved," *USA Today,* Dec. 11, 1996.

113 *the most licensed:* Interview with Kearns.

68 percent: Sesame Workshop 2004 Annual Report, p. 55.

Sesame Beginnings: Interview with Kearns. Product descriptions were culled from Amazon.com and other retail venues.

The promotional materials: Sesame Workshop Web site: http://sesamework shop.org/sesamebeginnings/new/dvds.php.

the Workshop had concluded: Interview with Truglio, May 2006.

114 *When the Walt Disney Company:* Background on Disney's marketing of Mickey Mouse was supplied by Dave Smith, director of Walt Disney Archives, via e-mail to Maryanne Buechner, who helped me with additional research. See also Cross, *Kids' Stuff,* pp. 104–7.

115 *Although Pooh began:* A. A. Milne's first story about Winnie-the-Pooh was published in the *London Evening News* on Christmas Eve 1925; Disney recognizes this as the official anniversary date, making Dec. 24, 2005, the eightieth anniversary.

Pooh is second: The retail sales figures here are derived from the list (published annually) "Top-Earning Fictional Characters," *Forbes,* Sept. 25, 2003, and Oct. 21, 2004; also Buechner's interview with Disney Consumer Products' corporate communications manager Clint Hayashi.

Disputes over: "The Curse of Pooh," *Fortune,* Jan. 20, 2003.

Retailers offered: The examples of eightieth-anniversary Pooh products were culled from online retail outlets, such as Amazon.com; Disney Store details are from Buechner's interview with Amy Hawk, the general manager of merchandising, April 2006.

116 *The success of licensed:* Much of this section was informed by Cross's description and analysis of the tension between an incipient American commercial culture and "play" purists; see *Kids' Stuff,* pp. 105–46. Details about Fisher-Price are from my visit to the company's toy museum in East Aurora, New York.

119 *Disney licensed Mickey's:* Buechner's interview with Hayashi.

In 1982 Fisher-Price: Fisher-Price's Toy Museum.

LeapFrog, for example: Interview with Melanie Bell, the head of licensing at LeapFrog, March 2004.

compelled Fisher-Price: Interview with Stan Clutton, senior vice president of licensing and new business at Fisher-Price, August 2005.

the word "toyetic": Stan Clutton discussed what makes a property toyetic and how Fisher-Price has negotiated that terrain.

121 *At the 2004 International Toy Fair:* Guided tour of Fisher-Price's exhibition at the 2004 Toy Fair.

by 2005 Dora had made: Sales figures are from Buechner's interview with Kagan Research analyst Derek Baine. The $1 billion figure was also reported in a *Business Week* article and confirmed by an anonymous Nickelodeon PR representative.

Paramount and Nickelodeon: USA Today, Apr. 4, 2005.

Viacom's 2004 filing: Viacom Annual Report, 2004, p. II-5.

122 *In a 2005 report:* Viacom Annual Report, 2005, p. II-13.

"Nickelodeon [reached]": Ibid., p. I-8.

It's the same story: Disney 10-K report, 2005, p. 48.

There is big money: I paid to attend this Geppetto Group workshop (and was upfront about my reasons for attending), which followed the Kid Power conference in 2005.

125 *Speaking on the phone:* Buechner's interview with Siegel, July 11, 2005.

as much as $100,000: Center for a New American Dream (www.newdream .org), quoted in "Toddler Temptation," *News-Leader,* Feb. 21, 2003.

126 *Chris McKee speaks passionately:* Buechner's interview with McKee, Aug. 12, 2005.

128 *"Although public opinion":* Sabrina M. Neeley and David W. Schumann, "Using Animated Spokescharacters in Advertising to Young Children: Does Increasing Attention to Advertising Necessarily Lead to Product Preference?" *Journal of Advertising,* 2004. Additional details come from Buechner's interview with Neeley, July 29, 2005.

131 *Iris Sroka and her team:* This section is based on a Hypothesis Group marketing seminar I paid to attend the day before the Kid Power 2005 conference, as well as several interviews with Iris Sroka. In addition, in April 2005 Sroka spent an entire morning with me describing her research for Disney and others. Buechner also interviewed her on July 25, 2005, and I consulted her notes from that conversation. In August 2006, Sroka confirmed by phone all the material in this section.

6. The Princess Lifestyle

137 *Within a year of Mooney's:* Background on Andy Mooney and his success with the Disney Princess brand was culled from business press reports, Buechner's interview with Mooney on April 6, 2006, and e-mail correspondence in 2006 with DCP's Hayashi (especially concerning sales figures); also Disney press releases. Especially useful articles include "Transformer of a Mickey Mouse Outfit," *Financial Times,* May 27, 2003; "Princesses Rule! Armed with Jewels and Lace, Fantasy Femmes Are en Route to World Domination," *Los Angeles Times,* Aug. 31, 2004; "Love the Riches, Lose the Rags," *New York Times,* Nov. 3, 2005; "Marketing Is King for Disney's Princess Line," *Daily Variety,* Dec. 12, 2005.

141 *The classic business textbook:* Philip Kotler, *Marketing Management,* 9th ed. (Englewood Cliffs, N.J.: Prentice Hall, 1997).
"A brand is said": Kevin L. Keller, "Conceptualizing, Measuring, and Managing Customer-based Brand Equity," *Journal of Marketing* 57 (1993): 1–22.

142 *There are essentially two ways:* Here I have tried to synthesize several themes that seemed to emerge from the extant research; Michael Brody, M.D., reviewed my synthesis to confirm its plausibility.
In a 1998 article: Taylor Randall, Karl Ulrich, and David Reibstein, "Brand Equity and Vertical Product Line Extent," *Marketing Science* 17, no. 4 (1998): 356–79.

144 *WonderGroup's "Millennium Mom":* WonderGroup's Dave Siegel presented these highlights of his firm's model at the Kid Power 2004 conference, which I attended. Also, see "Gen X Moms Take Back Purchasing Power from Kids," *KidScreen,* June 1, 2004.

146 *average Gen-X adult spends:* "My Generation: Hope I Shop Before I Get Old," *New York Times,* Aug. 14, 2005.

147 *"The emerging code":* David Brooks, *Bobos in Paradise: The New Upper Class and How They Got There* (New York: Simon & Schuster, 2000), p. 85.
One study, conducted by Neeley: Siegel discussed WonderGroup and Neeley's study about what he called the "four-eyed, four-legged consumer" in an interview with Buechner, July 11, 2005.

148 *Take a walk through:* These observations are my own, based on reporting, visiting these stores, reading the magazines cited, and watching television. I found Courtney Rubin, "Reality Bites," *Washington Monthly* (Oct. 2002), a terrific read on the zeitgeist. Details of *Harvey Birdman* episodes may be confirmed at the Adult Swim Web site, Harvey Birdman episode guide: http://www.adultswim.com/shows/birdman/index.html.

151 *By 2005, many of these:* Care Bears data came from Debra Joester, president of the Joester Loria Group, a licensing and marketing agency for American Greetings and other companies and the licensing agent for the Care Bears, in a phone interview with Buechner, May 3, 2006.

152 *Strawberry Shortcake followed:* Strawberry Shortcake data are from an American Greetings/DIC press release at Toy Fair 2006.
With the spring 2005 release: The description is based on my own observations, as well as my review of Amazon.com and www.shop.com/op/aprod-p20771309-k12-g-~Star+Wars+Playskool-nover.

153 *In promotional appearances:* Lucas quoted in "Taking Pre-Schoolers to See Star Wars," *San Jose Mercury News,* May 20, 2005.
He was hired to manage: The information about Richard Dickson and his success with the Barbie brand is based on his thorough and fascinating keynote speech at Kid Power 2004, as well as a conversation I had with him at the conference after that presentation. See also "Wanna Dress Like Barbie?" *CNN/*

Money, June 14, 2004; "Mattel Launches Barbie Clothes for Women," Reuters, Oct. 15, 2005.

159 *"We feel parents are more willing":* Buechner's interview with an executive who wished to remain anonymous, July 2004.

7. Anything to Get Them to Read

160 *Wander into the kids' section:* The description is based on my own observations. David Jacobs graciously spent a very long lunch in January 2004 talking with me about his career in the edutainment business, as well as his particular strategy for Thomas & Friends. I also consulted notes from Buechner's interview with Jacobs on April 28, 2006.

what "Thomas," or "Gordon": See www.just-thomas.com, "Meet the Characters."

As a brand, Thomas: Sales figures are from Buechner's interview with Jacobs. HIT's North American president, Pat Wyatt, could say only that overall sales in North America of toys, books, and everything else was "in the hundreds of millions" and "we've had eight consecutive years of double-digit growth." HIT is privately held.

Thomas books have sold: See www.just-thomas.com.

161 *by the late 1990s:* My interview, and Buechner's, with Jacobs.

163 *As HIT North America's president:* Buechner's interview with Wyatt, April 27, 2006.

John Newbery regularly bundled: Daniel Hade, "Storyselling," *Horn Book Magazine,* Sept. 1, 2002.

baby book category was born: I am indebted to Daniel Hade, associate professor of children's literature at Pennsylvania State University, whose presentation on the commercialization of the children's publishing industry at the 2004 Campaign for a Commercial Free Childhood (based on "Storyselling") was so penetrating that I sought him out for further exposition. He graciously spent an afternoon in 2004 at Penn State's campus in State College, discussing with me the origins of the baby book market and media conglomerates' influence on it. See also Hirsh-Pasek and Golinkoff, *Einstein Never Used Flash Cards,* pp. 100–102.

164 *The publishing industry came up:* Information on "chewables" came from marketing executives in children's publishing. A great number of executives were willing to discuss the nuances and complexities of making money in children's publishing on condition that the information they offered be used for background, not for specific attribution.

165 *Natasha Cane:* Buechner's interview with Cane, July 15, 2004.

166 *That was the opinion:* Hade, "Storyselling," and my 2004 interview with Hade.

I found the additional examples of Curious George merch on Amazon.com and at Toy Fair 2006.

169 *"Reading may be harmful":* Harper's Magazine, June 1991.

Like many readers, Hade: Hade, "Storyselling," and my 2004 interview with Hade.

170 *it formed Scholastic Entertainment Inc.:* Scholastic's Web site, www.scholastic .com.

171 *"The Company develops":* Scholastic, Annual Report, 1999, p. 1.

Four years later: Scholastic, Annual Report, 2004, p. 6.

Baby's First Book Club: Ibid., pp. 1, 3.

172 *ten most popular board books:* Ipsos BookTrends.

By 2004 HarperCollins: Publishers Weekly, July 26, 2004.

Board books based on popular: Information on the state of the business is from marketing executives in children's publishing.

175 *In 2001 Borders:* "Borders Adopts Category Management," *Publishers Weekly,* Feb. 5, 2001; "Group Protests Borders's Category Management Policy," *Publishers Weekly,* July 1, 2002; "Category Management at Borders," Publishers Marketing Association Web site, Nov. 2002.

176 *The baby genius trend:* Publishers Weekly, July 26, 2004.

Wal-Mart can order: Information about Wal-Mart's power in the publishing business comes from marketing executives in children's publishing.

177 *Amy Cohen:* This writer agreed to speak on condition that her name not be used.

8. Developing Character in Preschool

181 *Iris Sroka and her counterpart:* The information on Sroka's consulting is based on my interviews with her in April 2005 and July 2006.

182 *"Clifford's Ten Big Ideas":* Interviews with Sroka; see also pbskids.org/clifford/ bigideas/.

Since it debuted: Scholastic's Annual Report, 2004, p. 5.

"brand extension for infants": The quote is from a 2005 e-mail to Buechner.

"Clifford became a full-fledged": Ibid.

183 *Using the "Ten Big Ideas":* The head of Scholastic's academic division, Francie Alexander, spoke with me over lunch in 2004 about the Clifford curriculum and how it was designed. Contents of the Clifford package are listed at http:// shop.scholastic.com.

"When it comes to preparing": Quoted in "Targeting the Toddler Market," *New York Times,* July 11, 2003.

184 *Scholastic began to receive:* My interview with Francie Alexander. Scholastic's Kate Treveloni spoke with me at the 2004 National Association for the Educa-

tion of Young Children (NAEYC) conference about Clifford's popularity with very young children at daycare and preschool.

It might work: My interview with Church, August 2005.

185 *More than half:* National Research Council and Institute of Medicine, Jack P. Shonkoff and Deborah A. Phillips, eds., *From Neurons to Neighborhoods: The Science of Early Childhood Development* (Washington, D.C.: National Academy Press, 2000), pp. 297–98.

not legally required: Web site for the National Resource Center for Health and Safety in Child Care and Early Education (NRCHSCC): http://nrc.uchsc.edu/ STATES/states.htm.

186 *"Licensing is not":* Gwen Morgan, quoted in Joan Lombardi, *Time to Care: Redesigning Child Care to Promote Education, Support Families, and Build Communities* (Philadelphia: Temple University Press, 2003), p. 74.

National Health and Safety Performance Standards: http://nrc.uchsc.edu/ STATES/states.htm.

"Virtually every systematic": Cited in Shonkoff and Phillips, *From Neurons,* p. 320.

187 *"Both correlational":* Deborah Vandell and Barbara Wolfe, *Child Care Quality: Does It Matter and Does It Need to Be Improved?* (Washington, D.C.: U.S. Department of Health and Human Services, 2000), Executive Summary: http:// aspe.hhs.gov/hsp/ccquality00/execsum.htm.

Another report: Ellen S. Peisner-Feinberg et al., *The Children of the Cost, Quality, and Child Outcomes Study Go to School* (Washington, D.C.: National Institute of Early Child Development and Education, June 1999), Executive Summary: www.fpg.unc.edu/nced/PDFs/CQO-es.pdf.

188 *The problem, according to:* My 2005 interview with Joan Lombardi, as well as her book, *Time to Care.*

According to the Urban Institute's: Lombardi, *Time to Care,* p. 6.

"market failure": Vandell and Wolfe, *Child Care Quality,* Executive Summary.

189 *Today, as in the 1990s:* All data on NAEYC was culled from the organization's Web site, www.naeyc.org and from information at the NAEYC 2004 conference.

191 *"Character Education":* See www.whitehouse.gov/news/reports/no-child-left-behind.html.

The gulf between: See "The Littlest Test-Takers," *New York Times,* Nov. 9, 2003; "Pre-K Prep: How Young Is Too Young for Tutoring?" *Wall Street Journal,* Oct. 13, 2004; "Falling 'Behind' at Age 3: The Hazards of Pushing for Accountability in Pre-K," *Wall Street Journal,* Aug. 18, 2005.

193 *"even federally supported":* Lombardi, *Time to Care,* p. 80.

It seemed as if the Clinton and Bush: My discussions with Scholastic's Francie Alexander and early childhood educators at the NAEYC conference in late 2004, as well as marketing executives.

194 *"Let me start"*: My interview with Joel Ehrlich, June 1, 2004. Ehrlich left YMI in 2006.

195 *"long been an award-winning"*: www.youthmedia.com.

196 *"targeted, effective"*: www.youthmarketingint.com.
    YMI promotes its clients': My interview with Ehrlich; Ehrlich's presentation at Kid Power, May 2004.

197 *One of YMI's most successful*: www.youthmarketingint.com; Care Bears and *Boobah!* curriculum packets (downloadable at this site, as well as at www .youthmedia.com).

198 *The company had purchased*: My interview with Ehrlich; Cover Concepts' Web site; and "Advertisers Take Pitches to Preschools," *Wall Street Journal,* Oct. 28, 1996.

200 *Disney had a problem*: At the NAEYC conference in November 2004, I was introduced to Lauren Rees by Pam Abrams, a Scholastic executive at that time. Rees very kindly spent nearly an hour talking with me about Scholastic's consulting and curriculum packaging for Disney's preschool television programs. We followed up with several more phone conversations and e-mails, and Rees sent me the full curriculum package for *Jojo's Circus.*

201 *In addition to developing*: My interview with Pam Abrams; see http://www .scholastic.com/aboutscholastic/divisions/six_and_under.htm.

202 *When Disney signed on*: My interviews with Rees. Scholastic provided me with a spreadsheet of daycare facilities in the New York area to which Disney curricula had been sent, and I phoned them to find out how they had been used. Most directors (as Rees said) just hung up the poster and kept the video for a rainy or restless day.

205 *Another client of Scholastic's*: Alice Cahn met with me at her offices in the Time Warner building in Manhattan on July 23, 2004, to discuss preschool television in general, her career, and her plans for her new role at the Cartoon Network.
    In a presentation titled: Brochure advertising the 2004 Youth Marketing Mega-Event.
    Cahn lined up: My interview with Cahn, as well as information on the Cartoon Network Web site.

Conclusion: A Defense of "Nothing"

207 *Oberlin has the lowest*: Statistics on Oberlin are from the U.S. Census of 2000.
    If you live in Oberlin: Nancy Sabath and the OECC teachers spent an entire day speaking with me in late July 2005, letting me poke around their classrooms and ask questions to my heart's content. It was a privilege. I was introduced to them by Sonya Shoptaugh, a Reggio educational consultant in the United States, who has done most of her work in Ohio. In a morning with her

and several e-mails, I learned about her career putting the Reggio philosophy into practice.

216 *The Children and Media Research:* See http://clinton.senate.gov.

217 *Children's Advertising Review Unit:* See www.caru.org.

"CARU, frankly, has become": Tom Harkin spoke at the FTC/HHS workshop on marketing, self-regulation, and childhood obesity on July 14, 2005; see http://harkin.senate.gov.

218 *"Television commercials and Internet":* The study can be found at www.commercialexpliotation.org.

In a 2005 study: See "Subadolescent Queen Bees," *New York Times,* Dec. 11, 2005.

221 *As the journalist Nina Munk:* "My Generation," *New York Times,* Aug. 14, 2005.

222 *"The 'marketer within'":* "Merchants of Cool," *Frontline,* 2003.

223 *In his 2004 book:* David T. Z. Mindich, *Tuned Out: Why Americans Under 40 Don't Follow the News* (New York: Oxford University Press, 2004).

224 *Sales of minivans:* "How Long a Drive? 'Finding Nemo' or 'Harry Potter'?" *New York Times,* Nov. 21, 2003.

Supermarket chains have also: "Now Playing in Aisle 7," *Washington Post,* Jan. 29, 2003.

226 *"Since infancy, they have been":* See Wendy Watson, "X-treme Parenting," on the Porter Novelli Web site.

228 *Nearly 75 percent:* Cited in Joan Blades and Kristin Rowe-Finkbeiner, *The Motherhood Manifesto* (New York: Nation Books, 2006), excerpted in *The Nation,* May 2006.

Bibliography

Acredolo, Linda, and Susan Goodwyn. *Baby Signs: How to Talk with Your Baby Before Your Baby Can Talk.* New York: Contemporary Books/McGraw Hill, 2002.

Acuff, Daniel, and Robert H. Reiher. *What Kids Buy: The Psychology of Marketing to Kids.* New York: Simon & Schuster, 1999.

Allen, Kimberly. "Baby Videos Aim to Stimulate Young Brains." *Video Store,* Dec. 5, 1999.

Anderson, Daniel R., and Marie K. Evans. "Peril and Potential of Media for Toddlers." *Zero to Three* 22 (2001): 10–16.

Anderson, Daniel R., and Tiffany A. Pempek. "Television and Very Young Children." *American Behavioral Scientist* 48 (2005): 505–22.

Atlas, Riva D. "Milken Sees the Classroom as Profit Center." *New York Times,* Dec. 18, 2004.

Bailey, Maria T., and Bonnie W. Ulman. *Trillion-Dollar Moms: Marketing to a New Generation of Mothers.* Chicago: Dearborn Trade Publishing, 2005.

Barker, Teresa. "Parents Are Rarin' to Start Infants on the Fast Track." *Chicago Sun-Times,* Apr. 17, 1986.

Barr, Rachel F., and Georgetown Early Learning Project. "Infant Attention: Baby Mozart and Sesame Street." www.elp.georgetown.edu, Apr. 23, 2004; "Can I See That Again?" www.elp.georgetown.edu, Oct. 28, 2003; "Cartoon Sound Effects." www.elp.georgetown.edu, Dec. 11, 2002.

Bedford, Karen Everhart. "*Teletubbies* in Britain: Craze, Controversy and Consumer Frenzy." *Current,* Dec. 15, 1997; "Eh-Oh!: Bridging Real World and Toddler Fantasy, *Teletubbies* Reaches Youngest Audience." *Current,* Feb. 16, 1998; "Alice in Blunderland." *Current,* Mar. 16, 1998; "Tubbies Bring New Charges of

Commercialism to PBS." *Current,* May 4, 1998; "CTW Finds Its Cable Outlet: A Venture with Nickelodeon." *Current,* May 4, 1998; "Is Tinky a Gay Role Model for Boys or a Purple Toddler in Full Play?" *Current,* Feb. 22, 1999; "PBS Kids Said to Need Clearer Focus on Learning." *Current,* June 24 2002.

Bellafante, Ginia. "The Littlest Clotheshorse." *New York Times,* Nov. 4, 2003; "Cover Baby's Ears: Mommy's Online." *New York Times,* Mar. 21, 2004; "Celebrity Parents: Brad, Jen and Hollywood's New Morality Tale." *New York Times,* Jan. 16, 2005; "Trafficking in Memories (for Fun and Profit)." *New York Times,* Jan. 27, 2005.

Belluck, Pam. "With Mayhem at Home, They Call a Parent Coach." *New York Times,* Mar. 13, 2005.

Berrett, Dan. "These Days It Has to Do a Lot More Than Roll." *New York Times,* July 3, 2005.

Better, Nancy M. "How Long a Drive? 'Finding Nemo' or 'Harry Potter'?" *New York Times,* Nov. 21, 2003; "Greetings From Vanuabalavu!" *New York Times,* Dec. 19, 2003.

Bhatnagar, Parija. "Wanna Dress Like Barbie? Mattel Is Gearing Up to Launch a Barbie Line of Clothes, Accessories and Perfume for Adult Women." *CNN/ Money,* June 14, 2004.

Bing, Jonathan. "Marketing Is King for Disney's Princess Line." *Daily Variety,* Dec. 12, 2005.

Brazelton, T. Berry. *Touchpoints: Your Child's Emotional and Behavioral Development, Birth to 3 — The Essential Reference for the Early Years.* Cambridge, Mass.: Perseus Books, 1992.

Brenner, Susan. "The Littlest Test-Takers." *New York Times,* Nov. 9, 2003.

"Bringing Up Baby Entrepreneur: Julie Aigner-Clark Hits the Tot-TV Jackpot with Baby Einstein." *People,* May 22, 2000.

Brody, Michael. "Kids' Popular Culture: The Selling of Childhood." *Brown University Child and Adolescent Behavior Letter,* Jan. 1, 2003.

Brooke, Jill. "Mommy Rebellion; Tracking the Course of Mutiny Against the Tyranny of Parental Expectations." *Chicago Tribune,* Dec. 21, 2004.

Brooks, David. *Bobos in Paradise: The New Upper Class and How They Got There.* New York: Simon & Schuster, 2000.

——. *On Paradise Drive: How We Live Now (and Always Have) in the Future Tense.* New York: Simon & Schuster, 2004.

Bruer, John T. *The Myth of the First Three Years: A New Understanding of Early Brain Development and Lifelong Learning.* New York: Free Press, 1999.

Buckleitner, Warren. "It's Baby's First Video Game, No Joystick Required." *New York Times,* May 4, 2006.

Callaway, Libby. "Haute Tot: Label Crazy Moms Turning Kids into Mini Fashionistas." *New York Post,* Dec. 1, 2003.

Calvert, Sandra L., et al. *Age, Ethnicity, and Socioeconomic Patterns in Early Com-*

puter Use: A National Survey. Children's Digital Media Center and the Henry J. Kaiser Family Foundation, May 10, 2004.

Calvert, Sandra L., Amy B. Jordan, and Rodney R. Cocking, eds. *Children in the Digital Age: Influences of Electronic Media on Development.* Westport, Conn.: Praeger, 2002.

Castleman, Lana. "Taking Your Hit from Redhot to Evergreen." *KidScreen,* June 1, 2004.

Center for a New American Dream. *Tips for Parenting in a Commercial Culture.* www.newdream.org.

Chatzky, Jean. "Mini Me Fashion." *Time,* Nov. 24, 2003.

"Children Read Their Scribbles." *Washington Post,* Sept. 17, 1987.

Chomsky, Noam, and Edward S. Herman. *Manufacturing Consent: The Political Economy of the Mass Media.* New York: Pantheon Books, 1988.

Cipolla, Lorin. "Licensed Products Still Prevail." *Promo,* Aug. 1, 2004.

Clark, Erin E. *"Blue's Clues* Trickles Down to Babies." *Children's Business,* Feb. 1, 2001; "Study Probes Generation Gap." *Children's Business,* May 1, 2004.

Cohen, Patricia. "Mothering and Its Cultural Discontents." *New York Times,* Mar. 24, 2004.

Comiteau, Jennifer. "First Impressions: When Does Brand Loyalty Start? Earlier Than You Might Think." *AdWeek,* Mar. 24, 2003.

Corwin, Tom. "Newborns to Arrive with Music." *Augusta Chronicle,* June 24, 1998.

Cotliar, Sharon. "Mothers of Invention: Sometimes Being a New Mom Can Spawn New Ideas, Which Just Might Make Someone a Small Mint." *Time,* Mar. 20, 2000.

Couglin, Ron, and Tom Wong. "Generation XO — From 'Slacker' to Vigilant Family Gatekeeper." *International Journal of Advertising and Marketing to Children* 4, no. 4 (Sept. 2003).

Cox, Billy. "Non-Talking Video Big Hit with Babies and Toddlers." *Denver Post,* June 26, 1999.

Crittenden, Ann. *The Price of Motherhood: Why the Most Important Job in the World Is Still the Least Valued.* New York: Henry Holt, 2001.

Cross, Gary. *Kids' Stuff: Toys and the Changing World of American Childhood.* Cambridge, Mass.: Harvard University Press, 1997.

———. *The Cute and the Cool: Wondrous Innocence and Modern American Children's Culture.* New York: Oxford University Press, 2004.

della Cava, Marco R. "The Race to Raise a Brainier Baby; Parents Clamor for Educational Toys — to the Tune of $1 Billion." *USA Today,* June 25, 2002.

DeLoache, Judy S. "Becoming Symbol Minded." *Trends in Cognitive Sciences* 8, no. 2 (Feb. 2004).

de Marneffe, Daphne. *Maternal Desire: On Children, Love, and the Inner Life.* Boston: Little, Brown, 2004.

Desjardins, Doug. "Kids TV Surpasses Film as Source for Branded Merchandise." *DSN Retailing Today,* June 7, 2004.

Dominus, Susan. "She Speaks 3-Year-Old," *New York Times Magazine,* Jan. 4, 2004.

Duenwald, Mary. "Child Rearing by the Book, but Which One?" *New York Times,* Aug. 3, 2004.

Dunnewind, Stephanie. "Scholastic Wins Numbers Game in the Schools, but Publisher Has Its Critics — Marketing Deals, Quality of Offerings Questioned." *Seattle Times,* Sept. 24, 2005.

Eaton, Leslie. "Where Half-Caf Meets Double-Wide." *New York Times,* Feb. 6, 2005.

ElBoghdady, Dina. "Now Playing in Aisle 7." *Washington Post,* Jan. 29, 2003.

Seattle Post-Intelligencer, Mar. 28, 1996.

Elkind, David. *The Hurried Child: Growing Up Too Fast, Too Soon.* Cambridge, Mass.: Perseus Books, 2001.

Elliott, Laura. "Studies Show the Brain Is More Alive with the Sounds of Music."

Epstein, Robert. "The Loose Screw Awards: Psychology's Top 10 Misguided Ideas." *Psychology Today,* Jan. 1, 2005.

Farley, Robert. "With Baby Video, Family Business Born." *St. Petersburg Times,* Oct. 8, 2000.

Fasig, Lisa Biank. "Oldies Favorites Are Big Hits at American International Toy Fair." Knight-Ridder Tribune Business News, Feb. 17, 2003.

Ferber, Richard. *Solve Your Child's Sleep Problems.* Rev. and expanded ed. New York: Fireside, 2006.

"Fewer Kids Attract Greater Spending." *Brand Strategy,* Nov. 2, 2001.

Fisch, Shalom M., and Rosemarie Truglio, eds. *"G" Is for Growing: Thirty Years of Research on Children and* Sesame Street. Mahwah, N.J.: Lawrence Erlbaum Associates, 2001.

"Fisher-Price 'Rescue Heroes' Animated Series Debuts on Cartoon Network." *Business Wire,* June 11, 2004.

"Games and Giggles Toward a Better Baby." *Washington Post,* Sept. 10, 1985.

Gardner, Amy. "New *Star Wars* Movie Isn't Kid Stuff." *News & Observer,* May 19, 2005.

Garretson, Judith A., and Ronald W. Niedrich. "Creating Character Trust and Positive Brand Attitudes." *Journal of Advertising,* July 1, 2004.

George, James. "For Toys 'R' Us, a Time to Re-Build." *New York Times,* Jan. 4, 2004.

Gladwell, Malcolm. *The Tipping Point: How Little Things Can Make a Big Difference.* Boston: Little, Brown, 2000.

Gobe, Mark. *Emotional Branding: The New Paradigm for Connecting Brands to People.* New York: Allworth Press, 2001.

———. *Citizen Brand: 10 Commandments for Transforming Brands in a Consumer Democracy.* New York: Allworth Press, 2002.

Goode, Erica. "Yes, Babies Do Watch TV." *New York Times,* Jan. 24, 2003.

Gopnik, Alison, Andrew N. Meltzoff, and Patricia K. Kuhl. *The Scientist in the Crib.* New York: HarperCollins Perennial, 1999.

Gore, Ariel. *The Hip Mama Survival Guide: Advice from the Trenches on Pregnancy, Childbirth, Cool Names, Clueless Doctors, Potty Training and Toddler Avengers.* New York: Hyperion, 1998.

Green, Jesse. "Can Disney Build a Better Mickey Mouse?" *New York Times,* Apr. 18, 2004.

Grela, Bernard G., Marina Krcmar, and Yi-Jiun Lin. "Can Television Help Toddlers Acquire New Words?" Paper presented at the annual meeting of the American Speech–Language–Hearing Association, Chicago, 2003.

Hade, Daniel. "Storyselling: Are Publishers Changing the Way Children Read?" *Horn Book Magazine,* Sept. 1, 2002.

Harmon, Amy. "First Comes the Baby Carriage." *New York Times,* Oct. 13, 2005.

Hawkes, Nigel. "Mozart Fails on Reasoning Tests." *Times* (London), Aug. 4, 1999.

Hays, Constance L. "Targeting the Toddler Market." *New York Times,* July 11, 2003.

Heard, Alex. "The Final Word — We Hope — on Parenting in the 80s." *Washington Post,* Oct. 19, 1986.

Heffernan, Virginia. "The Evil Screen's Plot to Take Over the 2-and-Under World." *New York Times,* Apr. 14, 2006; "For Your Highbrow in Diapers." *New York Times,* May 14, 2005.

Hill, Alma E. "Classical Is Right Tune for Baby, Studies Show Benefit to Brain, Calming Effect Cited." *Atlanta Journal,* Jan. 15, 1998.

Hirsh-Pasek, Kathy, and Roberta Michnick Golinkoff. *Einstein Never Used Flash Cards.* Emmaus, Pa.: Rodale Press, 2003.

Hochman, David. "Mommy (and Me)." *New York Times,* Jan. 30, 2005.

Hochschild, Arlie Russell. *The Time Bind: When Work Becomes Home and Home Becomes Work.* New York: Metropolitan/Holt, 1997.

———. *The Commercialization of Intimate Life.* Berkeley: University of California Press, 2003.

Holson, Laura M. "After 13 Years Judge Dismisses Case on Pooh Bear Royalties." *New York Times,* Mar. 30, 2004; "A Finishing School for All, Disney Style." *New York Times,* Oct. 4, 2004.

Hopkins, Brent. "For Tots Testing Toys, Picking Tomorrow's Winners and Losers Is Child's Play." *Los Angeles Daily News,* Aug. 12, 2001.

Horn, Caroline. "Build Your Pester Power: Children's Book Marketing Has Come a Long Way in the Past Few Years." *Bookseller,* Nov. 8, 2002.

Hulbert, Ann. *Raising America: Experts, Parents and a Century of Advice About Children.* New York: Alfred A. Knopf, 2003.

———. "Look Who's Parenting." *New York Times,* July 4, 2004.

Hwang, Suein. "Pre-K Prep: How Young Is Too Young for Tutoring?" *Wall Street Journal,* Oct. 13, 2004.

Ives, Nat. "Nickelodeon Tries a Hotel." *New York Times,* Oct. 5, 2004.

Jensen, Kurt. "A Brief History of Smart Toys." *USA Today,* June 25, 2002.

Johnson, Patrick. "Child Research Yields Clues to Behavior." *Springfield Union-News,* Apr. 7, 2003.

Kalb, Claudia, with Joan Raymond and Jonathan Adams. "Research Shows Intellectual and Social Benefits When Kids Rely on Their Imaginations for Fun." *Newsweek,* Sept. 8, 2003.

Kantor, Jodi. "Love the Riches, Lose the Rags." *New York Times,* Nov. 3, 2005.

Keeney, Carole. "Those Amazing Newborns Are Complex." *Houston Chronicle,* Feb. 14, 1986.

Khermouch, Gerry. "Brainier Babies? Maybe. Big Sales? Definitely." *BusinessWeek,* Jan. 12, 2004.

Kinzer, Stephen. "Dolls as Role Models, Neither Barbie Nor Britney." *New York Times,* Nov. 6, 2003.

Kirkpatrick, David D. "Shaping Cultural Tastes at Big Retail Chains." *New York Times,* May 18, 2003.

Kirkwood, Kyra. "Babies Are Bundles of Love, Joy — And Money; Give New Parents a Helping Hand by Stocking These Videos for Babies, Toddlers." *Video Store,* Oct. 12, 2003.

Klein, Naomi. *No Logo.* New York: Picador, 2000.

Kloer, Phil. "Kids Television Programs Step Up Emphasis on Toys." *Atlanta Journal,* Apr. 20, 1987.

Kluger, Jeffrey, with Alice Park. "The Quest for a Super Kid: Geniuses Are Made, Not Born — Or So Parents Are Told. But Can We Really Train Baby Brains, and Should We Try?" *Time,* Apr. 30, 2001.

Knox, Richard A. "Certain Music Can Enhance Brain Functions." *Boston Globe,* Aug. 14, 1994.

Krier, Beth Ann. "Some Coos Babble in the Making of a Superbaby." *Los Angeles Times,* July 1, 1986.

Kunerth, Jeff. "IQ Booster Is Teacher's Smartest Idea Yet." *Orlando Sentinel,* Nov. 27, 1987.

Langley, Monica. "Bringing Up (Bilingual) Baby — Marketers Rush to Meet Demand for Toys, Tapes and Classes." *Wall Street Journal,* Oct. 6, 1999.

Lareau, Annette. "The Long Lost Cousins of the Middle Class." *New York Times,* Dec. 20, 2003.

Lee, Carol E. "The Evolution of Women's Roles Chronicled in the Life of a Doll." *New York Times,* Mar. 30, 2004.

Leeds, Jeff. "We Hate the 80's." *New York Times,* Feb. 13, 2005.

Lewin, Tamar. "See Baby Touch a Screen, But Does Baby Get It?" *New York Times,* Dec. 15, 2005.

Ligos, Melinda. "The Pacifier Isn't for the Client." *New York Times,* May 3, 2005.

Linebarger, Deborah L. "Young Children, Language, and Television." *Literacy Today*, Sept. 2004.

Linebarger, Deborah L., and Dale Walker. "Infants' and Toddlers' Television Viewing and Language Outcomes." *American Behavioral Scientist* 46 (2004).

Linn, Susan. *Consuming Kids: The Hostile Takeover of Childhood*. New York: New Press, 2004.

Lombardi, Joan. *Time to Care: Redesigning Child Care to Promote Education, Support Families, and Build Communities*. Philadelphia: Temple University Press, 2003.

MacDonald, G. Jeffrey. "Smarter Toys, Smarter Tots? Parents Spend $2.8 Billion Per Year on Educational Toys for Infants and Preschoolers." *Christian Science Monitor*, Aug. 20, 2003.

Markey, Judy. "Whatever Happened to the Silence of the Womb?" *Chicago Sun-Times*, Feb. 20, 1986.

Marsh, Ann. "Can You Hum Your Way to Math Genius?" *Forbes*, Apr. 19, 1999.

Martin, Sandra. "Bringing Up Baby." *Globe and Mail*, June 4, 1983.

McCormick, Moira. "Holiday Title Wave Breaks with Kingly Lions, Barney, and Mozart." *Billboard*, Aug. 22, 1998; "Mom's Baby Vids Sharpen New Minds." *Billboard*, Oct. 3, 1998.

McGinn, Daniel. "Guilt Free TV." *Newsweek*, Nov. 2002.

McNamara, Mary. "Princesses Rule! Armed with Jewels and Lace, Fantasy Femmes Are en Route to World Domination." *Los Angeles Times*, Aug. 31, 2004.

McNeal, James U. *The Kids Market: Myths and Realities*. Ithaca, N.Y.: Paramount Market Publishing, 1999.

Menzies, David. "A Trip to the Toy & Hobby Fair Proves Kids Rule This Billion-Dollar Industry." *National Post*, Jan. 27, 2003.

Mitchell, Elvis. "For Parents, the Fear Factor Grows." *New York Times*, Dec. 7, 2003.

Mooney, Carol Garhart. *Theories of Childhood: An Introduction to Dewey, Montessori, Erikson, Piaget, and Vygotsky*. St. Paul, Minn.: Redleaf Press, 2000.

Moore, Angela. "Fisher-Price Takes Edu Toy Fight to the Crib." Reuters News, June 21, 2004; "Mattel Launches Barbie Clothes for Women." Reuters News, Oct. 14, 2005.

Munk, Nina. "My Generation: Hope I Shop Before I Get Old." *New York Times*, Aug. 14, 2005.

Murkoff, Heidi, Sandee Hathaway, and Arlene Eisenberg. *What to Expect in the First Year*. 2nd ed. New York: Workman Publishing, 2003.

Neeley, Sabrina M., and David W. Schumann. "Using Animated Spokescharacters in Advertising to Young Children: Does Increasing Attention to Advertising Necessarily Lead to Product Preference?" *Journal of Advertising*, 2004.

Nussbaum, Debra. "Kindergarten Can Wait." *New York Times*, Dec. 21, 2003.

O'Connor, Colleen. "Moms of the World, Unite! A New Generation of Mothers Is Seeking a Voice." *Denver Post,* May 3, 2005.

O'Donnell, Rose. "Making Baby a Shade Smarter." *Seattle Times,* Dec. 3, 1984.

Oser, Cindy, and Julie Cohen. *America's Babies: The Zero to Three Policy Center Data Book.* Washington, D.C.: Zero to Three Foundation, 2003.

Owens, Darryl E. "Babies Off to Smart Musical Start." Knight-Tribune News Service, June 28, 1999.

Parkes, Christopher. "Transformer of a Mickey Mouse Outfit." *Financial Times,* May 27, 2003.

Peisner-Feinberg, Ellen S., et al. *The Children of the Cost, Quality, and Child Outcomes Study Go to School.* Washington, D.C.: National Institute of Early Child Development and Education, June 1999.

Pereira, Joe. "Parents Turn Toys That Teach into Hot Sellers." *Wall Street Journal,* Nov. 27, 2002.

Poole, William. "School for Babies in the Womb: Hayward 'College' Seeks to Give Kids a Jump on Learning." *San Francisco Chronicle,* Aug. 26, 1987.

Postrel, Virginia. *The Substance of Style: How the Rise of Aesthetic Value Is Remaking Commerce, Culture, and Consciousness.* New York: HarperCollins, 2003.

"Preschools the Newest Forum for Advertising." *Washington Post,* Oct. 18, 2003.

Quinn, Michelle. "Taking Pre-Schoolers to See *Star Wars.*" *San Jose Mercury News,* May 20, 2005.

Randall, Taylor, Karl Ulrich, and David Reibstein. "Brand Equity and Vertical Product Line Extent." *Marketing Science* 17, no. 4 (1998).

Rawe, Julie. "A Smart Toy Guide (Parents Not Included)." *Time,* Apr. 30, 2001.

Rideout, Victoria J., Elizabeth A. Vandewater, and Ellen A. Wartella. *Zero to Six: Electronic Media in the Lives of Infants, Toddlers, and Preschoolers.* Menlo Park, Calif.: Henry J. Kaiser Family Foundation and the Children's Digital Media Centers, 2003.

Rohrlich, Marianne. "Setting Sail to Wynken, Blynken and Nod." *New York Times,* Jan. 20, 2005.

Rosenberg, Alec. "Toy Companies Battle for Talking Book Market." *Oakland Tribune,* Nov. 16, 2003.

Rosenfeld, Alvin, and Nicole Wise. *The Over-Scheduled Child: Avoiding the Hyper-Parenting Trap.* New York: St. Martin's Press, 2000.

Rotenberk, Lori. "Value of Touching: Contact Can Feed Human Psyches." *Chicago Sun-Times,* Aug. 17, 1986.

Rubin, Courtney. "Reality Bites: Why He-Man, Care Bears, and Miami Vice are Making a Comeback." *Washington Monthly,* Oct. 2002.

Rushkoff, Douglas. *Media Virus! Hidden Agendas in Popular Culture.* New York: Ballantine Books, 1994.

———. *Coercion: Why We Listen to What "They" Say.* New York: Penguin Putnam, 1999.

Ryckman, Lisa Levitt. "Doctor Teaches Parents to Talk to Unborn Babies." *Chicago Sun-Times,* Jan. 5, 1986.

Salmon, Jacqueline L., and Jay Mathews. "Smart Baby Products Reeling in Parents." *Washington Post,* Mar. 3, 2000.

Salmon, Jacqueline L., and Marylou Tousignant. "Educational Toys Losing Cachet Among Generation X Smart Set." *Washington Post,* Mar. 8, 2004.

Schlosser, Eric. *Fast Food Nation: The Dark Side of the All-American Meal.* Boston: Houghton Mifflin, 2001.

Schmich, Mary. "Magic of Mozart Is All in the Mind." *Chicago Tribune,* Oct. 15, 1993.

Schor, Juliet B. *Born to Buy: The Commercialized Child and the New Consumer Culture.* New York: Scribner, 2004.

Scott, Janny, and David Leonhardt. "Class in America: Shadowy Lines That Still Divide." *New York Times,* May 15, 2005.

Seabrook, John. *Nobrow: The Culture of Marketing, the Marketing of Culture.* New York, Alfred A. Knopf, 2000.

Sears, William, and Martha Sears. *The Attachment Parenting Book: A Commonsense Guide to Understanding and Nurturing Your Baby.* Boston: Little, Brown, 2001.

———. *The Baby Book: Everything You Need to Know About Your Baby from Birth to Age Two.* Rev. ed. Boston: Little, Brown, 2003.

Shellenbarger, Sue. "Falling 'Behind' at Age 3: The Hazards of Pushing for Accountability in Pre-K." *Wall Street Journal,* Aug. 18, 2005.

Sherlock, Marie. *Living Simply with Children: A Voluntary Simplicity Guide for Moms, Dads, and Kids Who Want to Reclaim the Bliss of Childhood and the Joy of Parenting.* New York: Three Rivers Press, 2003.

Shonkoff, Jack P., and Deborah A. Phillips, eds. National Research Council and Institute of Medicine, *From Neurons to Neighborhoods: The Science of Early Childhood Development.* Washington, D.C.: National Academy Press, 2000.

Slatalla, Michelle. "In a Lavish Layette, the Illusion of Control." *New York Times,* July 15, 2004.

Starr, Alexandra. "Subadolescent Queen Bees." *New York Times,* Dec. 11, 2005.

Stewart, Lianne. "Licensed Books for the Masses!" *KidScreen,* June 1, 2004.

Story, Louise. "Many Women at Elite Colleges Set Career Path to Motherhood." *New York Times,* Sept. 20, 2005.

Swain, Gill. "Pester Power — Focus." *Sunday Times,* Dec. 29, 2002.

"Talking With: Julie Aigner-Clark; Founder, the Baby Einstein Company." Bluesuitmom.com, Aug. 2000.

Tan, Cheryl Lu-Lien. "Toilets for Tots — Pint-Size Fixtures Are Latest Parental Indulgence; Ripping It Out in Two Years." *Wall Street Journal,* June 9, 2005.

"The U.S. Market for Infant, Toddler, and Preschool Products." Report highlights, MarketResearch.com, 2003.

Thomas, Paulette. "Advertisers Take Pitches to Preschools." *Wall Street Journal*, Oct. 28, 1996.

Tompor, Susan. "More Parents Just Say No to Pitches Targeting Kids." *Harrisburg Patriot*, Mar. 17, 2003.

"Toy Company Asks Kids for Their Opinions." *Washington Post*, July 17, 2003.

Vandell, Deborah, and Barbara Wolfe. *Child Care Quality: Does It Matter and Does It Need to Be Improved?* Washington, D.C.: U.S. Department of Health and Human Services, 2000.

"VEE Corporation Presents New Nationwide Tour: Care Bears Live!" *PR Newswire*, Sept. 20, 2005.

Walker, Rob. "Training Brand." *New York Times*, Feb. 27, 2005.

"Warm Welcome Program Delivers the Sound Benefits of the Mozart Effect to Colorado Newborns." *Business Wire*, Sept. 17, 1998.

Warner, Judith. *Perfect Madness: Motherhood in the Age of Anxiety*. New York: Riverhead Books, 2005.

Watson, Noshua. "Generation Wrecked; The So-Called Slackers Are Complaining (Again) About the Economy. This Time They Have Reason to Whine." *Fortune*, Oct. 14, 2002.

Weber, Bruce. "Scandal for School (Don't Try This at Home)." *New York Times*, Nov. 17, 2003.

Webster, Katherine. "Tots and Parents Share Play with Purpose." *Daily Oklahoman*, Nov. 5, 1984.

Wilcox, Brian L., et al. *Report of the American Psychological Association Task Force on Advertising and Children*. Washington, D.C.: American Psychological Association, 2004.

Winner, Ellen, and Lois Hetland. "Mozart and the SATs." *New York Times*, Mar. 4, 1999.

Wolfe, Alexandra. "Children and Moms at Play." *New York Times*, June 5, 2005.

Zigler, Edward F., Matia Finn-Stevenson, and Nancy W. Hall. *The First Three Years and Beyond: Brain Development and Social Policy*. New Haven: Yale University Press, 2003.

Zimmerman, Rachel. "The Carriage Trade: Stay-at-Home Moms Get Entrepreneurial." *Wall Street Journal*, Oct. 21, 2004.

Zinman, David. "Infants and Brain Growth: A New Study Contends There Is Neurological Growth After Birth." *Newsday*, Sept. 2, 1986.

Zissu, Alexandra. "For Baby, All You Knead Is Love." *New York Times*, May 15, 2005.

Zukin, Sharon. *Point of Purchase: How Shopping Changed American Culture*. New York: Routledge, 2004.

Acknowledgments

I have depended on the expertise and help of many people during the course of working on this book; I am deeply grateful to them all. Were it not for my editor, Eamon Dolan, who encouraged me to explore a wide terrain (showing an almost distressing degree of confidence in my ability to navigate it), this project would have had a far narrower focus. That it *has* focus is thanks to Eamon's meticulous raking of the underbrush in the wake of my bushwhacking.

My agent and friend, Tina Bennett, equal parts aesthete and shark, has been enthusiastic about this project from the start. Without her efforts and encouragement, it would have remained where it started, as kitchen table conversation.

I am grateful to all the people who shared their expertise with me, often submitting to long and repeated interviews. Of particular note are Pam Abrams, Francie Alexander, Kathleen Alfano, Julie Aigner-Clark, Dan Anderson, Rachel Barr, Lewis Bernstein, Adam Biehl, Michael Brody, Alice Cahn, Renee Chernow O'Leary, Stan Clutton, Gary Cross, Joel Ehrlich, Beth Gellert, Alison Gopnik, Jim Gray, Shelly Glick Gryfe, Daniel Hade, Craig Hendrickson, Kathy Hirsh-Pasek, David Jacobs, Brown Johnson, Nancy Kanter, Ann Kearns, Claire Lerner, Deborah Linebarger, Susan Linn, Jim Marggraff, Laurie Oravec, Lauren Rees,

Nancy Sabath, Juliet Schor, Sonya Shoptaugh, Iris Sroka, and Rosemarie Truglio.

I appreciate the patience and indulgence of all the moms and teachers at the Rivendell School and in our community of Park Slope, Brooklyn — especially my friends Tatiana Acosta, Caroline Batzdorf, Genina Berger, Jackie Christy, Cindy Cordes, Agnes Daigncourt, Melanie Judd-Porter, Amy Kass, Yuko Kodama, Patricia Martin, Heather O'Donnell, Jennifer Russell, Susan Smith, Marje Wagner, and Judith Wolochow. I would have been nowhere without the help of Maryanne Buechner, a friend, mom, and fantastic reporter. And I'm not sure what to say about the friendship of Nati Porat and Jason Wizelman, except that I rely on it.

The Brooklyn Writers Space offered priceless real estate for an apartment-dwelling mother of young children: a quiet place to write. Thanks to my foxhole buddies there: Scott Adkins, Tasha Blaine, Heather Chaplin, Matt Roshkow, and Annie Seaton.

Peg Anderson and Holly Bemiss at Houghton Mifflin did yeoman's work in cleaning up my prose and presentation. I would also like to thank my former editor at *U.S. News*, Avery Comarow, for pushing me to toughen up and to ask the obvious questions, which are often the hardest. I am indebted to my godmother and mentor, Joan Downs, who gave me my first typewriter and published my first real article; to her husband, Steven Goldberg, who always took my ideas seriously (even when I was a punk teenager); to my parents and parents-in-law; and to my Nana.

During the time I worked on this book, my Dad died, and my children and I got pneumonia — twice. Without my husband's unfailing health, culinary talents, and support in all things, it all would have seemed — and been — impossible. Mostly, I am grateful for our children: my schmushkies, my heart's delight. I'll never understand how I got so lucky.

Index